The Flame and the Light

Cover art by JANE EVANS

The Flame and the Light

MEANINGS IN VEDANTA AND BUDDHISM

Hugh I'anson Fausset

A QUEST BOOK

THE THEOSOPHICAL PUBLISHING HOUSE
Wheaton, Ill., U.S.A.
Madras, India / London, England

First Quest edition 1976 published by the Theosophical Publishing House, a department of The Theosophical Society in America.

Library of Congress Cataloging in Publication Data

Fausset, Hugh I'Anson, 1895-
  The flame and the light.

  (A Quest book)
  Reprint of the 1969 ed. published by Greenwood Press, New
York.
  Includes bibliographical references.
  1. Vedanta—Comparative studies. 2. Buddhism—Relations—
Hinduism. 3. Hinduism—Relations—Buddhism. I. Title.

B132.V3F35   1976   294.3'3'72   76-2081
ISBN 0-8356-0478-0

CONTENTS

FOREWORD

This book was originally conceived and sketched in outline some ten years ago as a course of lectures for an audience little acquainted with Oriental thought. The idea failed to materialize in that way. But to some extent that outline underlies what I have written here and provides its structural basis. In the intervening years, however, the subject has come home to me much more intimately and has woven itself into the fabric of my life. Not that it was ever a matter of merely intellectual interest. The discovery and exploration of this ancient Indian thought has been for me, for more than thirty years, an engrossing spiritual adventure, which has sustained and changed my life, which, I might almost say, has at times made my life possible and anchored my mind in meaning. It is this adventure of discovery and inward enrichment which I want to share with my reader. He should not look for any systematic exposition of Eastern thought in the pages which follow. I was drawn in the first place to the sages of India because they spoke the language, not of philosophers or of theologians, but of poet-seers. For the same reason religion only became significant to me when it ceased to be a form of organized belief and engaged my spirit, as the art of his choice engages the artist and compels him to seek in and through it the creative freedom, in which he can fully live.

It is in the search for that freedom that we learn to suffer life patiently and to let the inward truth, from which all creation flows, penetrate more and more the outward movements of mind and heart. Less and less, as this inwardness grows, like a lotus revealing its jewel in the hidden depths of our being, are we tempted to grasp at the world around us, as militant dogma grasps or argumentative opinion or all the emotions and sensations which bind men to what is fleeting and unreal.

Knowledge grows as the sense of being continually reborn out of darkness into light deepens. That is what we experience as we travel Eastward. Yet though truly we go into a world of light, a *world lit by the undying sun of pure intelligence, when we journey to the ancient East, we go, too, into a night in which the chatter of our conceited, opinionated Western minds must be silenced.*

For the majestic millenial conception of the days and the nights of Brahman, those vast alternating cycles of time, in which the infinite Being is said to flow forth, without diminishment of Itself, into manifestation and then to reabsorb the universe of forms into Its own changeless silence, is enacted day by day, hour by hour, moment by moment in our souls.

This is the creative mystery in which we are immersed and which impels us, as we grow older, to transmute action more and more into contemplation, not by ceasing to act but by purifying our acts of all that is meaningless and uncentred in the heart of the mystery.

Truly, as St. Aquinas said, it is necessary that there should be men who devote their lives to contemplation. Seldom, perhaps, has it been more necessary than to-day when so much action is merely restless movement, because it lacks inward direction. And seldom has the human spirit lived with a purer awareness in the realm of contemplation than it did in the pre-Christian seers and sages of India.

In them I have found, not only an authentic expression and interpretation of the Truth which we are all striving imperfectly to live, but a constant stimulus to rediscover that Truth in oneself, to adventure into it without any preordained or preconceived beliefs, and to grow by its light more and more aware of the divine unity in which we are meant wholly to participate.

This book, then, is not addressed to scholars who know, in their own field, far more than I do and to whose patient work, particularly in editing and translating texts, I owe so much. Its learning is of another kind and perhaps, without presumption, I may call it spiritual learning, which grows less out of industrious study of words and texts, necessary though this is in the search for truth, than out of life with its testing and failings.

To learn how to live well is the need of us all and I am convinced that these teachers of old who lived when the spiritual sky was clearer have much to teach us, Westerners though we be, bred and reared in another tradition and another spiritual climate. It is that teaching, as it developed from Vedic times to the later schools of Buddhism, a single revelation, renewing itself through

*the centuries in a wealth of varying insight, that I have pondered
here, confining myself to the two wells of Eastern wisdom from
which I have drunk most deeply, wells that drew their virtue from
the same primordial spring.*

The renderings of passages from the Upanishads *and the* Bhagavad-Gita *are my own, but in making them I have weighed the
merits of many translations and am particularly indebted, for the*
Upanishads, *to my friend, Juan Mascaró's,* Himalayas of the Soul,
*a version remarkable for the purity and simplicity of its diction,
to Sri Aurobindo's* Eight Upanishads, *Swami Nikhilananda's* The
Upanishads *and, as a foundation of literal translation and exhaus-
tive scholarship, R. E. Hume's monumental* The Thirteen Principal Upanishads.

In my study of the Bhagavad-Gita *I have found particularly
valuable the version made by a gifted Indian, A. Mahadeva Sastri,
many years ago in conjunction with Shankara's Commentary. The*
Message of the Gita, *as Interpreted by Sri Aurobindo has, also,
been of great help, while the recent translation by Swami Prabhavananda and Christopher Isherwood, entitled* The Song of God,
*has the virtue, if also perhaps the defect, of a brisk contemporary
idiom.*

*Acknowledgment of other debts is made in footnotes through-
out the book and in the short Bibliography at the end. I wish, too,
I could mention what, in the course of the years, I have received
from many interpreters who have preceded me and whose insight
has helped to quicken and strengthen my own. Though they must
be unnamed, I thank, none the less, these fellow-travellers along a
path so ancient and so new.*

H. I'A. F.

Little Walden, Essex.

CHAPTER ONE

The Flame and the Light

I

IT IS often assumed that people living in Europe are, psychologically, so different from people living in India or China that each can only profit by their own religions and scriptures. Christian missionary societies have, of course, thought otherwise. For them the heathen could only be saved by receiving the light of a Western religion. But if a cultivated Hindu had suggested that some Westerners, pining in the prison of Protestant or Catholic theology, could find release in the teachings of Vedanta, the missionary would have rejected the suggestion with at best a kindly smile. To-day the smile would, perhaps, be less assured. For during the last fifty years our knowledge of the comparative qualities and defects of different religions has grown considerably.

I would not underestimate the real differences between people who have been moulded by centuries of civilization peculiar to themselves, and not merely moulded. For each civilization reflects certain inherent qualities in the people who create and shape it, and also the stage in human evolution which they have reached. Until recently, a sharp division between Oriental and Occidental man may well have been necessary, so that each might develop intensively the particular bias which his civilization both expressed and induced.

But to-day it is sufficiently obvious that the integration, both of the individual and the world, depends to a great extent upon an inter-communion between the East, with its deep insight into the hidden world of the psyche, and the mentality of the West, which, by its one-sided conquests of the outer world, is endangering its own survival.

Less and less, too, to-day is Western man sustained or vitally guided either by the doctrines of orthodox Christianity or by the values and disciplines of classical humanism. The European civil-

ization of the last five hundred years is dissolving and can only be
renewed as part of a greater whole which will embrace the
world.

In such a time we are brought face to face with the inherent
nature of man, which, despite all the differences of race, tradition,
or spiritual development, is the same in us all. It is then, too, that
we begin to recognize how artificial and stultifying are many of
the religious or cultural prejudices which hitherto have been regarded, not as relative to an age or a race, but as ultimate.

My own experience confirms the truth of this quite convincingly
and contradicts the view that the only spiritual tradition in which
a Western man can feel at home is Christianity. With me it has
been just the reverse. Descended from a line of clerical ancestors,
I was brought up in a clerical home. I read or listened to the Bible
from an early age and was familiar with Christian teaching. Unlike some children of the vicarage I was innately pre-disposed to
take an interest in religious questions. Indeed, when I was taken to
a children's service by my nurse at a tender age and sat in the front
pew, I embarrassed her and doubtless amused the clergyman con-
ducting the service by becoming so absorbed in his address that
I began to enter into vocal debate with him, quite oblivious of the
silent congregation of which I was a part.

But though, as I grew older, I felt the appeal of Jesus's teaching
and recognized in his life and death a unique expression of an
ancient mystery, I never felt him to be my own distinctive Master.
Since he was presented to me by the Church as the only true
Master, this often worried me and made me wonder whether it
was due to some lack in myself. Why was it, I used to ask myself,
when some evangelizing person enquired whether I had entrusted
my life to Jesus as my Saviour, that I felt not only embarrassed
but critical of the assumption that salvation could only come to
me through him.

Yet I was never a rationalist or in revolt against the deeper
mysteries of the Christian faith, though I became impatient with
its conventions and its exclusive claims. I always felt that it was the
right religion for some people. This of course affronted those
who claimed that it superseded all others and was obligatory on
all. I believed, indeed, that the essence of Jesus's teaching, the
imaginative as distinct from the literal content of it, spoke, in its
eternal wisdom, to everyone with ears to hear, and could not con-

flict with truth, in whatever form it was found elsewhere. Indeed being universal, it must have existed from the foundation of the world, as St. Augustine suggested.

But Christianity is predominantly a Judaistic religion, particularly in its Pauline emphasis, and the primitive Judaism in which Jesus's teaching has been embedded, those 'Hebrew old clothes,' as Carlyle called it, was alien to me, though I was deeply moved by its poetry. I questioned, too, the tremendous emphasis laid upon sin and judgment by an ethical monotheism, nor could I accept the claim of any race or religious fraternity to be the elect of God, to whom He had entrusted the only true revelation of Himself. That the Truth should manifest variously and with more or less significance through different races and people was to be expected and also that the focus of its expression should shift as human consciousness evolved in time. But I could not admit that at any historical moment this process should have reached finality or that early revelations were superseded or wholly absorbed in later ones. Each, it seemed to me, corresponded with certain recurrent needs and insights of the human soul as it grew, and each could bring the kind of illumination most apt and necessary to some pilgrim on the way.

This illumination I had not myself received from orthodox Christianity or from the Greek and Roman authors studied in the course of a classical education. I had received much from both sources, but neither really touched my inmost spirit, except for what flowed from some of the Christian mystics. And since human wisdom, in common view, had hardly existed outside this much vaunted Western phase of history, I remained dissatisfied, seeking I knew not what.

Then, one day, in the course of my literary work, I received a curious book for review. It was called *The Dream of Ravan. A Mystery*, and had appeared many years earlier as a series of articles in an Irish magazine. Its author, the preface informed me, had studied the Indian epic, the *Ramayana*, in the original texts and was a master of Vedantic psychology. It consisted of translations in verse of passages from the *Ramayana*, with a running commentary, at times rather tiresomely facetious, but culminating in an interpretation of the mystical philosophy which underlay it and of the ancient methods by which man came to realize his true nature.

I had been warned in the preface that most people would dismiss the book as a mere phantasy full of strange conceits, but that a discerning reader would find many truths but slightly veiled and many a secret wholly disclosed. I needed no such warning. In reading it I found myself for the first time in a spiritual atmosphere in which I was completely at home. Here Plato's doctrine of 'recollection,' upon which he based his view that the art of education consists in recalling to the pupil's consciousness what he really knows but has temporarily forgotten, proved itself upon my pulses. This was my world. I was familiar with it as with a face that I had loved long since and lost awhile. It was as if previously I had been adapting myself to the creeds and customs of a country which always remained a little foreign to me. Now I had touched again the shore of my native land.

It may well be that a man's nature is determined more essentially by his spiritual than by his physical line of descent and that, as some mystical schools teach, each of us is intimately related to dwellers in the unseen world. Clearly our lives are part of a pattern of other lives and inseparable from them and just as we inherit physical and mental characteristics from parents or grandparents, we may, at a deeper level, owe the quality of our spiritual nature and aptitudes, in some measure at least, to hidden ties which have nothing to do with the tie of blood. Hence, perhaps, the fact that our closest spiritual sympathies are seldom with relatives.

There is an esoteric explanation of spiritual affinity, which I find suggestive. In the language of ancient symbol Consciousness is always identified with light, and human beings are regarded spiritually, as points of light on a Ray sent forth by a Creative Sun into the realm of darkness which we call matter, and destined to unfold eventually the pure light of their origin. The light of each individual is distinctive, but just as physically there are groupings of race and of family, so in the unseen world, to which our spirits most intimately belong, the Light travels down different Rays, to one or other of which each of us belongs.

Pre-eminent among these creative Rays are those transmitted through certain Masters who at different periods in human evolution brought light to mankind, having themselves uniquely realized the Truth with which they were entrusted. In so doing they set vibrating in the world a creative force to which countless other spirits, still to be born, have been attracted and by the distinctive quality of which their souls, as they descended into earthly existence, have been tempered and their spiritual type determined.

Jesus was one of these Masters, but there were others who preceded him, in India, Persia, and Egypt, for example, of whose earthly history little is known because only fragmentary records of their lives have survived. But the Life Rays, associated with and in a sense originated by them, are still active, and those with an inner vision can recognize the Ray with which they themselves or others are most closely associated.

To many of my readers, however, such an enlargement of Plato's doctrine of *anamnesis* must seem but idle speculation. And I have only thus digressed to suggest that such intuitive recognition as I experienced when the world of Vedanta first dawned on my conscious mind could not be accidental. It had a lineage behind and within it. Looking back upon my mental interests and the kind of thought with which I was most at home, before I knew anything of Indian philosophy, I can see that I had an inborn aptitude for its kind of metaphysic. I have always had a sense of breathing ideas as naturally as I breathe air.

F. H. Bradley described the metaphysical task as the attempt to know reality as against mere appearance, to comprehend the universe, not simply piecemeal or by fragments, but somehow as a whole. Some of us are drawn to this task, even in this anti-metaphysical age, because it is on the plane of this kind of reality that we live most vividly. Such a plane is just as actual, for those who are inwardly attuned to it, as the planes of fact and of feeling.

Just as we have a physical body which we can see and touch, so we have finer bodies through which we feel and think. Ideas have a form of their own which they impress upon the world of matter. True idealism, therefore, is not, as so often assumed, a kind of abstract haze in which vaguely aspiring people veil the poker face of fact. Nor is it a compensation for failure in actual living. Its thought is of a particularly intense order since it is directed to the essence, not the accidents of things, and the same is true of the values which it seeks to discover and vindicate.

Facts, insulated from ideas and images, are unreal. For they owe what reality they possess to the ideas which inform them. As Romano Guardini has suggested,

*ideas and images are perhaps one and the same reality viewed
from different realms of existence, that above or that within.
They are, as it were, radiated by the Logos who creates and
regulates all finite things through them, from above by the
clarity of consciousness, from within by the deepening of life.*[1]

As idealists, therefore, we do not merely exercise our everyday
mind on another, more interior plane. We are exercising another
kind of mind, which is as much at home in a world of ideas and
images as our practical, analytical mind is in a world of physical
phenomena. The mind which we focus upon the physical world
and with which we sort the messages received through the five
senses, is itself a sixth physical sense. The Hindus call it the lower
Manas. It is the instrument by which we see and handle alien
objects with more or less of rational self-interest and discrimination.

By contrast the mind which is active on a more interior plane
and is named by the Hindus *Buddhi*, is comparable to a creative
eye. It is the intuitive organ of the Consciousness which informs
all creation and makes it one. It perceives and acts within what an
ancient Hindu hymn has called 'that Unbroken Sphere which
pervades this world of separate things'.

It is, of course, in the great spiritual Masters that this creative
eye is wholly open and perfectly focussed. But it can be partially
or intermittently open in less exalted persons. An artist of genius,
for example, is distinguishable from an artist of talent by his
capacity for such creative seeing and even the artist of talent
may have moments when pure intuition supersedes a self-centred
sensibility. It is the same with thinkers. The creative thinker is
dedicated to the task which the old alchemists called 'the transmutation of the mental view itself', of working his way through
the dialectical conflict, which is the necessary method of a divided
mind, to the wisdom in which it is resolved.

Sometimes, as in such God-compelled thinkers as Pascal or
Kierkegaard, or in Simone Weil, in our own day, we have the
tragic but fascinating spectacle of proud intellects of great
power and precision being invaded by the spiritual force of intuition which they struggle to accommodate within the bounds of
a tense individuality which thinks to argue its way into the heart

[1] Quoted by Gabriel Marcel in *Homo Viator* from Guardini's commentary
on Rilke's 'Elegies'.

of truth. Ecstasy seizes them but only to plunge them into more agonising conflict until pride of mind is consumed in the fire it generates.

By contrast we experience in such a thinker as Plotinus a consciousness so little involved in the dialectic of the lower mind that it can move freely in the unconditioned world of ideas with a grace that is never disturbed by the conflicts and contingencies inseparable from attachment to the physical world. Such a consciousness may seem elevated too far above our humbler human needs and dilemmas. It is more of a light in a tower than a lamp to our feet. But unless the mind is illumined from within—and it is this which distinguishes a higher from a lower consciousness —it will be at the mercy of what is without.

The aim of all spiritual discipline and devotion is to focus on the intellectual and sensory planes a radiance from above and beyond them, which releases the true light within them. This was the persistent aim of the Vedic seers. They were not thinkers in the modern, specialized Western sense of the word. The *Upanishads* are the fruit of inspired contemplation and, though a speculative element is to be found in some of them, they are meant primarily for contemplation. To regard them as a primitive expression of philosophical idealism, as some Western thinkers have done, is a mistake. For they offer more than thought. They offer a key which opens some of the most secret doors in the cosmos and in the human soul. We are, in fact, in the presence of poet-seers for whom the Real was not abstract or reducible to some logical postulate, but eternally alive and present as a consciousness of Being in the human heart and mind.

In the Western world, as in much Western philosophy, a gulf has opened between knowledge and being, which existential thinkers are to-day trying to close with very different degrees of success. In fact, of course, the effort to reconcile self-conscious knowledge and the unfathomable reaches of being has never ceased throughout the ages, whatever the cultural tradition within which different philosophical systems have arisen or their religious or anti-religious trend.

The Christian religion has always claimed to bridge the gulf, and for long succeeded, within the limits of a prescribed knowledge, in doing so. But for many to-day its bridge fails to span the void which increased knowledge has opened in human experience or even the division in its own ranks between a primitive or adolescent 'fundamentalism,' appealing to the emotions, and the doctrinal severities of its theologians.

The efforts of Western psychologists on the other hand to resolve the conflict of conscious and unconscious are closer to contemporary human needs. But as yet they are insufficiently related to a spiritual order, in which alone this conflict can be fully understood.

The Vedantic seers were subtle psychologists, but their intuitive understanding of human nature was rooted in a direct vision of the inner nature of the cosmos of which man, they held, was a replica. The whole of Vedanta is based upon the conviction, tested and proved in actual experience, that our awareness can be deepened, purified and transformed, until it ceases to be a condition of conflict and separation and recovers the unity from which it has diverged.

The vision of the One, the intuition of an eternal Consciousness as the reality within and beyond all change, was vividly present to these ancient thinkers. It was a vision more universal and profound, if less palpably human, than the Judaic conception of the one God. The mind which conceived the one God and objectified Him as a supreme potentate, waging relentless war upon such false gods as dared to dispute His sovereignty and inflicting savage punishment upon those who were seduced from allegiance to Himself, was already caught in the conflict of the divided self. It had fallen into the dualism which is the shadow of that true duality through which the One manifests. Ethical monotheism always tends to reflect this fall, to be the creed of an individualized consciousness which feels itself threatened and insecure, and defensively reduces the mystery of Being to the scale of its own mental and moral will.

But in Vedanta the One remained enthroned in its superhuman and supra-personal mystery, out of which, indeed, It acted as a Creator, worshipful and knowable by man in various forms, which imaged aspects of Its greatness. The relation of this Fount of consciousness and being to the world of change and becoming was the primal preoccupation of the Vedic seers. And since man was conscious, however fitfully and partially, of both being and becoming, of eternity and time, it was in him that the mystery of this relationship could be explored and its meaning disclosed.

The ego was, it seemed, endlessly immeshed in the movement of becoming, so much so that under a critical scrutiny it could appear to have no existence of its own, but to be a mere point of acquiescence in a succession of momentary impulses, feelings, thoughts and sensations. Yet there was something that persisted and that could, in some measure, quicken or retard the movement and, superficially at least, control or direct it. Did this capacity derive from a Self in the individual independent of the movement, a Principle of being which, though present in the world of becoming, was unattached to it and which, in becoming, did not cease infinitely to be and to know?

And did the purpose of life consist in the gradual realization by individual men and women that this Self was the reality in which they might learn wholly to live? If so, the world of time might cease to be at war with the realm of timeless Being, and the illusive self which floundered blindly in the shoals of time, ignorant of its inmost divinity, might dwindle and dissolve like a shadow in the light of the midday sun.

II

This was the very heart of Vedantic experience and enquiry, as it has always been of Indian thought. It is the heart, indeed, of all religious experience. But how seldom have the religions of the West vindicated such an imaginative approach to life against the combative beliefs, typical of ethical and intellectual self-consciousness.

It may be argued that the phase in human development with which we are so familiar in the West, in which the conflict inherent in individualistic thinking and living has been perpetuated to the point of self-destruction, has helped man to acquire self-knowledge and to master not only the physical world, but the sub-human forces in himself.

Certainly much has been gained, however dubiously, on the level of material and moral achievement. Nor, of course, has the West lacked its contemplatives. Mystics, poets and artists and many a sensitive soul, unknown to fame, have passed beyond the warfare of a divided consciousness. Yet the moral and physical attachment to this warfare which has characterized Western religion and civilization has, to a large extent, thwarted the creative freedom which life intends.

We come into this world endowed with a determined will to live, which persists through all the blows of circumstance. Even if the blows are so severe that at times we become mentally indifferent to life or desire death, the primal will in the physical body maintains its grip. Quite early, too, in our lives this inborn impulse of our animal nature to preserve and assert itself begins to assume a distinctively human form, not only in the realm of action, but in the more inward realms of feeling and of thought.

We are taught, more or less successfully, to accommodate our will to the wills of others and urged to surrender it, if we are brought up in a religious family, to what is called the will of God. But this divine will, as it is presented to us, is itself dubiously domineering. Certainly the Jewish God, as He confronted us in the Old Testament in childhood, seemed a forbidding mixture of the barbaric, the judicial, and, in His blander moments, the paternal. Even the Man-God of Christianity, who had surrendered his own will on the Cross of Calvary to redeem the sins of mankind, was exultantly hymned as 'going forth to war' and luridly pictured in the Apocalypse, with suffering features erased and a sharp two-edged sword proceeding from his mouth, as he went forth to tread the wine-press of Almighty God.

In fact, though our self-will may be disciplined by the religion or morality we are taught as children or at school, it is only tempered on the surface. At a deeper level it persists unchanged, as it did, if we observed them at all closely, in most of our teachers and disciplinarians. Indeed it has to persist until we have discovered a better will to live by.

This discovery and the radical transformation which it brings have been the professed goal of all the higher religions. But it has been left to those artists of the spiritual life, the saints and mystics, to pursue it wholeheartedly and to accept the price which must be paid for it. Organized religion has acknowledged their exceptional virtue, but it has generally regarded any tendency to follow their example with some suspicion.

This is understandable, since pseudo-mysticism is much more demoralizing than an orderly, if self-centred, morality. The ego defends iteslf behind a morality against the danger of regression into the formless abyss from which it has emerged and which it fears. For the light of consciousness, in the early phases of its un-folding, as the myths reveal, is at the mercy of the maternal dark-ness which envelops it. The ego is the first partial and transitional form which consciousness assumes as it struggles to break from the womb of primordial night and to challenge the negative power of the Great Mother.

This stage in the evolution of consciousness, reflected historically in the transition from a Matriarchal to a Patriarchal age, is the one upon which modern psychology has particularly concentrated its attention. For it is re-enacted in the struggle of every adoles-cent to cease to be dominated by his instincts by consciously con-fronting them. In this he slays the ancient dragon anew and re-leases the captive maiden, his soul, from the blind grip of primor-dial nature.

The masculine ego has thus to free itself from the unconscious depths of the feminine before the sun of creative consciousness can begin to shine in the human soul, redeeming the ancient dark-ness in that marriage of the above and below, in which the mascu-line and feminine principles meet as equals and so beget the divine child, the enlightened consciousness, in which wisdom and love unite.

For imaginative understanding is the child of eros as well as of logos. It is both lunar and solar, both psychic and spiritual. Though it originates in the ideal realm, consciousness would be barren, were it not everlastingly nourished in the bosom of the great Mother, whose soul is pregnant with wisdom as her body is the vessel of life.

But Her reality, as divine Sophia, has to be released from the dark womb of blind instinct. And the ego, in separating the light from the darkness and maintaining the conflict of the opposites through which a discriminating self-consciousness grows, serves this purpose. By deepening the rift between the conscious and un-conscious, it eventually compels a recognition that the rift can and must be healed.

It is with this later stage that I am concerned throughout this book, as were the masters whose teaching I shall study. I had better, therefore, state emphatically at the beginning that to point beyond the ego is not to deny its necessity as the knot which Nature first ties and tightens to ensure the growth of a specifically human consciousness. It is only to insist that this knot needs to be untied as we develop spiritually.

Pseudo-mysticism, in which must be included much so-called nature-mysticism, may seem to loosen the knot by temporarily inflating or deflating the ego. But ecstasy is not re-birth and the normal bounds of consciousness may dissolve in ineffable sensations without enlightenment ensuing, as drugs and mania prove.

Religions, therefore, which profess to initiate their followers into the secrets of a true re-birth, are right to reject pseudo-mysticism and even to be wary of the utterances of their own enthusiasts.

Nevertheless the lack of appreciation which priestcraft has generally shown for spiritual adventure beyond its dogmatic confines has, to some extent, one suspects, been due to a fear lest those who entered into a direct relationship with the creative mystery might cease to need the services of professional mediators. A religious organization on its worldly side can hardly escape being tainted by some interested motive. And since union with reality involves a total abandonment of self-interest, however elevated its professed purpose, it is not surprising if priesthoods have deprecated too ardent a pursuit of it.

Those of us who reject professional or official compromise with truth are just as subject to impulses of self-interest. But we are, perhaps, more on guard against making them respectable. We know, too, that a merely discreet control of them, 'competition regulated by ethical restraint,' as Ananda Coomaraswamy has called it, is not enough; that our own lives and the life of the society to which we belong will continue to be riven by conflict, hidden and apparent, until not only crude selfishness but 'enlightened self-interest,' a contradiction in terms, are outgrown.

Admittedly little of human existence as we know it would survive if ordinary self-seeking could be forthwith replaced by utterly mindful acts of love. But indiscriminate miracles do not occur. If they did, the tense spring of life for the majority of mankind would snap and the whole structure of society collapse. In countless individual lives the same would happen, as, indeed, it has happened when some aspirant or some disillusioned worldling has thought to cast out Satan before he has learnt to reintegrate the power which Satan perverts.

But obviously there is no danger of any such premature release of mankind at large into the freedom of the Sons of God, though there is a real danger of catastrophic collapse into chaos for the opposite reason. The creative and destructive forces in human life are more than ever precariously balanced. Man has grown slowly out of his animal origins. Slowly he climbs the ladder of evolution which at a certain point becomes a ladder of involution, a turning inward upon himself to discover consciously what he is and in the finding of that to become a new being, freed from the compulsions, but not the empowering, of ancient instinct. Slowly does self-seeking change into Self-seeking as the blind life-impulse in his blood meets and acknowledges the guidance of a Light-impulse. The Consciousness, which creates and informs the universe, call It what we will, has begun to awaken him to a knowledge of Itself.

Yet the first awakening to such Consciousness brings 'not peace but a sword.' For the force which impelled and still impels his physical being through its roots in earthly life seems, as he first wakes to self-awareness, opposed to the knowledge which descends into him from a supra-physical realm. Essentially instinct and intelligence are not in conflict. They are the channels through which two currents meet in man, one springing up from a dark abyss, the other descending from a heaven of light. Together they form the river within which his vital and spiritual development flows. And slowly, how slowly, through recurrent changes in its course, though never, in the long view, of its destined direction, through placid reaches, rapids, pools of conservation, and convulsive whirlpools, the rays of that heavenly Sun, which is Consciousness Itself, pentetrate the muddied waters, as increasingly they run clear and clean.

By a change of metaphor the Light, informing the darkness, may be pictured as a vital fire which devours everything that is less alive than Itself, everything which tends to relapse into inertness and to harden into what we mistakenly call dead matter.

This life-fire is what Boehme called the 'flaming love-fire' which rejoices to take possession of 'something that is standing still and at rest . . . even as the sun doth in the visible world.' As a fire it consumes to recreate in the eternal rhythm of death and life, by which continual death is the condition of continuing life. On the level of insensate life, matter is completely and, from a self-concious view-point, abysmally obedient to this primal law. But man, as he develops, appropriates the fire to serve and to feed his own desires. Yet its purpose remains the same. It continues to devour everything which disturbs the bridal harmony of life and death.

'Thou shalt feel it,' says the Master to his disciple in Boehme's dialogue,[1] 'in the burning up thyself, and swiftly devouring all egoity,
or that which thou callest I and Me, as standing in a separate root,
and divided from the Deity, the fountain of thy being.'

In this burning up of that in us, which asserts itself against the
unity of the whole, the fire in the dark depths of sub-conscious
being is gradually transmitted into the half-light of self-consciousness. In primitive animal man the fire burns primarily in the
opaque or semi-opaque elements of earth and water, in the realm
of physical instinct and of vital energy and feeling. But as conscious intelligence awakes in man, it burns increasingly, also, in
the element of air, an element which, though often clouded by the
fumes and mists rising from the lower being, is transparent to the
light. And the more the fire consumes the ignorance of the ego as
it manifests in elementary desire and blind passion, the clearer
grows the air in which his intelligence breathes and grows. The
stronger, too, shines the divine Sun in the heaven of his awareness,
making him conscious, not only of the perversity of his ego, but
of an undivided Being or Selfhood, in Which he can find That
which he veritably is.

These are but metaphors through which to image the mystery
of man's ascent from division to wholeness, from bondage to freedom. Yet, as symbols, they correspond on all levels of life with
cosmic law. That is why the worship and invocation of Fire and
its association with a sacrificial ritual is the most ancient in the
world.

One of the great hymns to 'Agni' in the *Rig-Veda*, the oldest
invocations of the sacred Fire which have come down to us, begins
with the verse,

> *O Fire, thou art born with thy lights,*
> *flaming out on us in thy effulgence; thou art born*
> *from the waters and around the stone, thou art born*
> *from the forest and born from the plants of the earth*
> *Pure art thou in thy birth, O Master of man and his race!*

In another we read,

> *Thee, O Fire, ever with one passion the gods have sent in-*
> *wards, the divine Traveller (or Worker); with the will they*

[1] *Of the Supersensual Life* by Jacob Boehme.

*sent thee in; O master of sacrifice, they brought to birth the
immortal in mortals, the divine who brings in the divinity, the
conscious thinker, they brought to birth the universal who
brings in the divinity, the conscious thinker.*

In the first of these two verses the creative Fire is conceived as
the elemental flame of life, burning in the veins of nature and of
man as a natural being; in the second as the genius of Truth, informing the inner man, awakening in him the divine power of
conscious thought and a realization of his immortal essence. But
it is the same Fire which burns in the instinctive love of the flesh
and the intuitive love of the mind, in the obscure depths of primal
nature as on the lucid heights of pure intelligence.

The poet-seers of the *Rig-Veda* worshipped the divine Fire
under these two aspects, as the Gods 'Agni' and 'Indra.' 'Agni,'
for them, represented in the words of Sri Aurobindo, from whose
rendering of these Hymns I have quoted, 'the pole of Force instinct with knowledge that sends the current upward from earth
to heaven; "Indra" the other pole of Light, instinct with force,
which descends from heaven to earth.'

Man is thus polarized by the divine Fire from above and below,
and his physical, vital, and mental being is the womb in which his
essential godhead grows. It grows by a process of refinement of
the grosser elements, by which they become more and more transparent to the light of intelligence and spiritual insight. We have a
simple example of this process to hand each time that we kindle
a fire, as the poet Kabir has reminded us. At first we cannot see
the fire for the smoke. Then smoke and fire intermingle, and
eventually we cannot see the smoke for the fire. It only remains
by some process of concentration to refine the fire into light. For
always fire is a manifestation of light. We distinguish it from light
when its function is to destroy what is contrary to itself. But when
it is free to express its essential nature in creation, it irradiates
the world and the souls who can receive it purely and lovingly.

Hence the age-old symbolism of the sacrificial flame burning,
not merely in some priestly ritual, but on the altar of the soul.
The outer, visible sacrifice was but an emblem of and occasion
for an inner self-offering. Yet the Gods who were invoked in the
Vedic hymns were 'living realities,' as Sri Aurobindo points out,

protagonists in the cosmic struggle in which the human soul, as microcosm, was engaged, a struggle between destructive and creative powers, the Demons and the Gods.

In the blind depths of the physical universe the struggle has not entered upon its crucial phase. There the demonic and the divine are fused. The fire of sacrifice never falters, by which the unity of life and death is preserved. But self-conscious man fights against death and darkness for his own separate life and in so doing falls a prey to demonic or divisive powers and loses the support of the Gods. He fails to maintain on the higher level of intelligence the essential sacrifice which instinctive life accepts. Then the flame languishes on the altar of his soul, but it burns destructively in his body and his mind and in the wilful impulses which draw their perverted power from the immortal fire which is insufficiently sanctified in the sacrifice.

Truly, as Krishna declares in the *Bhagavad-Gita*, 'This world is not for him who offers no sacrifice' nor any other world that we can conceive. Of that sacrifice the Cross is the ancient symbol and one which long ante-dated the exclusive appropriation of it by Christianity to its own myth and historical Saviour. On the cross of sacrifice, of a true self-offering in mind and body, the divine polarity of the fire and the light, of 'Agni' and 'Indra,' is ultimately re-established.

Thereby the individual regains his true alignment on the Tree of Life, both vertically and horizontally, his true uprightness between the heights and the depths in the realm of being, and his true relation, both of freedom and dependence, to the world of time and becoming.

In his interpretation of the hidden meaning of the hymns of the *Rig-Veda*, Sri Aurobindo has described more figuratively what this restoration involves.

> *We have to invoke the Gods*, he writes, *by the inner sacrifice, and by the word call them into us—that is the specific power of the Mantra,[1]—to offer to them the gifts of the sacrifice and by that giving secure their gifts, so that by this process we may build the way of our ascent to the goal. . . . We give what we are and what we have in order that the riches of the divine Truth and Light may descend into our life and become the ele-*

[1] Mantra = incantation or ritual.

ments of our inner birth into the Truth—a right thinking, a right understanding, a right action must develop in us, which is the thinking impulsion and action of that higher Truth, and by this we must build up ourselves in that Truth. Our sacrifice is a journey, a pilgrimage and a battle—a travel towards the Gods and we also make that journey with Agni, the inner Flame, as our path-finder and leader. Our human things are raised up by the mystic Fire into the immortal being, into the Great Heaven, and the things divine come down into us.[1]

Viewed from a less celestial angle, human life is a vale both of 'soul-making,' in Keats's phrase, and of spirit-finding. For the soul grows as it awakens more and more to the presence of spirit in its depths and thereby to awareness of its own essential nature. The myth of Eros and Psyche, so beautifully retold by Apuleius, images this awakening by which primordial nature becomes conscious in man as an individual soul.

For Psyche, in breaking the bondage of darkness imposed on her by Aphrodite, the devouring Mother and Mistress of all that is born and lusts and dies, and in claiming her right to see and to suffer, initiates a new order of relationship in which spirit and soul meet as contraries and through the stresses of their encounter may accomplish at last that marriage of the opposites, in which the flame feeds the light and the light irradiates the flame, and the mystery of creative love, that unites life and understanding, is fulfilled between them.

[1] *Hymns to the Mystic Fire* by Sri Aurobindo.

CHAPTER TWO

Two Birds on one Tree

I

MOST PEOPLE at present participate in the sacrifice unconsciously or semi-consciously. It is the flame of 'Agni' rather than
the light of 'Indra' which burns on the altar of their souls. The
Light which descends from heaven to earth is never, indeed, absent from its counterpart in the subconscious depths. But, in the
evolution of human consciousness, man is for long more strongly
'earthed' than 'heavened,' a creature of life rather than a creator
and distributor of light, though always he is rooted in both kingdoms. 'Earth' and 'heaven' are symbols of contrary modes of experience, but they are, also, the poles between which all life is
magnetized in varying degrees of material grossness and fineness, of
ignorance and awareness.

As, with awaking intelligence, we begin to be conscious of ourselves and of the nature of the world in which we move, we seem
to divide inwardly into two beings, one of whom is able to observe with detachment what the other does, how he feels and the
impulses to which he yields. This power of self-scrutiny varies
very much in different people. Some possess it hardly at all. In
some it exists as a moral directive and principle of control. Others
are reduced by it to indecision and worse. These two beings, the
Mundaka Upanishad, quoting a stanza from the *Rig-Veda*, describes as 'two birds, close friends, who dwell on the same tree.'
One eats the fruit of the tree, the other looks on in silence. The
first is the human self, who, though active, is bewildered and sad.
'But when he sees that other, his Lord and beloved, his sorrow
passes away.'

Ultimately this is so. But it is long before the distracted eater of
the fruit of the tree of life knows his other Self to be his close
friend. More often, indeed, he acts towards him as an enemy.
There is a passage in the *Maitri Upanishad* which employs a dif-

28

ferent imagery to suggest how the soul, which is like 'the drop of water on the lotus leaf,' is overcome by Nature's moods and so is confused and does not see 'the blessed Lord, the causer of action, who stands within oneself. Borne along and defiled by the flux of life, unsteady, wavering, bewildered, full of desire, distracted, it falls into a state of self-conceit. In thinking "This is I" and "That is mine," he binds himself with his self, as does a bird with a snare.'

In each of us, the Masters teach, a fully conscious and undeluded being waits to be known. In that realization we shall be reconciled with ourselves and also with life. We shall no longer be subject to blind alternations of attraction and repulsion as we grasp at the fruit of life. For we shall contemplate life truly and lovingly in the act of living it.

But in the early stages of our education through experience the eternal onlooker or, more accurately, 'inlooker,' in each of us is not consciously recognized as the beloved Lord of our being, since in the first phases of self-consciousness he manifests as little more than a critical overtone of the personality which seeks to possess and enjoy, an overtone which sounds clearly enough in times of satiety and frustration, when the enjoyer is thrown back upon the emptiness of himself and of his quest, and glimpses the anguish beneath the habitual mask of life.

It is then that we begin to be spectators of our compulsive activities, to examine them anxiously, to question their worth or their wisdom and even to repudiate them. Though we are far from realizing that the whole of life which is lived possessively and so under continual tension is a source of pain, our capacity to view life and ourselves with detachment begins to grow. The spectator in us begins to exist in his own right and not merely as a mental reaction to the follies and excesses of feeling. In the language of the mythological archetypes, we have begun to master the 'Terrible Mother,' or the primeval 'Dragon.'

Yet we have hardly begun to be truly Self-conscious. Our awareness is still so undeveloped and precarious, so involved, too, in the pleasure-pain process of egotistic living, that even when we cultivate and seem to have attained mental objectivity, our vision of things is still conditioned and coloured by unconscious impulse and subjective preference.

This dualistic condition of the self is characteristic of all of us, when we first awaken from the sleep of instinct. Whether in the

moralist who has learnt in some measure to control his more reck-
less impulses, but whose self-willed balance is always liable to
be upset by some unusual trial or temptation that releases hidden
forces from the deeper levels of his personality, or in the sensualist
who swings between indulgence and abstinence or who succeeds
apparently in compromising between them, there is a rift in the
being.

The greater Selfhood, 'the Lord and the beloved,' in whom
alone the rift can be healed, is still to be known. At best He is
conceived as an ideal, external to the self and set apart from the
actual, or as a divine ruler whose commands have, with continual
effort and watchfulness, to be imposed on a rebel will by a faulty
servant who strives to execute his orders.

Clearly then, an ethical discipline is for long necessary to maintain some sort of balance between the dark and the light sides of
our nature and between our own desires and the desires of others.
This is as far as most of us get on the path of development. But
for a few it is not enough. For them, either because the balance
breaks down or because they divine a truer kind of life beyond
it, merely to control selfish impulse is to perpetuate a feud, which
arrests the creative purpose of life at the very point in human
evolution at which further advance is essential.

The men of old clearly defined the various stages through
which human life, fully lived, should pass. The successive stages,
for example, which they laid down, of the student, of the householder, and of the *sannyasin* who renounced worldly property
and position and devoted himself entirely to the spiritual life, did
equal justice to man's physical, mental, and spiritual faculties and
to what he owed both to earth and heaven. Something of the
same recognition is implicit in the suggestion of a modern psychologist that we may divide human life into three main phases, 'a
phase of settling in, a phase of unfolding, and a phase of transformation.' But somewhere within these three phases lies a crucial
change of direction, a change which divides what Ananda Coomaraswamy has called 'the Pursuit' from 'the Return.'

There is a tidal rhythm in the spiritual life, as in the physical
world. But the turn of the tide in the life of the soul,

> *When that which drew from out the boundless deep*
> *Turns again home,*

though it involve a death, is not away from life, but towards its heart, is, in fact, an affirmation of life on a new, organic level. It is the gathering up of life into light.

The outflowing life of self-assertion can seem, indeed, to be immensely affirmative. But from the standpoint of the soul which has reached this crucial turning-point, its affirmations are seen to be negations of an altogether deeper and more comprehensive order of being. Caught up in the flux of conditioned existence, man's actual state is one of continual restlessness and agitation from which he cannot escape so long as he identifies himself with the blind thirst of phenomenal life to renew itself.

Yet the tide of life which flows out of primal depths and rises and falls in the veins of man is as necessary a part of the order of creation as the primordial sun which irradiates his consciousness when he has learnt how to receive it. In an ancient Gnostic fragment Hermes is bidden to understand the Light as Life and so make friends with it. Indeed the vision of the abyss from which life eternally springs, of hell with its devouring jaws, would be overwhelming if there were no vision, however clouded or remote, of a lucid heaven to counterbalance it, that vision of Hermes in which he sees 'the cosmos in its finished beauty, when all things in it are full of Light and nowhere is there Fire.'

Of the other vision, the vision of the abyss, Mr. Evola writes finely,[1]

> *There are some who, at certain moments, are able to become detached from themselves, get beneath the surface, down into the dark depths of the force which rules their body, and where this force loses name and identity. They have the sensation of this force expanding and including 'I' and 'not I,' pervading all nature, substantiating time, supporting myriads of beings as if they were drunk or hallucinated, re-establishing itself in a thousand forms, irresistible, untamed, inexhaustible, ceaseless, limitless, burning with eternal insufficiency and hunger.*

This is the elemental force which Melville imaged in his great white whale, and which moves with dreadful majesty through primitive myth and drama. And truly he who has looked into the deathly face of life, if only for a moment, knows that his little

[1] In *The Doctrine of Awakening* by J. Evola, from which this is a quotation.

self-assertive ego is as impermanent and unsubstantial as a fleck of foam on the heaving surface of the sea.

Providentially few have this experience until they are ready for it or the necessary world of self-assertion which floats, in constant danger, over these depths, would founder in them. But this vision or something like it happens to those who have come to the turning-point, to the change of the tide, of which I have spoken, when a knowledge of what we are and are not begins to dawn and we no longer ignorantly identify ourselves with the blind process of living in the body which we delusively believe to be under our control. Then and only then we begin to seek within for a real freedom, which, something tells us, we have abdicated, and for a Principle of being, which, like the force of the abyss, is 'not I,' but which, instead of sucking us down into depths of hungry insufficiency gathers us up into itself and invests us with its own gift of comprehensive awareness.

Yet in this inward turning we are not meant to deny our physical senses or the outer world, but only our attachment to them, and to restrain our out-going impulses only in the degree necessary to establish us in that inward reality from which we can act outwardly with the freedom of a conscious consent.

Another symbolism which has often been used to describe this crucial change of direction in a human life can be equally misconceived. The terms of this symbolism are 'descent' and 'ascent.' The divine spirit is pictured by the seers of old as descending into the primal matter which It has emanated as the necessary medium for Its creative and informing activity. And man, in his spiritual essence, is pictured as making the same descent through planes of increasingly denser matter, until he reaches the densest of them and is born in a physical body, 'not in entire forgetfulness' of the celestial mansion from which he comes, but enveloped in the darkness of ignorance. Nor is he only enveloped, but through some mysterious 'fall' or 'fault,' as some say, he identifies himself with this ignorance, so that the Light can only reach him obscurely or in a perverted way.

In the terms of this symbolism man's salvation lies in a continual ascent out of this ignorance, and from the delusion that his darkened will and personality are free to shape his destiny, into the Light from which he came. Here again the error which is so often associated by aspiring people with this symbolism is in supposing that ascent is exclusive of descent and darkness at war with light, not relatively through man's error or, at a certain stage, to further his evolution, but absolutely. In the logic of dualistic thought this is so. But in creative experience a true ascent necessarily involves at the same time a true descent. Each is an exact measure of the other. We are not at one with heaven until we are also perfectly reconciled to hell, and the ancient war between them in our souls and the soul of man is over.

When we awake to the higher worlds of consciousness, the Light breaks also in those veiled realms of the unconscious. As we soar, we need also to sink. If we fail to do so, we become unbalanced or even lose our reason in an excess of light that is not sufficiently grounded in the darkness. For when the balance between the two poles is not maintained, the deeds of mental elation can be as destructive as those of brute stupidity.

The soul must be prepared, as a bride for her bridegroom, to receive the light of the numinous, if she is not to be injured or consumed by it. The various journeys and testings of myth and legend image the initiations by which the soul fits herself to conceive and bear the divine child, the spiritual consciousness. For to appropriate the light selfishly may be more fatal to ourselves and others than to be blindly possessed by the power of the darkness. Neither consciousness nor life are our own. Each is a mode of the divine. By accepting our lowliness as creatures we are at once saved from being lost in the emptiness of the Godhead and raised up to share in the divine activity of a creator who lives in His creation.

The darkness, to which we fearlessly commit ourselves, is not evil. When we accept it in ourselves and allow what is within us to become calm and clear and fathomless, we find that what we feared as self-loss is the gateway to a life beyond the lure of gain or the threat of loss. By rejecting or recoiling from the darkness through which the light must shine, we had perverted and falsely empowered it and, by tearing being apart from non-being, had fallen into a pit of our own making.

It is to a realization of this truth, however faint, that we begin to awaken, when we reach the crucial turning-point in our lives, from which there follows a change of tide in the deep current of our being. Some are even at birth innately nearer to this awakening than others are at death, and not, as might be suggested, through a mere lack of physical vitality. Rather, these, it may be surmised, are older souls who, in ways of which we have no certain knowledge, have already assimilated many of the lessons so painfully learnt in the self-assertive cycle of human experience. Or they may owe their knowledge to their spiritual ancestry. Unlike younger souls, still avid for the pleasures and pains of sense-experience, such older souls, even when they yield to the allure of life, are haunted by a knowledge of its illusoriness. At present this kind of disillusion compels comparatively few to a life-long effort of transformation. But in the coming cycle their number is likely to grow, since the threat of self-destruction which hangs over every individual who has become conscious of the conflict in himself and fails to resolve it, hangs now over the whole of mankind.

What in past cycles has been an exceptional vocation has become a task to which every man and woman of understanding must try to contribute. To be aware of the necessity of this task and to commit oneself to it gives new meaning to the whole of life.

Even when I was a young man, I was obscurely aware that something of this kind was required. Doubtless a leading of this kind springs from deep roots in our spiritual history. We are born with it, as an artist is born with the need to recreate the world in the form of his vision or to evoke the harmonies of another dimension in his music. We come into this world, bearing in our souls the impress of past experience, whether exclusively our own or received from those who have preceded us on our Ray of spiritual descent to this earth. Whatever the pattern of this hidden background may be, it determines the situation into which we are born here and within which we live our human lives.

Because this situation is largely hidden from us as our lives begin to unfold, we react to it in all sorts of faulty ways. But later, when we are able to survey our journey and have become all too familiar with the kind of person we are and the problems we have repeatedly had to face, we discover a surprising consistency in what had seemed, often enough, tragic mischance.

The great Masters, who appear in different ages and civilizations to point the way, are born on this earth with an awareness of being which transcends the ordinary human condition. Their truth and example reinforce the truth within ourselves and strengthen and direct us in our quest. But the quest must be our own. A great teacher can only quicken in us a Light which waits the moment when we will allow it to shine in all its purity. That moment of inward revelation, which is also one of release from the false tensions of the divided human state, is the goal of the quest.

But it is unlikely to be sought with a sincere persistence or the prizes of the world foregone, until that 'Inlooker' in ourselves, of whom I have spoken, has begun to be more than a detached observer of the engrossed ego as it pursues, in a genial, sullen or extravagant manner, its own delusive interests.

This 'Inlooker' has always been more than a detached observer. For what we call our 'conscience' is, at least partially, a reflection of His pure consciousness. But our conscience is seldom, if ever, untainted by self-interest, because it is, in some degree, attached to the ego, if as its higher principle. Indeed with Freud, we might call conscience the voice of the Super-ego, though, with a characteristic bias, he derived it almost exclusively from the parental or other influences which inserted themselves into the growing psyche.

In the view of the Eastern teachers the higher ego acts as a bridge between the self, still attached to the realm of instinct, and the creative Selfhood which will eventually supersede it. But, being a bridge, influences traverse it from both ends or, if we visualize it as a ladder, from below as well as from above. That is why men are so often driven by their 'conscience' to do terrible or misguided things. Nevertheless 'conscience,' or what we define more superficially as our sense of what is right, reflects, however faultily, the idea of unity.

It is through the pain of conflict that we learn more and more to detach ourselves from blind enjoyment and the spectator in us begins to manifest as an organ of pure reason or intuition. This faculty of direct perception is what the Indian scriptures call the *Buddhi*. It is beyond self-interest or compulsive attachment to external things, being transparent to a Light which informs it from within. This Light, no longer hidden within the flame or obscured by the smoke of an ego which endlessly burns in the flame, begins to shine clear in a heart pure and simple enough to receive the truth and an intelligence rendered wise by love.

This is the beginning of that experience of release (*Moksha*, the Hindus call it) which is the aim of *Yoga*, an experience attained at

present in all its fullness only by a few, but revealing its transforming possibilities long before it takes possession of the whole
nature. For something of any ultimate attainment shows itself in
the first step we sincerely take towards it. In the five-finger exercise, rightly played, there is a faint intimation of the piano con-
certo.

I have in my own journey through life travelled far enough to
verify some at least of the preliminary phases in the transformation
of an ego-centric person into a unified being. And few, looking
back, can fail to be impressed by the way in which the circumstances of their lives, many of which, particularly in their early
years, were quite out of their control and, outwardly, not of their
choosing, are seen later to have been in character, typical of and
perhaps necessary to the kind of person, whom, all unknown,
they were meant to be or at least to struggle to be.

Significantly my birthday is in June, when the sun is moving
through the constellation of Gemini. For this third division of
the Zodiac, with its symbol of the two Pillars through which
the soul on its journey must pass, is supposed to represent that
splitting of man's nature into two parts, by which he first became
mentally self-conscious in the cycle of time when, through the
precession of the vernal equinox, the sun was in this Sign in its
periodic circuit of the Zodiac.

Gemini is pictured as 'The Twins,' Castor and Pollux, and is
associated in ancient records with a story of two brothers who
built the first city. Though opposed to each other they work together, as the higher and lower self, often in conflict, yet building
slowly and painfully stone by stone, until towards the end of
their labour they combine in harmony to transform the city of
their building into a Holy City, the city of spirit, soul, and body
made one.

In this myth I recognize a profound truth of my nature, as of
all human nature, at a certain stage in its growth. And it may help
to explain why I should have been absorbed throughout my life
and in my writings with this dual condition of man's being.

The outer pattern of my life conformed in this closely with the
inner. Certainly the loss of my mother, a few days after I was
born, which broke my father's heart and enveloped my childhood
and boyhood in an atmosphere of sorrow and strain, was exactly
calculated to bring out an inherent division in my nature. In such

circumstances what should, ideally, be a gradual organic adjustment between instinctive needs and spiritual aspirations, is liable to become a painful conflict.

There is, of course, nothing exceptional about such a struggle. It is the normal one for all of us when we reach a certain stage of development as self-conscious beings. I differed only from the majority in having been made particularly conscious of it through what was denied to me in my upbringing and my human relations. This it was which made me precociously attentive to that bird on the tree of my life, the silent 'Onlooker' or 'In-looker,' in whose serene awareness all conflicts are resolved and the wounds that time and circumstance inflict are healed.

CHAPTER THREE

Sin and Judgment

I

I HAVE touched on my personal background, because it will help to explain why the vision and thought of India appealed to me so strongly, not merely as an object of intellectual study, but as a rope thrown to a drowning man, or, at least, as a door through which I could find peace of mind and, even more, peace of heart. But before we begin to ponder the wisdom of Vedanta, something more needs to be said about my Christian affiliations, if only to explain why I had to turn elsewhere for help.

As I have said, the Christianity in which I had been reared as a clergyman's son never made a comparable appeal, nor could I ever accept the claim that Jesus was the only real mediator between God and man, who broke into history at a certain point in time and absolutely transformed the human situation. The profound inner meaning of the Christian mystery, the eternal descent of the Godhead into the realm of limitation, and the crucifixion of the divine on the Cosmic Cross is not singular to Christianity and, as such, is universally acceptable. For many this mystery lives most vividly and powerfully in the person and the life-story of Jesus. And so inevitably and rightly they choose him as their Master.

A true Master, according to the Eastern tradition and practice, embodies the truth for the disciple and transmits it directly, as a lit candle can light another. He represents the reality which is present, but as yet imperfectly released, in the disciple, and his purpose is to help the disciple to realize, in the Indian phrase, the eternal Guru or Teacher in himself. When he has succeeded in doing this, the need of external Master and mediator is over. In short, the aim of the Master is to prove himself superfluous, since what he essentially is, the disciple is too.

Among Jesus's sayings are a number which suggest that he, too, regarded this as his vocation, such sayings as that his disciples would do greater miracles than he. As a historical individual Jesus was a relative being and as such could not limit the expression of absolute truth to himself. As the Divine Word, made flesh, he could declare 'I am the Way.' But this eternal Way passed through him and extended beyond him. It was not exclusive to him.

One, too, who said, 'Why callest thou me good? There is none good but one, that is God,' can hardly have encouraged the kind of exclusive personal attachment to himself which is so prominent in Christian devotion except as something which must eventually be surpassed.

I do not wish to be misunderstood in this. The Godhead speaking through Krishna in the *Bhagavad-Gita*, invites an equally absolute love and faith as a condition of ultimate union. 'Of all men,' says Krishna, 'I deem him who loves Me in faith, with his inward Self dwelling in Me, to be My very own.' It is still commonly believed in India that liberation depends on the grace of the Guru, as in a true sense, too often misconceived with fatal consequences in doting subservience, it does. But, in principle at least, the Eastern genius has succeeded better than devotional Christianity in blending without prejudice in the enlightened teacher the human and the divine.

For though Krishna speaks with a human voice, the love He invites is something that transcends all emotional or intellectual preference. It is a surrender of the whole being to a Light which is the divine birthright of every human soul. This was the Light which such great Christian mystics as Meister Eckhardt saw in Jesus and which saved them from wrongly deifying the man. But too often Christian zealots, while stressing his humanity and claiming that in all respects, save that he was without sin and was born of a virgin, he was a man like other men, have exalted him into a God, to whom every knee must bow in exclusive devotion, and without whose intercession at the judgment-seat of the Creator, mankind would be irretrievably damned.

I cannot reconcile such a belief, except in an esoteric and symbolic sense which would destroy its exclusive claim, either with the teacher and sufferer of the Gospels, with the wisdom and insight of the men of old, or with what we know of the divinely impersonal laws of the cosmos. The Redemption, M. Schuon has written,[1]

---

[1] In *The Transcendent Unity of Religions* by Frithjof Schuon.

is an eternal act which cannot be situated either in time or space, and the sacrifice of Christ is a particular manifestation or realization of it on the human plane; men were able to benefit from the Redemption as well before the coming of Jesus Christ as after it, and outside the visible Church as well as within it. If Christ had been the only manifestation of the Word, supposing such a uniqueness of manifestation to be possible, the effect of his birth would have been the instantaneous reduction of the universe to ashes.

With this I cannot but agree.

A good deal of the exclusiveness embedded in Christianity derives from the Old Testament. For Christianity took over the exclusive Judaistic claim and it rooted itself in the Jewish scriptures, in which 'the fear of the Lord' of a sin-haunted people weighed heavily upon their sense of the divine omnipresence and overshadowed the joy and wonder in which wisdom grows most happily. Above all Christianity absorbed into its Mystery the Judaistic blood-sacrifice.

Such a sacrifice is to be found in most primitive religions. But in the *Vedas* the juice of the Soma plant was drunk as the life-essence of the sacramental ritual, which symbolized, not some cruel and penal sacrifice, but a joyous free-will offering to Gods who were more trusted than feared and who, as Surya, the Sun God, for example, or Varuna, the god of the wide sky, participated with their worshippers in the love-feast of life. In Christianity, however, the Judaic blood-sacrifice, exacted by God in atonement for sin, reappears as the Eucharistic feast, in which the body and blood of the Saviour are consumed, not only symbolically, but also, through the mystical faith of the communicant, in actual substance.

I recognize the deep meaning of this rite, but for me the emphasis laid upon body and blood has always seemed disproportionate and to belong to a time when man was much more engrossed in the physical than many of us are to-day. Certainly man's body needs to be redeemed as well as his mind and soul. That his blood is tainted is proved by the fact of disease. But his physical body is only the most external of his spiritual sheaths and of itself neither good nor evil. All such forms are subject to the change which we call death. Hence the necessity, as the

Eastern teachers have always insisted, for a man to cease to attach himself to his body in any of its forms, since by so doing he disturbs its unconscious harmony and forgets what he really is.

The redemption of body and blood, as of heart and mind, will inevitably ensue when he has ceased to be enthralled by any of the forms in which, as a spiritual being, he is clothed. Only then will he have truly awoken from that sleep of nature with its delusive dreams and fearful nightmares into which he sank when he was born in the flesh. For, as the *Bhagavad-Gita* says, 'in what is night to the ignorant the wise man is awake (e.g. in the *Atman*, the hidden sun of his being); what is bright day to the ignorant (e.g. *samsara*, the life of conflict and sensation) is night to the true seer.'

For me, at least, myths and rituals of sacrifice which lay such realistic stress upon the flesh bind those who cling to them to a primitive past which it is necessary to outgrow.

The strong primitive roots of Judaism and Christianity, their passionately personal and existential emphasis, have enabled them to appeal particularly to those still deeply immeshed in the physical and sensory world. Each of the three Semitic faiths (for it is true, also, of Islam) is deeply earthed. This gives them a strength on one level of life which Oriental metaphysic may seem to lack. But they are by comparison inexperienced on the more interior planes where Hinduism and Buddhism are subtly informed. It also ties Christianity for good and ill, both ethically and emotionally, far more closely to the grosser material plane. The age-long conflict in Christian thought between the supernatural and the natural worlds, valid only on an individualistic level, and the insistent stress upon sin and judgment indicate clearly how tenacious that tie is.

No such hostility to the world of instinct shadows the Eastern mind; no guarded frontiers frown between the divine, human, animal, and vegetable kingdoms. All are seen to be interdependent. The need to awaken from the illusion which the external world casts over us from birth, the need to be weaned from a blind craving for life if we are truly to live, is indeed a basic tenet of Eastern wisdom of all schools.

But for the East the disability to be outgrown, devotedly and disinterestedly, is ignorance. For Christianity the burden to be cast off, in an agony of repentance, is sin. There is truth in both conceptions; for each is an expression, at a different level, of the same truth. But while real enlightenment wholly transforms, crystallizing in a man his essence and releasing light through him into existence, the salvation which the Christian claims to have found through belief in and dependence on his Saviour, seldom in fact seems to open fully the eyes of the mind.

When I think, for example, of the clergymen of different persuasions whom I have met or listened to or observed, almost all of them were kindly, upright men, many were devoted pastors, some were pious, a few were learned, but how seldom did one see in their faces that unmistakable inward light, which characterizes the man of creative vision and awareness. May not this be due, to some extent, to the shadow that the doctrine of original sin and redemption through a personal Saviour has cast over their minds, as over most modern books of Protestant theology? Indeed exoteric Christianity, as an expression of the activist West and the professed guardian of the interests and needs of the average man, has spent far more of its energy in stressing the fact of sin than in exploring disinterestedly its nature and ways to outgrow it.

Admittedly the pure Christian doctrine of sin is not thus morally biassed. Sin, in Christian theology, is only secondarily an ugly act or failure to act. Primarily it is a state of deprivation and disunity through loss of vital contact with the Ground or Centre of our being. For the Christian, therefore, salvation from sin is, in principle, the same as the Vedantic release from bondage. But, in practice the moral emphasis has unduly predominated over the imaginative vision, which suggests that the underlying conception is, in some degree, positively one-sided.

Clearly the possibility of altogether ceasing to live separately is beyond the reach of most of us. Yet all true humility is rooted, however unconsciously, in the knowledge that there is no limit to the human emptiness which we may offer and the divine fullness which we may receive. The doctrine of sin and judgment does express, in homely terms with which we are familiar from childhood, a dependence upon something divinely other than our childish selves and a failure to acknowledge that dependence in all we do and are, which is the truth of our condition. There can be few of us who, in the course of our life and particularly in its tragic moments of failure or dereliction, have not cast ourselves upon God's mercy and strength in this way or found an echo in our hearts of the words for which Bach composed one of his grave and noble Choral Preludes, 'O Man thy grievous sin bemoan.'

Yet this very personal and too often sentimental or sensational way of relieving the tension of egotism is surely appropriate only to a comparatively early stage in our spiritual development. Moreover it is often associated with a morbid sense of the heinousness of sin and a dread, equally morbid, of its consequences. The love of the self-conscious sinner is inevitably riddled with fear. Frequent professions of sin tend, too, to perpetuate the condition which we deplore, but which, if we look more deeply into ourselves, we are not prepared to pay the unemotional price of changing. This is evident in the kind of arrogant abasement, for example, which the narrower sort of Christian mistakes for humility and to which the 'converted' intellectual is particularly prone. An authentic humility is quite unobtrusive and totally devoid of self-satisfaction, because it is a spontaneous and habitual expression of a nature that rests in the real.

For the Eastern teachers there was, in the true nature of things, no conflict between the sensory and the spiritual worlds, though they regarded the sense-bound view of the world as an illusion. They may have insufficiently acknowledged the conflict, which the individual has to live through before he can resolve it. But they saw truly how illusory it ultimately proves to be. It was primarily to break this illusion that the science of Yoga was developed. And it embraced all levels of the being, excluding none. The body and mind, the emotions and will, the sexual impulse itself—all were accepted as faculties of experience and communion to be harmonized and ultimately transfigured when the body, as the sensible manifestation of power, is wholly irradiated by a spiritual consciousness.

By contrast the professing sinner, who casts himself on the mercy of a God outside himself, turns his back on his 'shadow.' And this repudiated 'shadow' will continue, like the ghost of Cathie in 'Wuthering Heights,' to beat upon the windows of his soul until it is accepted and forgiven by the God within himself.

Similarly, in the Eastern tradition, what a man regards as his virtues are quite as likely to be bonds which need to be broken as his vices. The aim is not to take sides with virtue, but to awaken from the night of ignorance. Morality, as ordinarily practised, is secondary to this. It is a necessary crutch when we are learning to walk. But it is a fetter when we have truly found our feet. By morality I do not mean, of course, such essential qualities as humility, charity and truthfulness. For these, when pure, loosen the grip of all self-centred virtue and vice.

Equally the aim of classical Yoga was neither to submerge the moral sense in nature's amoral depths nor to fortify it in its self-defensive codes. It was to purify and transform it, like all the other senses, and thus to translate into the values and directives of a discerning love the blind forces of nature, which, on their own level, as in healthy human instinct, serve the creative purpose.

There are necessary correspondences between natural law and spiritual grace, between humility, for example, and gravitation, charity and animal love of kind, though natural law is so crude a reflection of spiritual grace that it may often seem to contradict it and in no sense determines it. All the beauty we divine in creation does not belong to creation itself but comes from the uncreated spirit which informs it. This is equally true of all moral beauty which, in essence, owes nothing to the ethical systems in which men have tried to codify it. The purpose of a true Yoga is to free this essence, this infusion of the divine will, from all that cramps and distorts it.

It is frequently argued, however, by Western theologians and moralists that these men of old evaded or at least failed fully to face the fact of evil, which has weighed so heavily upon the mind and conscience of Western man in the last two thousand years. When we think of a representative man of the Christian era we picture not only a being inspired and often enslaved by his imaginative, intellectual and physical passions, but also a creature patiently enduring the pains of earthly existence, humbled by his close struggle for life with the natural world, persevering through disaster and disappointment, tenacious of his gains, resigned to his losses, labouring doggedly to better, if only to some small degree, his human lot, content to regard any lifting of the judgment of Eden as irrelevant to his day and hour.

This hard apprenticeship to earth, this recognition of the sadness and transience of our mortal day, half enveloped in the folds of night, this dumb acceptance of the pains and limitations of the fallen self, has not, of course, been peculiar to the West. All men, the world over, and particularly the poor and unprivileged, have lived beneath this shadow.

It is the distinction of Christianity to have spoken more intimately for and to these chastened children of earth than any other religion. Christ's saying, 'Come unto me, all ye that labour and are heavy laden and I will give you rest,' has its parallels in the words of other Masters who teach release from the bondage of a self-centred life through an inward change of consciousness. But the peace they promise differs in more than idiom and imagery from rest in the arms of a loving Saviour.

Christianity is predominately a religion of the soul despite the masculine over-emphasis of some of its doctrines. Heaven, we may say, symbolizes the plane of eternal spirit, earth that of evolving soul. These two planes meet in man. But the marriage of spirit and soul cannot be consummated until the soul has truly suffered all that the material realm can teach. Spirit has to be known and lived in the depth and the height. And every soul that truly attains to freedom in union with its spiritual counterpart, and so rests in that Creative centre in which eternity and time are folded within each other, has descended into hell as a condition of ascent to heaven.

More than any other religion, perhaps, Christianity has been faithful to this descent, of which the death, resurrection and ascension of its Saviour is for it the supreme and unique example. But it has done so at a cost. We may regard the soul as a well of feeling, of varying depths, the spirit as intelligence manifesting at different levels. The two are never separated, but they do not realize their union until they meet in what the Eastern seers call 'the Buddhi,' in the intuitive mind which is also the heart.

In this great heart of understanding, feeling is no longer fevered by selfish attachment, while intelligence sheds whatever was cold or abstract in its impersonal regard of truth. In 'the Buddhi' the fire and the light feed and transmute each other in a still splendour of loving awareness. Then, indeed, is the mystery fulfilled in which soul and spirit truly blend in divine intercourse.

Christianity has, in its myth and its teaching, concentrated more on the evolving soul of man than on his eternal spirit. Hence its insistent anthropomorphic emphasis. But it has been unwilling to accept as fully the complementary truth that man is meant to outgrow his partial manhood and realize his divinity. It is true, as M. Schuon has written, that 'whoever entertains this ideal without first having overcome the consciousness of the physical ego . . . deceives others and deceives himself' and that 'it is useless to seek to realize that "I am *Brahma*" before understanding that "I (in my partial selfhood) am not *Brahma*".[1]

Christianity has guarded against this danger by interposing the person of Jesus between man and God, not merely as an embodiment of the eternal Principle in man, which is always present in the human soul and which in Jesus, as in other Masters, revealed itself uniquely, but as consubstantial with God Himself, Who can only be fully known and loved in the person of this one incomparable Son. The anthropomorphism which, in consequence, dogmatic Christianity has imposed both on its Father God and its earthly Saviour, have humanized the Divine at the cost, it seems to me, of cramping and even distorting man's relation to the spiritual realm.

And though the greatness as well as the blindness of Western man, his nobility and his pathos, have derived during the last two thousand years from his fidelity to earth and the temporal realm, from his sense, too, of the humbling bounds of the human, these bounds and attachments have more and more within the modern era shut off the soul from the quickening which it needs to receive, at every stage of its growth, from the interior plane of spirit.

For in proportion as men have become self-conscious, they have lost the instinctive fidelity to those spiritual depths in nature and themselves which ensured, within limits, an organic growth. But they have not become newly sensitive to a supra-conscious and supra-natural dimension.

The result is obvious in the outlook and practice of modern man. Instead of the old fruitful intimacy with nature and the dignity and wisdom which are nature's gift to the humble, man, like a clever schoolboy, has learnt to exploit mentally the field of gross matter. With this has gone a reduced sense of the personal values which grew out of a recognition that man was created in the divine image. More and more are these imperilled in a world of uniform mechanism and scientific abstraction. Through neglect of the supra-personal realm of spirit man is in danger, not so much of lapsing into the sub-personal (for he is too self-conscious to return to the primitive) as of having nothing but sentimentality with which to counter the impersonal mechanism of science.

We have, in fact, reached a stage when our greedy attachment to the lower kingdom, the realm of ignorance and of power,

[1] *Spiritual Perspectives and Human Facts* by Frithjof Schuon.

threatens human survival. We need a sacred science, which will transform our self-interested mentality into true self-knowledge. For though we may seem to have learnt in the last two thousand years many secrets about the lower kingdom of nature, which the men of old overlooked or failed to exploit for the relief of toiling mankind, we cannot know what is to our real benefit until we have discovered what we truly are and have begun consciously to live in and by that knowledge.

II

Admittedly the doctrine of sin even in its cruder forms, implies a recognition of a whole to which the sinner is meant to belong. But this sense of sin differs in quality in different people, as do the doctrines and practices in which they seek relief from it. Some people experience sin more mentally than emotionally, others more emotionally than mentally. Some feel it physically as uncleanness.

To-day, it is sometimes said, people are less sin-haunted than they used to be. I doubt if this is so. Our sense of division only takes another form and is expressed in another idiom, usually a psychological one. Yet this change of idiom, so far as it reflects a more detached approach to what used to be called 'sinfulness,' is important and even encouraging.

There are, doubtless, many who no longer concern themselves with sin and judgment, because they are unconscious of any centre, false or true, in themselves which relates them to a universe of meaning. But there are others who repudiate the old jargon of sin, bcause they see in it an antiquated barrier to that transformation of 'conscience' into consciousness which is required of us.

As a child and at school I was taught that I was a sinner for whose redemption Jesus had died. But even when I was being prepared for 'Confirmation,' I felt that there was something unhealthy in the emphasis of such a belief, particularly in its reference to desires which were part of a profound upheaval of my nature and an awakening of new sensibility. Certainly I was often remorseful over acts or thoughts which I knew to be mean or dishonest and I increasingly realized how tenacious was the force of selfish impulse. But I never believed that this force was really myself. Even in adolescence I viewed it with a good deal of rueful detachment, as a sort of monkey whose clever and sometimes despicable tricks failed to take me in, though part of me seemed to consent to them. To concentrate so much emotional attention upon this trickster and to identify the individual so closely with it seemed to me, even then, a curious disability in religious people.

Later I came to realize that the ancient image of the serpent was much more appropriate to this subtle, guileful entity which, through the reiteration of perverse habits and states of mind, had coiled itself round the real being of people, in that mystery of 'the sad-eyed serpent of darkness,' to quote a Hermetic text, 'wrapping itself round the lower limbs of the Light.'

For in the old mythologies the serpent symbolized something much more comprehensive than the Satanic ego. Cosmically its coils represented the path of the earth in space and her revolution round the sun. And as the snake ascending the rod or tree, it symbolized the raising of the instinctive life-energy from the loins to the head and its transformation into wisdom. The serpent of wisdom is the tempter redeemed. Indeed the image of the serpent on the tree of life is metaphysically analogous with that of the God-man suffering on the Cross.

The serpent of Eden figures that mysterious moment in human evolution when darkness and light fall into conflict. Then it is that the self-conscious ego emerges. The ego *is* this conflict. It consists of nothing else. It contains at once the shadow which seems to deny the light and the Light which obscurely affirms itself in the darkness. Hence in the ego intelligence and ignorance meet and, in their striving with each other, they often deceptively combine. For they hunger to be reconciled in the eternal Subject, yet cannot be so until the long fight between them has been fought out.

In this conflict the darkness has ceased, as man becomes self-conscious, to be a fathomless well-spring of rest from which life flows unknowingly in constant renewal of the physical being and the collective soul. It has become, instead, an abyss into which the half-formed individual dreads to fall and lose his precarious hold upon independence. He fears the Light, too, lest its glory should consume the little spark which flickers in his own skull. Between the two he exists anxiously, now clinging to, now repudiating the breast of the dark mother, the realm of instinct and sensuous experience, within which self-conscious thought began to stir.

But the dawn has broken, the sun climbs; his mind, kindled by its rays, awakes to a sense, at once valid and delusive, of its own freedom, and eventually the descent of spirit into matter, of which man is so meaningful an expression, becomes a re-ascent of spirit, ensouled by its sojourn in the unconscious depths, but less and less veiled in the mists of ignorance, to its creative Source.

As thus the Light grows and heart and mind and body are suffused by it, a man feels less and less the primitive compulsions of the blood. It is then that the Semitic conception of the wrath of God, of sin and atonement and the like, seems too crude and sensational an idiom to represent the subtle alchemy of reality. It is as if the individual who hitherto had been engrossed in the struggle with the darkness and with his involvement in the flesh, began to realize that his spiritual roots in life were less real, though no less necessary, than his roots in Light. At such a moment in the soul's history the teaching of the Eastern Rishis, for whom ignorance and enlightenment, not sin and salvation, were the keywords, can bring to a Western seeker of to-day a sense of emancipation from ancient bonds.

For the vision of these sun-lit seers had not been clouded, as our Western vision has been, by the smoke belched from the chimneys of a thousand Satanic mills. The mental fight with the material world, which Western man was to wage so avidly, had not begun. And though they possessed a primordial knowledge of the underworld of death, they lacked that self-interested pre-occupation with the matter and the mechanics of nature which is the pride and menace of our contemporary Western society. The realm, too, of personal relationship, with its tragic conflicts and its rare, but radiant realizations, was little explored by them. Their consciousness was chiefly concentrated on the vertical arm of the Cross, the arm which connects man with eternity in the height and the depth.

Admittedly human life, though it can only be valued in relation to timeless values, is historical. It is governed by cycles, within which certain realizations are possible and others impossible. We see this in the art of different times. The arts of ancient India and China, of Egypt and of Greece could only have flowered when they did. Christianity itself has developed and declined within one of these cycles and much of its strength has lain in its historical emphasis, even if this has led it to divide human history in a far too arbitrary fashion and to attribute to one event, of which the historical evidence is uncertain and the spiritual consequences very mixed, a cosmic importance transcending any other in the history of man.

During the last thousand years we have seen European man becoming more and more immersed in history, until to-day he may be almost said to be drowning in its political and economic shallows. For the off-shore shallows of an ocean are notoriously the most storm-tossed. The direct relationship with the divine which can only be fostered in the inner life of the soul has everywhere been diminished, while in the mass societies of to-day it is necessarily repudiated or simply disregarded.

Yet within this vertical vacuum a new importance has come to be attached by the psychologist and by perceptive people generally to personal relationships, to their difficulties and conflicts and to the possibility of resolving these creatively. Thus Jung writes that 'the whole weight of what ails humanity has lately transferred itself to the sphere of human relationship.' In the climate of our age, he suggests, the numinous is entering life through the mediation of such relationships. The healing self-release, which used to be invoked directly through religion, is now sought indirectly through them.

Yet human relationship is only fruitful as an expression, in terms of 'I' and 'You,' of that hidden mystery which unites what is twofold in ourselves to its unseen creative principle. Growth in divine knowledge and being can come through human relationship only to the degree that such relationship is an outward expression of the inner relationship of each person to That which makes unity in diversity possible. So far as our human relationships distract us from a dedicated attention to the reality within and the practice, in a form suitable to our particular needs, of the presence of God in our souls, they hinder our real growth. To be really fruitful they must be rooted in and continually enriched by that solitary communion between the Creator and His creation which holds the universe together and without which the atoms would disintegrate and meaning dwindles and dies.

If, too, relationship with others dims our sense of that essential aloneness which death enforces on us at every moment of our life, when we truly recollect and accept our human condition, it is a form of social distraction, however agreeable and apparently harmless. And it may and often does encourage the very attachment to which we are called to die. But of this there will be more to say.

The Eastern Rishis concentrated, as I have said, upon the vertical relationship and we, in our distracted day, need to concentrate upon it as never before. But they were not blind to the meaning of the horizontal movement through time and space and rejected it only so far as it bound man to an external necessity and blinded him to the realm of inner freedom. To them man's tragedy was one of immaturity and so, in no sense, final or irretrievable.

Western poets and dramatists have regarded it as inevitable that men should be possessed by their passions and that the more godlike they were, the more were they torn between the noble impulses and the base in themselves and in others. This is a true picture of man at what the Eastern scriptures call the *rajasic* or passional phase of his development. But it is a phase which could and should be outgrown. From the more mature standpoint of these wise men much that is tragic in the human lot is akin to the pains of childhood and adolescence and as such a fit object for compassion, but not for thrilled absorption.

To many Western men and women, hitherto, to whom a state of combative tension is normal to life, such serenity has seemed an escape from the real, as inevitably it must seem until a greater reality has begun to dawn in minds capable of perceiving it. But to-day we are ripe to learn from these teachers anew, we who have plunged deep into the abyss at the bottom of which lies an infinite force which can destroy us. If we are not to perish, we must learn how to live in the light of an infinite Consciousness which is the true counterpart and complement of that force. We need to know the *Atman*, the divine Self, if we are to survive our knowledge of the atom.

The immense development, too, of a certain kind of scientific thinking which has occurred in the West during the last two hundred years, has made a too personal and emotional expression of religious truth unacceptable to many people. They are seeking for a new orientation of head and heart. Yet this can only be 'new' in the sense that it will be rediscovered and rearticulated.

The phase 'perennial philosophy' does not adequately convey the quality of the original gnosis, the ancient wisdom, around which organized religions later built their different structures of doctrine and dogma and which they so often perverted. For it was not a philosophy in the modern meaning of that word. It was rather a primordial insight and a way of life, which enabled those who had deviated from reality to return to it and wholly to *be* from moment to moment.

The world is becoming outwardly unified through aeroplanes and radio, those crude mechanical equivalents of extra-sensory perceptions, which swallow up time and space. It has to become, with all its enriching and endangering differences, inwardly one. In the past the traditions of race and civilization may have made it impossible or at least unprofitable for the West to learn of the East or the East of the West. But that is no longer so.

The differences remain. The kind of consciousness through which an un-Westernized Indian of to-day lives and thinks is still profoundly different from that of an active, logical individual in the West[1]. We need all the more to enlarge our experience by discovering that neglected or impoverished centre in ourselves. These are differences which, far from dividing, invite a mutual intercourse from which the individual and the world may become whole. Always there have been innately Oriental souls in Western bodies and innately Occidental souls in Eastern bodies. This has become increasingly clear in the last hundred years. It is particularly such souls, feeling the division in themselves, who are drawn to resolve it.

It was just this division which I recognized in myself and which drew me so compellingly to this ancient wisdom for my healing.

Yet even so luminous a pattern of truth is only a means to an end, a bridge by which one may cross from the unreal to the real. 'The soul in its nature,' wrote Plotinus as he approached the end of his great work, 'loves God and longs to be at one with Him in the noble love of a daughter for a noble father; but coming to human birth and lured by the courtships of this sphere, she takes up with another love, a mortal, leaves her father and falls.

'But one day coming to hate her shame, she puts away the love

---

[1] For an extremely penetrating study of the difference between the mental structures of Eastern and Western civilizations the reader may be referred to *The Destiny of the Mind, East and West* by William S. Haas.

of earth, once more seeks the father and finds her peace. . . . The soul takes another life as it approaches God; thus restored it feels that the dispenser of true life is There to see, that now we have nothing to look for but, far otherwise, that we must put aside all else and rest in This alone, This become. . . . Thus we have all the vision that may be of Him and of ourselves; but it is of a self wrought to splendour brimmed with the intellectual light, become that very light, pure, buoyant, unburdened, raised to Godhood or, better, knowing its Godhood, all aflame'.[1]

In those memorable words, spoken so many centuries later, an Alexandrian of unknown race, settled at Rome, reaffirmed the vision of the Indian Masters and the goal of all their seeing. For nothing less than this is the end or consummation of knowledge of which Vedanta is the name.

[1] *Plotinus On the One and Good. The Sixth Ennead,* translated from the Greek by Stephen Mackenna and B. S. Page.

CHAPTER FOUR

⟨That you are

I

THE AIM of all religions is essentially the same. It is the reunion of the self-conscious with that supreme Principle of consciousness and being which is known metaphysically as the One and religiously as God. Since the aim is the same, the bitter conflicts between those who pursue it in different ways are the more deplorable. It is significant that such conflicts are fierce in the degree that the contestants worship a personal God. However much they may conceal the fact under doctrinal systems of an impersonal kind, their God is an image of themselves, sublimated doubtless and at best impersonating their highest conception of the good and true, but reflecting their bias and that exclusiveness which is the sign and bane of a one-sided personality.

How can He be other? it may be asked. How can we conceive God except in our own human terms? Indeed we cannot. That is why all the great teachers have insisted that God is ultimately unknowable and that no image can contain Him. The theologians, too, acknowledge that their personal God is wrapped in a cloud of mystery. But this does not prevent them from presenting to us their image of Him, as if it were wholly real. Inevitably those who make this claim repudiate any other image than their own and strive to repress it. In this we see the working of the same dualism which governs the whole of secular life. From such dualism the teaching of Vedanta, as of all ancient Gnosis, offers deliverance.

For Vedanta the eternal 'I,' the absolute Subject, in which the maximum of being and the minimum of non-being meet, is beyond all form and, as such, is inconceivable by any form-dependent mind. The habit of Western thought is to conceive of a personal God who embodies its highest values and then invest Him with transcendence. He remains thus a transcendent person or even, in the Christian doctrine of the Trinity, three persons in one God.

This is crudely put and theologians have, of course, found a place in their conception of a personal God for what is more and other than personal. But the personal image has remained central and dominant. The plunge into That Which is beyond form as our partial minds conceive it is not taken, except by the mystics, and so the dualism in which man confronts God as an object of devotion and affronts him as a self-tainted sinner, is never surpassed.

This plunge into a Reality beyond the mind's partial defining and the heart's binding attachments, is the first requirement of the Indian teachers. The ego will resist it to the last possible moment, since it means the dissolution of itself. Yet even its resistance is a tribute to the inescapable truth of That Which it fears and Which, its own insufficiency obscurely tells it, must triumph when the resources, which it has borrowed from reality and squandered in its attempts to enlarge itself, are exhausted.

The aim of Vedanta is to undermine this resistance. It does this by an appeal to understanding, believing that in the deepest sense there can be no final release from the error which the ego perpetuates until we see the authentic Self-revealing truth. Short of this, there can only be relative adjustments on the moral and intellectual planes, though these may bring us nearer to this truth than we were.

It is, therefore, on the purest reality we can imagine, a reality beyond the capacity of our ordinary minds to conceive, that the Hindu sages invite us to concentrate. To the question, 'What is that which, when known, all is known?' they answer,

> *We know not, we cannot understand how That can be explained; for It is other than the known and above the unknown. Thus have we heard from the sages of old who taught It to us.*
>
> *What cannot be spoken in words, but by which words are spoken—know that alone to be Brahman and not what people here worship.*
>
> *What cannot be thought by the mind, but by which the mind can think—know that alone to be Brahman and not what people here worship.*

> *What cannot be seen by the eye, but by which the
> eye can see—know that alone to be Brahman and
> not what people here worship.*
>
> *What cannot be heard by the ear, but by which
> the ear can hear—know that alone to be Brahman
> and not what people here worship.*
>
> *What cannot be breathed with breath, but by
> which breath is indrawn—know that alone to be
> Brahman and not what people here worship.*

The essence of this passage from the *Kena Upanishad* finds expression again and again in other *Upanishads*, in the *Mundaka*,
for instance,

> *He is the Self-luminous and formless Spirit, un-
> born, within all, outside all, above life and mind and
> beyond this creation's Creator . . .*
>
> *Radiant, the Brahman dwells in the secret place of
> the heart and is known to shine there. In It is all this
> universe centred, all that moves and breathes and
> sees. Know It as the Is and Is-not, adorable, supreme,
> beyond the knowledge of creatures . . .*
>
> *Vast is That, Its form unthinkable, yet It shines
> smaller than the smallest. Far and farther than far-
> ness is It, yet It is very near, resting in the heart's
> heart.*

In such words did these seers try to express the inexpressible.
Here is no God with human characteristics raised to a divine or
demonic pitch. Here is mystery, divined but undeified. Within
this mystery of beyondness and inwardness, they say, all that exists
is. And we shall not understand either existence or ourselves aright
until we lose and find ourselves in This.

This mystery for Vedanta is no vague 'infinite' with which we
are invited to put ourselves in tune. For it contains, but is not contained by every finite form and thing. It is neither abstract idea
nor concrete fact. When we call it the Supreme or Absolute Principle, we are as far from realizing it as when we give it the name
of a personal God. It is equally beyond our mental and our sensory reach. Yet it thinks in us and feels, even in the distortions of

our feeling and thought. It speaks in us and hears and every breath we draw is a ripple on the surface of its unbreathing calm.

But, it will be asked, if we cannot know it or feel it with our ordinary faculties, if it is beyond any form within which we may try to enclose it, how can we come to it or be sure that it is not a mirage born of longing out of emptiness?

The Indian teachers answer this question with another. How, they ask, should you know That by which you are known or see the seer of seeing, or hear the hearer of hearing or think the thinker of thinking? The Subject of all objects cannot be known objectively whether in the Cosmos or in ourselves. Yet It can be known in another way than that of a subject confronting an object. We can know It through our identity with It in the formless centre of our being. In that centre we and the purest transcendental Reality are one.

> *This Knower*, says Death, as he instructs Nachiketas in the *Katha Upanishad*, *this Atman is never born and never dies. It has neither sprung from anywhere nor become anything. Unborn, unending, timeless, and everlasting, it is not killed in the killing of the body* . . .
>
> *Smaller than the small, greater than the great, it dwells in the secret heart of beings. A man who strips himself of self-will and is tranquil in his senses beholds the greatness of the Self-being and is weaned from sorrow.*

Or again later in the same dialogue,

> *When a wise man realizes that it is through the great and omnipresent Self that we are conscious both in waking and dreaming, he grieves no more.*
>
> *When he knows the Atman, the ultimate subject of all experience and enjoyer of its fruits, who is ever near and Lord of past and future, he shrinks thereafter from nobody and nothing. This in truth is That.*

Finally, in the *Chandogya Upanishad*, a father teaches his son, who has returned home as a rather conceited student, what the true knowledge is 'whereby the unheard is heard, the unthought

thought and the unknown known.' He bids him bring a fruit from a banyan tree and break it open, and then break open one of the small seeds he finds in it. 'What do you see in it?' he asks. The son answers, 'Nothing at all, sir.'

Then his father says, 'My son, from the subtle essence in the seed, which you cannot see, comes this vast banyan tree.

'Believe me, my son, in that invisible and subtle essence all that exists has its Self. That is Reality. That is Atman. That are you.'

Tat Tvam Asi, 'That you are'—this is the basic affirmation of Indian metaphysic. And how crassly it has been misunderstood by God-habituated Western minds! For such minds with their dualistic bias it has seemed to represent a blasphemous claim by the individual to be God, or at least to deny the necessary distance between Creator and creature upon which they insist even in their most intimate communion.

But this is to misconceive the plane on which the affirmation is made and on which it can be realized. It is said in another Upanishad, the *Brihadaranyaka*, 'He who has the knowledge "I am Brahman" becomes all this that is; but whoever worships another divinity than the One Self and thinks, "He is one and I another," he knows not.' This truth is beautifully expressed in a Persian parable.

> *One came and knocked at the house of the Beloved. And a voice asked from within: Who is there? Then he who stood without the door replied: It is I. Then said the voice: This house will not hold Me and Thee; and the door was not opened. Then went the lover into the wilderness and fasted and prayed in solitude. And after many moons he returned again, and again he knocked at the door and again the voice asked: Who is there? and the lover replied: It is Thyself; and the door was opened unto him.*

The Beloved of this parable is not a sovereign God and the 'I', who acknowledges his identity with Him, has ceased to be a self-conscious person, as every true lover does. Through union with his spiritual Principle he has lost the illusion of separate individuality in an awareness of the timeless, transpersonal Being, in Which he uniquely is. Thus it is that the in-dwelling identity of the human and the divine is a Self-evident truth to a consciousness centred in the Atman, but it is hidden from the ordinary mind and the physical senses upon which it depends.

This identity in being, however, does not destroy the distinction between the soul and its Creator which is as much assumed by Vedanta as their divine kinship. The individual soul is named the 'jivatman' by the Hindu sages. Essentially, as an embodiment of the Atman, it is free and exists as a conscious centre in the field of nature. Thus it is associated with all the natural elements and with every grade of existence, gross or fine, and by falsely identifying itself with these, it loses the Unity in which it possesses itself and through which it can order and balance them.

This Principle of Unity is the Atman. And a man cannot begin to be free as an individual soul until, through knowledge of the Atman, which, spiritually, he is, he ceases to identify himself blindly with nature and recovers his true centre. All his struggle with multiplicity and all his conflict with his fellow-men is a striving of the finite in him to be centred and completed in this infinite. In achieving this a man breaks out of individuality as he has known it and realizes that all which seems finite in his existence, as in his thought and imagining, is in essence infinite, as the grain of sand was for William Blake, or a bird in flight.

As infants, we lived in close union with our infinite source, but day by day we drew imperceptibly away from it. We were passively at one with it in the organic life of the body. For our bodily life is rooted in the unconscious, which is the negative or maternal aspect of Brahman. The positive aspect of Brahman is pure Self-consciousness and to this we can only faintly respond, when our life here begins. Our life acquires meaning as this response quickens and deepens, until we grow through partial awareness into that unity of Light and Life, imaged in the Cosmos as Brahman, and present in our souls as Atman.

This integrity of consciousness and life, as of all the 'contraries' which are harmonized in and through the Atman, is unattainable by a self-centred individual. 'That you are' does not signify identity between me, as such an individual, and Brahman, however much I may enlarge or elevate my individuality. It is only beyond the opposed, if for long necessary, dualism of subject and object that Brahman, as Supreme Principle, and 'I,' as Atman, are known to be one.

That is what the Indian teachers meant by 'realization,' the

intuitive awareness of a reality which is non-dual and which, by
virtue of its non-duality, ensures a union of true relationship.
Brahman, they declared, is not two, but It is, also, not one as opposed to two. It is the Oneness which contains duality as a mode
of Its Being, whether in manifestation in the Cosmos, or in Its
hidden heart; a Oneness of such perfect and sufficient Being that
no expression can diminish or disturb It.

The realization of this undividedness, when it comes, is immediate and beyond all argument or theory. It happens in us when
certain conditions are fulfilled and certain barriers removed. One
condition is that we should reject all attempts to define it. Since
any positive definition excludes its opposite, while Brahman is all-
inclusive, the aspirant was advised to meet all such attempts, by
his own mind or the minds of others, with the phrase, 'netti,
netti,' 'not this, not this.'

To the question, already quoted, 'how should he know That
by which he knows all?' Yajnavalkya answers in the *Brihadaranyaka Upanishad*,

> *That Self is to be described by No, no! He is incomprehens-
> ible, for he cannot be comprehended, imperishable, for he can-
> not perish, unattached, for he does not attach himself; un-
> fettered, he does not suffer, he does not fail.*

The sage has used here a number of negative epithets to describe
the Atman, because a negative is less limiting than a positive. But
the phrase 'not this, not this' was not meant to imply any restric-
tion upon the power of Brahman to be or not to be. Brahman is
equally beyond any negative and any positive formulation which
abstract intellect can impose upon It. It is and It is not. For the
bliss of its total consciousness of Self includes as a necessary condition a total unconsciousness of a partial or restricted self.

The first condition, then, of realizing the Atman which we are
is the acceptance of That Which has no name though It gives all
names, Which is formless, as It is timeless and spaceless, but contains and creates all forms and enters time and space to enjoy and
be enjoyed. This is the Reality for Which man unconsciously or
consciously hungers amid all his temporal distractions and of
Which discursive reasoning can at best only catch a reflection in
the mirror of phenomena. But when, say the Indian sages, the
empirical ego is dissolved in the light of the Atman, the light, 'that

doth both shine, and give us sight to see,' to borrow Sir Philip Sidney's words, all fears and hungers die and the long feud between temporal individuality and eternal Being which underlies them, is ended.

The meaning of such realization is beyond our grasp until a way has been found to actualize it, a way, in other words, which enables it to grasp us. This, as we shall see, is the way of Yoga. It may, therefore, be argued that it is more practicable to accept the dualistic situation in which, as ordinary men and women, we find ourselves, sanctifying it on the religious level with a personal God Who is a projection of what is highest in our human consciousness and to Whom we can subordinate our selfish impulses, until gradually we conform, always imperfectly but more and more closely, to the ideal which our image of a personal God embodies.

The arguments in favour of this are strong and so long as such an approach to the supreme Reality can satisfy, it would be unwise and probably profitless to suggest its ultimate inadequacy. It is to those who have come to feel that theistic religion, however much it may ameliorate and sublimate their dualistic condition, can never wholly redeem it, that the Eastern teachings offer a way of release into the heart of Being which conform more truly, it seems to me, to the organic order of the universe.

Life proceeds from the unseen to the seen, from Mystery to meaning. It is, therefore, right that we should begin our new journey along the spiritual path, as we began our natural life, in an ignorance which is an act of faith, not involuntary as with the infant, not doctrinally determined as in the acceptance of a Creed, but in a willing suspension of the kind of knowing, with its attendant beliefs and unbeliefs, which we have acquired as we grew up.

The affirmation 'That you are,' if we fully understand and accept it, compels us to empty our minds of all images which reflect a self-interested relationship of subject to object, so that a new creative movement can begin in us, grounded in something other than the ego. It is true that the devotees of a personal God acknowledge that they are as nothing in comparison with their God. Yet they hold on to the fact that they are other than He. This is true of the empirical self to which we cling and by which we thereby alienate ourselves in some degree from the timeless Principle of our being Which we worship in the form of a personal God.

We may invest such a personal God with the purest qualities of wisdom and love we can conceive, but so far as he reflects our impure subjective needs, His image ties us to our temporal and even our physical selves and tends to perpetuate our belief in their immortality. We have an example of this in the Christian belief in Jesus's bodily resurrection which has led countless people to confuse resurrection with the resuscitation of a corpse. Truly to 'rise from the dead' is to rise from attachment to the body by which both body and mind are recreated spiritually. As Rudolf Bultmann has pointed out in his *Kerygma and Myth*, 'Christ's death was itself the victory over the power of death and did not need any physical resurrection to reverse it.' In this his death did not differ essentially from his life.

The same belief in a personal Deity creates, also, such insoluble problems as that of how an all-good and all-powerful God, conceived in limited human terms, can be the author or countenancer of apparent evil, even as a condition of ultimate good.

In short, a personal God, even when we invest Him with the highest human attributes, reflects in some degree the conflict between what we feel to be our eternal being and our temporal self and the opposition between good and evil, life and death, which originates in our struggle to break free from the negative embrace of the unconscious. When we bow our heads and bend our knees before such a God, however objectively we may regard Him, we reverence and supplicate the imperfectly realized divinity in ourselves which we have projected into this sacred figure. We are, in some measure, attached to him as we are attached to ourselves, and to him we cling when the transience of our existence forces upon us the terrible thought that in our separate selfhood we are nothing. Our personal God fights for us in this war between the timeless and the temporal, in which our ignorance or imperfect knowledge of what we are has involved us.

But though our God may help us to believe that we are essentially and unassailably His in our inmost essence, a part of us is left out, and so anxiety remains. It may be only a faint uneasiness which hardly penetrates the armour of religious belief which we have put on. But the necessity of such armour and the insistence that without it a man cannot successfully overcome the foes within and without, betray the persistence of a state of war. The feud between existence and being, between the conscious and the unconscious, is not resolved.

It is to resolve this feud that Vedanta begins and ends by affirming the non-duality of the divine Principle. Against all our habitual impressions and reactions it insists that the self and the not-self are centred in a Reality which makes them one. They are one in Brahman, the primordial Spirit of Which the whole universe is the Self-expression. They are one in Atman Which expresses itself in and through each of us and which makes possible a new unity of relationship.

To quote Yajnavalkya again, 'When there seems to be duality, then one sees the other, one smells the other, one hears the other, one thinks the other. But when all has become Spirit, one's own Self, how can one smell another, see another, hear another, greet another, know another? How can one know That which knows all? How, O beloved, can one know the Atman, the Knower?'

This and similar passages are easily misinterpreted. For they cut radically through our habitual experience and, seen from that side, may suggest that in a true Self-consciousness all relationship in which I and another meet is dissolved in a kind of spiritual vacuum.

This is not the meaning at all. After this change of consciousness to which Yajnavalkya is trying to lead his disciple, Maitreyi, the world of the not-self still exists, but it has ceased to be 'other' in the sense of being inwardly separated from me. I still see, smell, hear and know a world and people extended in space and time, but I experience them as an expression of the spaceless, timeless Being in Which I have learnt to live and which I essentially am. They are not swallowed up in my individual self-consciousness. Rather, they and I meet in a Consciousness which we share, in the Atman Which we are, and in which all, in their differences, are one.

That is why, when Yajnavalkya says that 'after death there is no consciousness,' he does not mean merely bodily death. He means the death of ignorance, of dualistic thinking and seeing. What is born of that death is so different from our ordinary consciousness that, compared with it, it is a sort of unconsciousness.

In Vedanta this condition of non-dual experience is compared with that of deep sleep. In such sleep it is said, 'there the Spirit sees not, but though seeing not, he sees. How could the Spirit not see, if he is the all-seeing, the imperishable? But there is no duality there, nothing apart for him to see.'

The eternal Self sees by Its own light. Beyond all objects, as within them, this divine Seer sees and is. Since all objects are expressions of Itself, It sees them in Itself and Itself in them. Dreamless sleep is a negative condition of this pure vision. In it we are withdrawn from the world of objects, and from our imperfect and often sorrowful relation to them, into a pure, but unconscious subjectivity. We return to the pre-natal Paradise, the womb of life in which the opposites were merged.

In dreaming, our ego is still active, fabricating forms out of its desires and frustrations and drawing equally upon racial memory and upon our waking experience for its material. When we are awake, we are bound to our bodies and the external world of the senses, which put a limit on our desires. But whether awake in a grosser world or dreaming in a subtler, and the two states often mingle and merge, we are, at best, in imperfect union with our source.

For Vedanta, dreamless sleep and the faint recollection of some pure bliss which we often bring back from it suggests only the negative aspect of non-dual experience.

But there is for It a fourth state of the soul, which It calls the 'turiya' condition, in which the partial states of waking, dreaming and dreamless sleep, as we know them, are integrated. To be awake in this condition is to be at one with the consciousness of the Atman, the eternal 'I'; to dream is to see the world imaginatively instead of self-interestedly; and to sleep is to spiritualize the body by no longer identifying the self with it, so restoring to it its native innocence. This state, in which we cease to be conscious of that shifting and precarious balance of opposites in which we ordinarily live and enter into a deep oneness with ourselves and with all, is indescribable, as the Upanishadic sages acknowledge. But it is none the less real and attainable, if the conditions requisite for its attainment are met.

Vedanta teaches that all relationship on whatever level, from physical touch to spiritual sight, originates in and depends on the Absolute Brahman which is Atman. This is the One in Which the seer, the seeing eye and the object seen are held together in one whole. In it the dualities of manifested existence are perpetually harmonized. I and you can only meet creatively in and through this unseen but all-seeing Presence. Whether we confront a human being or God, as our imagination pictures Him, we experience them but partially so long as we fail to give ourselves wholly to That Which knows us beyond all difference, Which is the eternal Truth equally of the 'I' and the 'you' and Which therefore makes it possible for me to be you without ceasing to be myself, indeed to be far more truly and fully myself, and for you to be me with the same enhancement of your own distinctive identity.

For to realize 'That are you' is to perceive the identity in all difference. It involves no hubristic claim 'to be God.' Rather, through a humble surrender of the self-will and partial knowledge that divide, it ensures a capacity to see the wholeness of each and all, even in those who are ignorant of it themselves or violate their own integrity. We have this perception in the exact measure that we live in the whole of ourselves through the indwelling light of Atman.

Of that light which lightens everyone who comes into the world Yajnavalkya said,

> *As a man in the arms of a beloved woman knows nothing that is without, nothing that is within, so the soul in the embrace of the* Atman, *the divine consciousness, knows perfect peace. This indeed is his true form, in which all desires are fulfilled, since the Self that is all has been attained, and there is no sorrow.*

Or again,

> *When a man knows the* Atman, *his true Self, when he can say, 'I am He,' what desires can attach him to the body?*
>
> *He who in the mystery of life has found the Self, the Spirit, and has awakened to its light, he truly is a creator. His is the world of the spirit, for he is that world.*
>
> *While we are here, we may know this. If we know it not, we are in darkness and destruction. Those who know it enter life eternal, but others are in pain and sorrow.*
>
> *If a man sees the* Atman, *the Self that is divine, the Lord of all that is and will be, he fears no more.*

Him, before Whom the years roll with the days,
the Gods adore as the Light of lights, as undying
time.

Him, in Whom the five hosts of being rest and the
vastness of space, I know as immortal Atman, *as*
eternal Brahman.

Those who know the life of life, the eye of the
eye, the ear of the ear, the mind of the mind, they
know the primordial Brahman.

By the mind this truth must be seen: there are not
many, but only One. He who sees diversity without
the unity goes from death to death.

But he who rests between the wings of that which is neither
born nor dies, 'the Bird of Life,' 'the Eternal Swan,' knows what
can never be proved and proves what can never be known. Such
enlightenment, in which death is moment by moment transformed
into life, and blindness into seeing, is not just a personal achievement. Were it so, the pursuit of it would be valueless and fore-
doomed to failure. It is, like all true acts of creation and recrea-
tion, a cosmic event, which changes the balance of forces in the
world, as it changes them in the individual and, to a less extent,
in all with whom he enters into relationship.

II

But how, it may be said, can we commit ourselves to a Reality
that is beyond all the forms we know or can conceive? And is it
not more seemly for us, with our human limitations, to approach
this Real through the vast hierarchy of forms in which It reveals
Itself? Certainly a self-intoxicated abandonment to the infinite is
as stultifying as any formal idolatry, indeed more stultifying,
since the study of forms is educative, even when it binds.

Vedanta implies no divorce between the formless and the world
of forms. But it recognizes that our formative imagination is so
self-centred and has spun in consequence such a web of partial or
distorted images around the mystery, of which we are meant to

live the meaning, that we need to commit ourselves anew to the unimaginable and allow it to recreate our imagination.

This is what the sincere artist does, in whatever province he works, when he dedicates himself to the task of integrating his vision. In the East this task was regarded as a branch of Yoga and involved, like every other spiritual activity, a discipline and a ritual, by which the artist might become identified with his creative source in the Atman. The method was similar whether the artist was a poet or a painter. Of Valmiki, for example, the author of the 'Ramayana,' it was written that 'seating himself with his face towards the East and sipping water according to religious ritual, he set himself to *Yoga*-contemplation of his theme.' It was by virtue of the *Yoga*-power which welled up out of the stillness of this contemplation that 'he clearly saw before him the protagonists in the epic he was to write and all that was to come to pass.'

The contemplation practised by Buddhist artists emphasized more explicitly the basic need of an initial emptying of the mind of all images. 'He must meditate' a *Tantra* reads, 'on the original Purity of the first principle of things and . . . on their emptiness. . . . By the fire of the idea of emptiness there are destroyed beyond discovery the five elements which compose the individual consciousness. Only when the personality of the individual is thus set aside is he able to invoke his Deity.'

To the ordinary Western mind the idea of consciousness without any content, of being aware by ceasing to think, is a contradiction in terms. Yet such a state of pure consciousness is the goal of Eastern Yoga. To be wholly empty of partial concepts, to be, in this sense, conscious of nothing, is for the Eastern sage the necessary condition of being truly conscious of anything, of experiencing it purely and immediately.

Because we cannot assent to this emptiness, fearing the loss of our singularity, we cling to the images which reflect our separateness. Nor, it must be admitted, do we do this without reason. If the only alternative to an individualistic half-life were total nonentity, we should have reason enough to prefer the former.

But the nothingness which we are asked to accept does not involve this bleak alternative. Indeed it is from just this misconceived alternative that it frees us. The popular notion that for Vedanta the universe of forms is a mere play of unreal shadows is untrue. The Vedic seers never repudiated the world of nature. They gloried in it as expressing in its countless forms the joy of the Lord of Creation, the play of the divine Lover with his bride who is the physical counterpart of his spiritual self.

Experienced as such, the universe of change is not a mere phenomenal show, projected on to the screen of matter by some celestial film-operator. It is reality itself unfolding with eternal newness in time. In the revealing there is also a concealing. The universe of forms is drawn, like a veil, over the face of the formless Brahman. For that face we can never see direct. In this sense it is eternally true that 'no man has seen God at any time.' But God can see through us the forms of His creating and when we see them even partially with His eyes, we see the essence of Being in the ceaseless flow of becoming. For those who have attained this vision Time is no longer a turbid stream but a succession of moments, each one of which contains a possibility of spiritual realization.

The finite aspect of the forms around us, our own physical and mental form as well as those of our fellows, can be thus transfigured. We can see them not merely as windows opening at different levels into the infinite, though they are this, but as expressions of a Creative power which possesses an infinite capacity for Self-embodiment and which integrates thereby every particle in the body of life. It is only when we see the forms about us or our individual selves as less than expressions of this Being that we are deluded. Then, indeed, we see a world of phenomena, not of creative forms, and such a world is partial and illusory, is 'maya,' to give one of the meanings of that often misinterpreted word.

There is a passage in W. Hale White's (Mark Rutherford's) *More Pages from a Journal* which suggests vividly what it can mean to awake, if only partially and for a brief moment, from habitual self-imprisonment. 'When I was in the wood,' he wrote, 'something happened which was nothing less than a transformation of myself and the world, although I "believed" nothing new. I was looking at a great, spreading, bursting oak. The first tinge from the greenish-yellow buds was just visible. It seemed to be no longer a tree away from me and apart from me. The enclosing barriers of consciousness were removed and the text came into my mind, *Thou in me and I in thee*. The distinction of self and not-self was an illusion. I could feel the rising sap; in me also sprang the fountain of life uprushing from its roots, and the joy of its outbreak at the extremity of each twig right up to the summit was my own: that which kept me apart was nothing.'

Such an experience, like that of many other nature-mystics of whom Richard Jefferies is an obvious example, is little more than a sensational anticipation of a truly integrated vision and would have been so regarded by the Indian sages. In such dissolutions of self-consciousness the atonement experienced is primarily through the roots in earth and with the unconscious realm of instinct. It is insufficiently balanced and completed on the super-conscious or super-natural level in a realization of identity with the pure Mind of the Creator.

It can, therefore, only suggest in an elementary and partial way what true non-dual awareness means, an awareness in which the formless is not preferred to, still less exclusive of, the formal.

The worlds within and without, of mind and of what we call matter, interpenetrate each other. We need to relate ourselves attentively to both as aspects of a greater whole. But the seen is rooted in an Unseen, which no form can wholly comprehend, though within its limits even the humblest form contains It entirely.

And since we, through fear of self-loss and perverse habit, have become attached to forms, whether by attraction or repulsion, and view them one-sidedly as concrete or abstract objects, we need, if we are to make contact with the real, to allow the Unseen to possess us and create, in and through our faculties of perception, distinctive images of Itself.

To surrender thus to the Eternal means that we do not wait for death to convince us of our temporal transience. As the Upanishad says, 'while we are here, we may know this.' Yet with pathetic persistence we try to eternalize ourselves in time, not by yielding up each moment to the timeless Power which is our reality, but by investing time itself with an absolute power, so that we are at the mercy of its movement, hurrying in mind from the past into the future or recoiling from a dubious future to the securities of the past, and never experiencing the present as the meeting-place of the timeless and the temporal and the occasion of a pure awareness which it is meant to be.

Time is never dead, but always dying. It is thus that it reflects the deathless will of the eternal. But if we hinder the dying of time

by clinging to it and to the temporal self which we have built up
by such attachment to fleeting images, this self will hide from us
the eternal Being in which we do really, moment by moment, live.
Our very thirst for temporal life kills our realization that we do
eternally live.

Yet 'while we are here, we may know,' now, at this moment
wholly lived, that we are at once in time and in eternity. The feud
between them is not real, but of our own making. The Indian
sages did not say, 'What That is you *will* be,' but 'That' which
makes of all the contraries a loving union of opposites, 'you are.'
The whole science of Yoga was directed to removing the false
habits which blind us to this truth and prevent us from entrusting
ourselves wholly to it.

When we 'enter and become the Self, the Seer, Who is without
quality,' but Who is eternally active in creation, the estranging
veil between us and objects is lifted. For centred in this 'Seer,'
Who 'sees all beings in his own Self and his own Self in all beings,'
we are as conscious of another as we are of ourselves and know
that, though different, we are essentially one. Subject and object
are united in a mutual exchange and affirmation of being in which
it is natural to see ourselves objectively and the object subjec-
tively. For now the within and the without no longer exclude each
other, as in a dualistic relationship, but are realized as complementary aspects of the same whole.

Only a vision thus imaginatively transformed can make us and
all we contemplate wholly real. In the light of it the world of
changing forms no longer ensnares. Its magic, its *Maya*, is that
true enchantment which we experience when, in contemplating
any form, we see its essence shining in and shaping its temporal
substance. Then, indeed, we are freed from what Shankara called
'outward imaginings,' but only to be possessed by that inward
imagination which creates instantaneously and with such subtle
simplicity the true form of things.

So, too, it is with the forms of the God-head in which we embody our conception of the Divine. The Divine unceasingly mul-
tiplies images of Itself and delights in them, yet, loving each, is
bound to none. And the nearer man comes to knowing the Divine
in himself, the less is he attached to the Gods of his imagining or
to any other images. So far as the images which he creates and
which express his joy in creation reveal the non-dual in the dual,

they can be means of communion with That Which eternally trans-cends the bounds within which, instant by instant, It recreates Itself.

The Atman could not assume any form, were It not free from form. Nor would It be free to change, were It not in essence un-varying. Otherwise each change would limit Its creative spon-taneity. To be incapable of change is to be dead. That is why time, though always dying, always lives. And it is the changeless-ness of the Atman which ensures an infinite capacity for vital be-coming as an expression of fathomless being. The Atman is eternally now, instantaneously changing and changeless in each form It assumes and in each moment of time.

And 'That Atman,' Vedanta declares, 'you are.' When you rea-lize It, nothing will be alien to you and falsely other. You will see the world as if it were within yourself, and yourself as if you were within the world. The forms which your imagination creates will then be true expressions of your formless essence, even as the cos-mos is an expression of the creative power which goes forth from Brahman. For the birth of a universe and of the universal man obeys the same organic laws and reflects the same divine pattern. What this cosmological pattern is, as Vedanta conceives it, we will now briefly consider.

CHAPTER FIVE

The True Trinity

I

THE MYTH of Creation, as the Vedic seers conceived it, was like all such myths, a myth of sacrifice. The existing universe is born of the willingness of the Creator, Brahma, to submit to dismemberment, not in His limitless essence as Brahman, but in His formal substance. Through this sacrifice Brahma creates in a passion of love, delight and self-giving a world of forms, of which the crowning manifestation on this planet is Man. For in Man Brahma awakens a creative consciousness akin to His own and a faculty to create forms which express his spiritual nature. Brahma consents to be dismembered and diffused in nature, so that He may be assimilated by His creatures and they may conceive by Him. They in turn must consent to dismemberment, if they are to fulfil His purpose and become creators in their turn.

The Creator cannot wholly inform the man whose mind and senses are as yet turned away from the inward light of His presence. Yet that light is the Eye by which such a man sees the outer world as a whole and as a reflection of something within. But he sees that something dimly through the opaque or distorting lens of his egoism. Day by day this outer man denies the Inner Man, his real Selfhood or Being. In the Sacrifice, as it was ritually performed in Vedic times, the sacrificer by pouring a libation into the sacred fire, as into God's mouth, enacted the reunification of the divided members of the deity through the surrender of the outer Man to the Inner.

Any reader who wishes to study the Myth and its significance in detail may be referred to Ananda Coomaraswamy's luminous analysis and interpretation of it in his *Hinduism and Buddhism*. But this brief summary of it is enough for my purpose. Brahma is thus conceived as being both primal Creator and primal Victim, and creation itself as an eternal process of death and re-birth on all planes of manifestation and supremely in the person who has awoken to the meaning of his life in Time.

Such a person needs no ritual to dramatize outwardly this meaning, though he may of course find such a ritual helpful and, by participating in it, he may collaborate, with others who share his vision of the creative design, and also with unseen overshadowers who can use the power of a true ritual for the furtherance of the redemptive work, in which they are, with fuller knowledge, continually engaged. The 'Mysteries' and the Mystical Brotherhoods which have maintained them down the ages are based upon belief in such communion with the higher or more interior worlds.

But participation in such rituals is not essential to deliverance from ignorance into the knowledge of the real. He who is alive to the true meaning of his existence sees every moment as ideally a burnt-offering in which the Dragon of the partial selfhood may be slain and the true Self brought to life. In every such moment the cosmos itself can become whole in him. For he thus aligns himself with the will of the Creator, Who eternally dies to separateness that He may live undivided in multiplicity, being Himself in His inmost nature neither separate nor multiple, and Who, through this union of apparent life and death, maintains the 'Ten Thousand Things' in harmony.

In the Myth, then, as in the later metaphysical expression of it in the *Upanishads*, there is no essential conflict in the soul of creation between eternity and time. There is a descent as a perpetual condition of ascent, and so far as the descent appears to be a fall, it is because the true relation between descent and ascent has for some obscure reason been disturbed in man's evolution out of the unconscious. How much man is responsible for this dislocation or how much it is a necessity of his peculiar destiny as a self-conscious being, no one really knows, despite the dogma of 'original Sin.'

But if the dislocation is not in the essential nature of things, it can be outgrown. The prophets and preachers of an eternal war between the darkness and the light, the antagonists which figure so prominently, for example, in the teaching of Zarathustra, have universalized the temporal war in themselves and seen the Cosmos as a reflection of it. The vision of the Vedic sages went deeper. So did that of Zarathustra. In his original teaching, contained in the *Gathas*, he conceived the two primeval powers, which he named Spenta Mainyu and Angra Mainyu, as meeting in the higher unity of Ohrmazd or Ahura Mazda and as being opposed only in the shadow world of existence. Characteristically the priests and theologians of a later Zoroastrianism travestied the Prophet's truth by making Ohrmazd and Ahreman, as God and Devil, eternal antagonists.

Union of the two in the One, as a marriage of contraries, not a conflict of opposites, is the ancient Trinity, truer, it seems to me, to the Cosmic pattern than the 'Father, Son, and Holy Ghost' of Christian doctrine. In the Vedantic view Brahman, Which is in essence non-dual, assumes the part of Creator, as Brahma.[1] As prime Actor, Brahma manifests two aspects or two equally balanced powers. These powers, inherent in the creative Principle, are positive and negative. They confront and complete one another and each is equally necessary. Within their primordial relationship are contained all imaginable contraries, such as heaven and hell, day and night, stillness and movement, man and woman, life and death. It is only in us or through us, in the degree that we have fallen into the dualism of the outer man, that the balance of these principles is upset.

In Hindu mythology these two principles of creation were imaged as Vishnu, the preserver of life, and Shiva, the destroyer, and they were balanced and reconciled in Brahma. In relation to Brahman, these three powers formed a creative trinity, each of them being necessary for the manifestation of the eternal in time. But as powers of creation Vishnu and Shiva are dual aspects of Brahma. Through the one he unceasingly breathes forth the world, through the other he draws it back, as continuously, into himself. Hence his secondary name 'Paramahamsa,' which denotes this act of respiration. Shiva is significantly both 'The Destroyer' and 'The Conqueror of Death.' For in his destruction there is perpetual resurrection and transformation. Similarly Vishnu is no negative preserver, but 'The Cherisher of Life.'

This trinity or triangle is found in one form or other in all the ancient teachings. It is of the greatest importance as a metaphysical basis both of a true cosmology and a true psychology. It is not a mental conception, which, even when highly spiritualized and per-

---

[1] I have used the name Brahma to denote the personal aspect of the Brahman throughout this book, because the two names suggest their intimate relation, although the Creator is more usually known in Vedanta as Ishwara.

sonalized, as in the Christian doctrine, betrays a recoil from the feminine depths of life. It is an organic realization of the true balance of forces in the Cosmos. As such it corresponds with the inner structure of our own being. Thus the equal-sided triangle was the traditional symbol both of creation and of creative man. As a symbol of the Cosmos the angle at the apex represented Brahma and the two angles of the base Vishnu and Shiva. As a symbol of the divine man, the apex stood for the creative Selfhood, while the positive and negative forces, polarized by this Selfhood, were represented by each of the angles at the base.

It is interesting to see what happens when the balance of this traditional trinity is upset, as it generally is in monotheistic systems of belief. In the male God of such systems the positive and negative principles are no longer reconciled in a third. There is war between God and Satan, Heaven and Hell, a war which cannot be resolved, but in which the predominance of the positive over the negative is the best that can be hoped and striven for. The creative triangle has become a vertical line dividing two points in opposition, God in the height, Satan in the Abyss.[1]

Such a dualism does in fact reflect the condition in which self-divided man exists. But he can find no deliverance in a similarly self-divided God. The moralities which derive from this distortion of the true metaphysical pattern can only perpetuate and even sanctify the war which God himself is pictured as waging. Indeed, during the last fifty years we have seen the leaders of the Christian religion pleading the necessity on these grounds of indiscriminate slaughter and repudiating as unrealistic the pleadings of creative pacifists. It was not for nothing that it was a Hindu, steeped in the wisdom of Vedanta, who proclaimed and practised a better way.

The West has for long equated such ethical dualism with religion. There is a sense in which God is purely positive. For what is negative in Him is a mode of the positive. But He is not positive in any sense which excludes or denies the negative. Minus, as its sign (—) indicates, does not contain plus, but plus (+) contains minus, and when this plus which is also minus is itself contained in a circle (⊕), in which Henry Vaughan named a 'great ring of pure and endless light,' it signifies the whole mystery of creation in time

___

[1] See *The Supreme Doctrine* by Hubert Benoit for a lucid analysis of this perversion.

and in eternity. The true creator as we know in our own human experience, can only give in the degree that he can receive, and receive as an expression of giving.

As Dr. Hubert Benoit has shown, the only superiority of the
active and positive force over the passive and negative lies in the
fact that 'the play of the active force *causes* the play of the passive
force.[1]

In all creation the active force initiates, the passive responds. Yet
creation depends upon their inter-action, and the re-action of the
negative force, when it is rightly related to the action of the positive force, is itself creative. Equally the positive force, if it falls
out of its true relation to the negative, is destructive. We have a
familiar example of this in the sexual and spiritual relationship of
man and woman. But it is equally present, though usually less
apparent, in the manic or depressive tendencies in every individual,
whether man or woman. When the balance is maintained on whatever level, there is health and wholeness; when it is disturbed
whether by a predominance of spirit over body or of body over
spirit, there is disease.

In Time, then, the positive force has a relative superiority over
the negative as initiating the interplay which makes creation possible. For this reason God as Creator has usually been regarded as
masculine, though in many of the Mysteries He was invoked as
'Father-Mother.' In most of the ancient Myths, too, He is indis-
solubly wed to His feminine counterpart, the Moon of His Sun,
the eternal *mula-prakriti*, as the Hindus call her, the primordial
matter, itself eternal spirit in its negative mode, without which He
could not generate a world.

Each, too, of the principles of the Brahmic trinity has a consort,
who represents his feminine and manifesting aspect. Brahma's is
Sarasvati and she, as partner of the Creative power, is the patroness
of the arts. But, archetypally, she is much more than this suggests.
In her elementary aspect Brahma's consort is 'Maya,' the enchant-
ress who engulfs the soul in the ocean of existence and 'muffles the
universe in her darkness.' But in her fully evolved form as 'Tara,'
she is the Mother of all wisdom, the redeemer and transformer of
souls, who have become conscious of her as 'the pristine spirit, . . .

[1] See also *The I Ching or Book of Changes*. The Richard Wilhelm Translation. Rendered into English by Cary F. Baynes, for an ancient Chinese
interpretation of the same truth under the symbols of *Yang* and *Yin*.

the ultimate nature and the clear light of heaven.' Vishnu's consort is Sri or Lakshmi, fittingly the goddess of wealth. Shiva's is Paravati or Uma, and, as consort equally of the power of death and the Lord of the cosmic dance, she is in aspect both terrible and benign.

But in Brahman, in that absolute realm beyond Time, to which all manifestation perpetually returns and in which no causal action or complementary reaction is necessary, the positive and negative principles are conceived as residing in a perfect inward communion, that rapt contemplation by the Supreme Self of Its own infinity of which the unknown author of the ancient 'Hymn of Creation' in the *Rig-Veda* wrote,

> *THAT, the primal fount*
> *Of light—immobile—rest and action joined—*
> *Brooded in silent bliss.*[1]

In the perfect act of creation in Time, then, the act of Brahma eternally forming and informing the universe or of those human beings in whom a universe can be truly generated from moment to moment, undistorted by egoism, creation is not at war with destruction. In such Masters the union of the two forces in the Supreme THAT is so true that there is no negativity, whether as self-assertiveness or self-recoil. There is only creativeness and receptiveness enlivening and sustaining each other. The action of the liberated man springs out of a profound passivity. And when he is apparently most passive, he is most richly active. In this sense the divine life is, indeed, pure activity.

Such action is of a wholly different order from that of the man who takes sides in his mind and his will with 'good' against 'evil.' Such a man is never really good as creation is good in Itself and Its acts. In real goodness, good forgives evil as Jesus did on the Cross. What appears to us in our dualistic condition to be an unending war between them, as between energy and inertia, is not in the true nature of things. Every act of true creation restores the lost polarity. And this creativeness, the Hindu sages taught, is the condition into which we are meant to grow through a realization of the Atman in ourselves.

We can make little advance towards it so long as we are *attached* either to good or to evil. And to be attached to one is to be at-

[1] As translated by Swami Prabhavananda and F. Manchester.

tached to the other, though we may not recognize it. This does not mean, of course, that we should cease to acknowledge that good and evil exist as one-sided antagonists in ourselves, as in the unenlightened world, and that what moralists call good is often, though by no means always, more constructive than what they call evil.

Yet such constructiveness may, in fact, be a self-interested defence against experiences which would aid, though it be through pain and error, the unfolding of meaning in our lives. For this we need to be free to act and to suffer creatively.

Consequently ethics for Vedanta are only a means to the attainment of an end which surpasses them, that union with Reality in which we can realize the perfection for which our hearts long. That this impulse is most deeply implanted in our nature and survives every disappointment and failure proves that we are meant to realize it. The nearer morality comes to this perfection, the more are its laws transformed into the inspired acts of imaginative love.

Those who are capable of such acts are not blind to the distinction between the creative and the destructive. But by committing themselves to the adventure of creative living, which involves letting go of their moral preconceptions and preferences and being hospitable to all experience, they can begin to live morally in the truer and deeper sense of the word.

We cannot, of course, do this merely by recognizing its necessity, though that is an essential first step. Most of us are too much involved in the battle of existence, not so much outwardly as inwardly, to transform recognition into realization. For we *are* that battle, as Krishna shows Arjuna so convincingly in the *Bhagavad-Gita*. The bright and dark angels are at enmity in us on such different levels, in some crudely and obviously when the dark angel is the repressed and alienated satyr of our lower nature, but often, as in Arjuna, more subtly, when contrary impulses are bewilderingly mixed.

But if, as we range ourselves on what seems to be the better side in the battle, we realize that this temporal choice is due to our failure and the failure of our world to recognize the timeless Truth, in which our good and evil are redeemed, we shall be gradually preparing ourselves for the moment when the scales fall from our eyes, when we become creative both in what we do

and refrain from doing, responding to circumstance with a spontaneous rightness, our feet set at last on that 'Perfect Way,' of
which the Zen Patriarch, Seng-ts'au, wrote that it

> *knows no difficulties*
> *Except that it refuses to make preference:*
> *Only when freed from hate and love*
> *It reveals itself fully and without disguise.*
> *A tenth of an inch's difference,*
> *And heaven and earth are set apart:*
> *If you want to see it manifest,*
> *Take no thought either for or against it.*[1]

The Buddhist patriarch who wrote this poem lived in the
seventh century A.D. But what he realized with such inward
subtlety is implicit in the cosmogony and metaphysics of Vedanta.
The 'Perfect Way,' which mediates between the conscious and
unconscious, and reconciles them, can be trodden by man because
the ultimate Principle of his being is non-dual. Only a non-dual
Principle could create through duality without falling into dualism.

In Vedanta there is a primordial syllable in which this Principle
and the mystery of its triune nature is immemorially enshrined, and
through which, it was held, the cosmic harmony might be invoked. This is the syllable A U M. It is, the Vedic seers affirmed,
the most basic and all-inclusive of sounds, its first letter A being
the root sound, pronounced without any contact of tongue or
palate; the U filling the sounding-board of the mouth, and the M
completing the sound through the closed lips. To speak it, therefore, involves the whole process of human sound-production.

The significance of the word A U M in Vedanta is, of course,
much more than phonetic. It is the word in which, supremely,
silence and sound are felt to combine, the vibrating silence of the
unmanifest Brahman, the very pulse of Being, expressed through
the harmonizing chord of the Brahmic trinity. Thus the A is the
creative Brahma, who, in ancient Indian writings, is named 'the
first singer,' his song the singing world; the U is Vishnu the preserver, and the M is Shiva the destroyer; while the whole syllable,
truly spoken, sounds, as it symbolizes, the unceasing act of creation.
A Master, it is said, when he intones this word of power and peace

[1] Quoted in D. T. Suzuki's *Essays in Zen Buddhism* (First Series).

and directs it towards some troubled person or realm, counters the destructive vibrations, as Jesus did the storm on the Galilean lake.

This eternal word, as it is called in the *Mandukya Upanishad*, symbolizes, also, the three states of, waking, dreaming, and dreamless sleep, which, in the truly awakened, blend in a fourth state that 'is neither outer nor inner consciousness, neither semi-consciousness nor sleeping consciousness, neither consciousness nor unconsciousness. It is Atman, the Spirit itself.'

II

This brief analysis of some of the inner meanings discovered by the Hindu sages in the syllable AUM shows how their conception of the triune pattern, which informed all manifested life and made it One, was no abstract idea. But where in this Trinity, it may still be asked, is there a place for the divine Son, of the Christian Trinity?

For the Vedic seers, as I have said, he who realizes that he is Atman, is reborn as the divine Son, which in reality he always is. This surely, is the Son of whom Jesus said:

For the Father judgeth no man, but hath committed all judgment unto the Son; that all men should honour the Son, even as they honour the Father. He that honoureth not the Son honoureth not the Father which hath sent him.

To honour the Son is to reverence the divine image implanted in each one of us and to labour to make it wholly real in our lives and the lives of others. But the Christian Church has read into Jesus's words here and elsewhere the claim that those who denied, not the divine imagination in their hearts which Jesus supremely exemplified, but certain doctrines about him as the only Son of God, formulated by early Church Councils, would be condemned in the Judgment.

There are dangers, admittedly, in the Eastern conception of Self-realization in the Atman, temptations to pride and to the pursuit of a bodiless ecstasy, despite the wisdom and warnings of the ancient teachers. But the dangers of exclusive attachment to a personal Saviour, however helpful this may be to some at one stage in their struggle with the impersonal forces of the abyss, are quite as great. For the ancient teachers the disciple who truly loved his Master loved the Atman which the Master uniquely embodied and could thus realize his own identity in and through his Master's. By contrast any element of false attachment in devotion to a Master, as, indeed, to anyone else, sullies the pure imaginative understanding by which we can be wholly ourselves in intimate communion with another.

It is this principle of identity in difference that we are meant to love and so often fail to recognize even in those most dear to us. 'Verily,' as the *Upanishad* says, 'not for the sake of the husband is the husband dear, but for the sake of the Self. Verily, not for the sake of the wife is the wife dear, but for the sake of the Self.' We love even the imperfections of people because they give us partial glimpses of the perfect and we forgive the injuries they do us as lapses from the real goodness which we divine within them.

If this is true of our human relationships, how infinitely true it must be of our relation to Brahman, the Principle and Source of all perfection. And since such a relation cannot subsist with emotional or mental ties, Vedanta seeks to free us from these. Whether we claim to love God or some person who is dear to us, it bids us ponder that love to see if there is in it any desire that binds. If there be, we have not learnt the reality of love, however much we may protest our devotion. The 'living, loving, personal God' understandably dear to Christian believers is less than real, so far as he is the reflection of our need and not the image of our truth.

Vedanta does, indeed, discourage belief in such a 'personal' God. The ideal of relationship which it holds before us, primarily with That Which we are and through That with our fellow beings and the natural world, is one of wholeness in ourselves. Only when there is nothing unrelated to the Atman in ourselves can we be truly in union with the God Who in wisdom, love and power creates, preserves and destroys. The prayer, 'Lead me from the unreal to the real, lead me from darkness to light, lead me from death to immortality' is addressed to a Mind and a Heart, omnipresent in the universe, which answers from the depths of our being.

As Sri Aurobindo wrote, 'to see the truth does not depend on a big intellect or a small intellect. It depends on being in contact with the Truth and the mind silent and quiet to receive it.' Or, in the words of the *Mundaka Upanishad*, 'the Atman (the Self) cannot be won through learning nor through the intellect nor by much study of Scripture. He who chooses Atman is chosen by Atman. To him the Atman reveals his true nature.'

It is as simple and as difficult as that. We need only to consent to be possessed by That which we truly are. And all systems of Yoga are no more than means by which we may learn to do this, breaking down in the process the barriers of self-centred intellect and feeling which divide us from undividedness. Non-duality has never been for me, as it never was for these ancient seers and sages of India, a metaphysical theory. As knowledge, it was and is a realization of the nature of reality from which inevitably flows a non-dual way of life, and with it a transformed experience.

> *When the mind is overcome by its own radiance*, says the *Prasna Upanishad, then dreams are no longer seen: joy and peace come to the body.*
>
> *Even as birds, O beloved, return to their tree for rest, so all things find their rest in Atman, the Supreme Spirit.*
>
> *All things find their final peace in their inmost Self, the Spirit: earth, water, fire, air, space and their invisible elements; sight, hearing, smell, taste, touch and their various fields of sense; voice, hands, and all powers of action, and their spheres of action; mind, reason, the sense of 'I,' thought, inner light and all their objects; and even life and all that life sustains.*
>
> *It is the Spirit of man who sees, hears, smells, touches, and tastes, thinks and acts and has all consciousness. The Spirit of man finds peace in the supreme and deathless Self.*
>
> *He who knows that Eternal Self, bodiless and shadowless, luminous and everlasting, attains. He knows, O beloved, the all and becomes the all.*

This it is to live wholly the ancient affirmation *Tat Tvam Asi*, 'What That is, you are'.[1]

[1] I owe this rendering of the Sanskrit words to Professor Ernest Wood in his book, *Practical Yoga.*

CHAPTER SIX

Approaches to Yoga

I

THE ART of Yoga is based upon the conception of the universe and of man's part in it which I have outlined in the last chapter. It is an attempt to act out this conception and to conform to reality by living it. The philosophical fashion to-day, particularly among the logical positivists, is to assert that metaphysics are meaningless because metaphysical statements cannot be tested empirically. This may be true of a purely abstract idealism, but not of organic Vedanta. Its metaphysics grew out of real experience and the practice of Yoga is a proving in actual living of the pattern of reality which has been spiritually seen. To grasp fully the pattern and assent to it initiates a new way of life.

By assent is implied something more than mental assent, valuable as that can be as a preliminary to a deeper commitment. Between such assent and a vital realization there is a gulf to be crossed as wide as life and as deep as death. That gulf is primarily in ourselves, though it divides us also from real intimacy with our fellow-men. That the gulf is, from the standpoint of reality, an illusion does not make it less formidably actual, though it may tempt us to take short cuts across it.

Vedanta has never countenanced such short cuts whether physical or mental, by breathing exercises, for example, or gymnastics of the mind. True it is that realization will change our very breathing as well as our mental habits. But the Indian sages taught that enlightenment of mind and heart was a pre-condition of all fruitful change on the instinctual or semi-conscious and sub-conscious levels.

In this the Yoga of Vedanta differs from the 'depth psychology' of our own day in which release from conflict is sought through images projected from the unconscious in dreams which, if rightly interpreted and accepted, may become transforming symbols.

This apparent difference of approach is primarily due to the contemporary assumption that the lower can sufficiently explain the higher. But it, also, results from the fact that analytical psychology is a medical science. The modern psychologist's theories have grown out of his practice in treating unbalanced people. He is almost exclusively concerned with the conflicts which occur at that stage of evolution in which an individual is emerging from unconscious subservience to instinctive forces and struggling to become independent.

A relatively stable ego is, in fact, a necessary basis for any advance towards deeper integration. The psychologist seeks to resolve his patient's quarrel with primordial nature. And so he concentrates on those archetypes or primordial images which are, as Erich Neumann has well put it, 'the pictorial forms of the instincts.'[1]

The Masters of Yoga, on the other hand, begin where the psychologist ends. At least they insist that only the responsibly adult should undertake intensive practices which conduce to outgrowing the ego. They do not, therefore, neglect to affirm and reaffirm the basic moral principles upon which any healthy unfolding of spiritual consiousness depends.

The psychologist suspects and avoids all moral teaching, not only because his approach is experimental, but because a negative or Puritan morality has played havoc with many of his patients and is part of the disease from which they are suffering. The moral teaching of Yoga, however, is universally relevant, because it conforms to the creative pattern. It ensures, disinterestedly, the bounds within which the miracle of transformation can occur.

In brief, contemporary psychology concentrates on the self-conscious individual's relation to the instinctive plane and the 'collective unconscious' from which he is painfully emerging, while the teaching of traditional Yoga is addressed to a more fully conscious individual, whose soul is ready to open to the super-conscious realm and complete thereby his integration in the height as well as the depth. Admittedly the analytical psychology of Jung has thrown valuable light on this stage in human development, too, to which it has given the name 'centroversion.'

Unquestionably, too, dreams can be a means of communication

[1] In *The Origin and History of Consciousness* translated from the German by R. F. C. Hall.

with super-conscious as well as with sub-conscious life and a method based on dream analysis need not conflict with the ancient Yoga, may, indeed, corroborate it. But it represents a different approach to the centre in which unity lies. Modern psychology explores the feminine depths of the psyche, its instinctive roots. This is appropriate to an age which has witnessed the disruption ensuing from centuries of masculine assertiveness both on the mental and physical planes. The patients of the psychologist are victims, as we all are in different degrees, of a civilization in which the self has ceased to draw, either through instinctive faith or intuitive knowledge, upon That which sustains and completes it. It is contact with this 'More,' as Jung calls it, which psychology to-day seeks to restore through the symbols which arise in the dreaming mind, when self-consciousness is in abeyance.

Under skilled guidance this technique is of proved value for the individual who is still at the mercy of forces of which he is unconscious, forces which are potentially of the greatest creative value. Until these are consciously recognized, they are more often than not forces of negation and destruction, dark monsters that intensify in the depths the conflict being waged by the ego on the surface. The initiative in changing the centre of our life may, however, come directly from the conscious and super-conscious level or indirectly through the sub-conscious and unconscious. Any opening to the primordial depths must be at least dubious unless it is balanced by an equally dedicated opening to the spiritual heights. On those heights Reality manifests Its nature through a pattern of ideas which, as Plato and Plotinus taught, signify the essential form of things, just as in the depths It reveals Itself darkly through archetypal images.

These ideas provide a metaphysical framework and sanction within which any 'experiment in depth' may be conducted and its findings evaluated. They are not arbitrary notions, but reveal themselves to the kind of intuitive understanding, named *Buddhi* in Vedanta, of which I have spoken. Through this faculty we apprehend the Divine Wisdom, and the enlightened spirit sees the ideal form of truth, when consciousness is detached from the sensory plane, just as the soul gives birth to archetypal images, when allowed to dream.

But while the human soul in its primordial dreaming is embedded in the realms of nature, the awakened spirit is conscious of a super-human and angelic world with which it is intimately related. Spiritual vision without depth is thin and ghostly. But the soul cannot fully awake from that vegetative sleep which Blake anathematized, until Consciousness has descended into it from a supernatural realm—a truth which many myths have pictured. The intentions of the creative spirit may be imaged in dreams, but it is only in minds awake in the ideal realm that it reveals the pure form of its wisdom.

The Masters of the ancient Yoga did not overlook the feminine kingdom, in which the serpent of life lies coiled, awaiting its ascent and transformation into the serpent of wisdom. Some schools of Yoga, such as the Tantric, concentrated attention upon it and in all schools its importance was recognized. How, indeed, could there be 'union,' if one of the contraries was disregarded? In all true meditation the body meditates as well as the mind, even as a forest meditates beneath the sun or a flower beneath the stars. But while the Tree of nature has its roots in the earth and the nether abyss, the Eternal Tree, in the words of the *Katha Upanishad*, 'has its roots in the sky and its branches falling on earth,' branches which, like those of the BoBo tree under which the Buddha found enlightenment, root themselves in the soil of existence.

Man's roots in the darkness of earth are not in doubt, though often, alas, violated. But he is even less conscious of his roots in the Kingdom of Light. Admittedly the Light does not only shine in its own Self-luminous kingdom. It also lies hidden in the dark unconscious. Hence the patterns of universal significance which emerge from it in dreams for the psychologist and his patient to interpret. But in the traditional Yoga, as in the traditional practice of mystics of all faiths, the devotee seeks his true centre, not in a trance or a dream, but by a process of mindful concentration, which embraces more and more of reality as it enlarges and deepens its content. Such practice was based on the belief that only when the individual has clearly recollected what he is as a being unattached to, though immersed in, the natural world, can he descend into the lower kingdom in freedom, not de-natured but re-natured.

Doubtless in some of the ancient Masters of Yoga and in the schools they founded this descent happened very imperfectly. This, indeed, is the popular conception in the West of what Yoga means. Its practice has seemed to many to be based on an ideal of total abstraction, of a perpetual flight of the alone to the Alone, of withdrawal without return. Pictures of emaciated Fakirs, lost to the world in an intoxicated state of 'God-consciousness,' have encouraged this notion. Nor can one deny that the East has erred as grievously in its pursuit of a bodiless spirituality as the West in its materialism.

But a true art and science is not invalidated by its corruptions or excesses. India has taken much more seriously than the West the injunction of its spiritual teachers that a man must renounce the world as a possession to receive it back as a gift. Jesus said the same. True renunciation is an inward act which alters and eventually transforms one's relation to what is within oneself, one's divided faculties and impulses, and to what is without, one's fellow-creatures.

We grow by the grace which is given to us, when we have ceased to want to grow by our own effort or for our own profit. It seems to contradict all our active habits, but the deeper law of life is that we cannot find the truth until we have ceased to *want* knowledge, or experience real love until we have ceased to *want* love. Only then are we in a condition to receive and to give it.

In Yoga we learn to surrender this 'want' in the discovery of an omnipresent reality. Even the desire to be free from desire, if it contains within it any recoil from suffering, is a denial of Yoga, which aims to transform the instinctive faith, deep-rooted in our subconscious, that we are inseparably at one with That which acts and suffers in us, into a conscious awareness, an intuitive certainty which nothing can shake.

The first and last aim of a true Yoga is to teach us to live in a realization of our spiritual being. But though this requires that we should not identify ourselves with any of the vehicles of our spirit, it is equally essential that no part of our being, of which body and mind are modes, should be excluded from the transforming power of spiritual consciousness. Nor is it only our own bodies which are involved in this. For they are a part of the body of life, of the physical world to which they belong, just as our minds are part of the mental life of the world. It is through their redemption that the material world which has been infected and corrupted by our diseased living, as the mental world has been by our diseased thinking, will be restored to health and harmony.

This truth is implicit in the lives and teaching of those Saviours or Avatars, who, in the words of an Indian Scripture, 'descend from God eternally, like life-giving streams flowing in every direction from an inexhaustible lake,' or, 'like countless sparks from a great fire go forth eternally from God's ancient fire, the fire of love. In order to redeem, they descend upon the earth and other worlds to remove the burdens of these worlds, and then return to their origin, the fire.'

There is darkness to be redeemed in the heavens immediately above the earth as well as in the hells below, in the superconscious as well as in the subconscious. For the divine and the demonic are in conflict in the realms of half-knowledge not less than in the abyss of human ignorance. It would seem that the ancient Masters of Yoga concentrated the light of their wisdom chiefly upon these higher levels, knowing that the 'below' is conditioned by the 'above' and must be approached through it. Nor was mankind then, as I have suggested, so deeply entangled in matter as it was later to become. But when, in later centuries, the cult of Yoga spread more widely among men of inferior vision, its integrity was often lost in various systems of training directed to perfect control of body or mind for its own sake. Thus separation found its way into the very heart of the sacred science of Union.

This, however, is typical of what has happened the world over, in the West as in the East, when the revelation of a Master has descended into self-interested minds. But the integrity of the real Yoga is secure against such violation.

I I

But before we ponder the Yoga which Krishna teaches in the *Bhagavad-Gita*, it may be well to consider briefly the nature of personal devotion to one who is held to incarnate the divine. We confront the issue in the Christian creed. For to the majority of Christians Krishna is no more than a myth, at best a dramatic impersonation of the divine wisdom, conceived by some seer or poet of old, while Jesus is an actual person, who alone can be loved as both God and man.

Yet this distinction, if indeed it is valid, since, in the belief of many of his devotees, Krishna, also, took human form as a living teacher, is to me of secondary importance. For their immediate disciples the presence in the flesh of Krishna or of Christ was a powerful aid to devotion. But even to them it was the spirit which each Master embodied in his own unique way that really mattered. One might say, that a man is only real in the degree that he is a myth. For that is his eternal image. And that is what survives the death of the actual man.

The archetypal figure, who transcends the personal Saviour of the Christian's worship, is a mythological re-creation of the man who taught and died in Palestine. The process, if we are to judge by what has invariably happened in the case of other teachers or martyrs whom their followers believed to be divine, began within a few years of his death, long before the Gospels were written or even the inspired, but prejudiced imagination of St. Paul created the Pauline Christ.

We see, too, the same process at work in the visions which men and women of different religions have of the particular Master whom they have been taught to reverence. There has been a recent example of this in the vision of Jesus which the Pope is reported to have had during his illness. It is possible to interpret such a vision as indicating the actual presence of that one Master, provided it is not claimed that only that image of the divine is authentic and that a Hindu who in similar circumstances has a vision of Krishna is deluded. For each of these Masters embodied the Supreme Spirit and it is this Spirit, in one of its manifestations which the devotee receives through the form most dear to him.

But it is equally true that many mystics have entered into communion with and received the Grace of the Supreme Spirit without any mediating figure or image. Sufficient for them was 'that God, who,' in the words of the *Katha Upanishad*, 'is always seated in the hearts of men and who is known by the pure in mind and heart.'

To the Christian, however, the person of his Saviour is of supreme importance, since he believes that in Jesus alone did the Divine Mind create the one entirely human image of Itself.

This belief, however, has borne very mixed fruits. That Jesus embodied a quality of the divine, distinct from the Masters who preceded him, is undeniable and that he gave a more deeply human expression to that side of the Divine nature which we may call personal. To the eye of the seer and the poet this personal quality is inseparable from the love imaged by Vedanta in Vishnu, which informs and cherishes all creation, without transgressing the impersonal rule of law, which can seem to be its opposite. In fact we have here but another example of the contraries through which the Creator manifests. But to over-emphasize the personal in our approach to Him, even if this does not involve, as it often does, an anthropomorphic conception of Him as a person, is to reduce His mystery and narrow our approach to it.

One result of the exclusive concentration on the person of Jesus in Christian belief and practice has been a tendency to reduce the emphasis which he placed upon seeking the Kingdom of Heaven within in favour of dependence upon the sanctified figure of the Master, the hero-Saviour by whom 'a sufficient sacrifice' has been made, once and for all. In this way Christianity may satisfy more completely than other faiths the deep-rooted need of humanity to deify its heroes. But it does so at a grievous cost as its arrogantly militant history has shown. Yet a personal relationship with the divine need not be exclusive and out of it has flowered so much of tender beauty in poetry and legend, folk-lore and homely custom, whether in the East or the West, that this alone proves how creative it can be.

In Hinduism the devotion paid to Krishna as an incarnation of Vishnu is a comparatively late development of Vedanta. It, too, has had its excesses. But love of one who for the devotee embodies the divine has never in Hinduism been exclusive. For it is believed that God has descended time after time to earth. Not one star in the heavens has beckoned the wise throughout the ages, but many. And each has a message of eternal value for someone.

As Krishna himself declares in the *Gita*, 'though birthless and unchanging of essence . . . whensoever the true order of existence fails, then do I reincarnate, to protect those who are in the right path, to destroy wickedness, to establish the divine Law, I am reborn from age to age.'

The stories of these incarnations are intertwined. The legend of Krishna's birth, for example, like that of Gautama Buddha, is similar in some of its symbolic incidents to that of Jesus. His birth, as related in the *Bhagavata*, was in a prison (stable and prison are variants on the the ancient cave), in which his parents had been confined by a wicked king, who, like Herod, planned to kill him. He, too, was Virgin born. At least his father is described as receiving the divine child first in his spirit and communicating the divine being to the spirit of his young wife. Instead of the celestial song of the angels to greet the birth of the holy child, there is celestial light which fills the prison, and instead of the flight to Egypt, there is the miraculous escape from the prison by the father who carries the child across a river to a pastoral country where he is entrusted to a shepherd king and queen for safety.

Such correspondences occur in the legends that grew up around the lives of all in whom humanity has recognized the divine. But they are different in quality because each Master has expressed a different note in the scale of divinity. For the Hindu, Krishna embodies the pure joy of the divine, of spirit rejoicing in its own light and radiating that light lovingly to the minds and hearts of men. For the Christian, Jesus embodies the divine spirit as it suffers in the growing soul and redeems it by the sacrifice of love on the cross of existence. We see this difference reflected in the story of the child, Krishna, playing with the Gopas and Gopis, the shepherds and milkmaids, who symbolize the natural senses, while Jesus argues with the Rabbis in the Temple or helps his foster-father at the carpenter's bench. All the tales of Krishna have something in them of tender playfulness, of a divine love and light at home in a human world that is not yet tormented by an ingrained sense of sin, or by the craving for self-torture which so ofter accompanies it.

The being who embodied on earth the divine teacher of the *Gita* lived long before historical records and what tradition tells of his life may well be fictitious. But it is untrue that God can only be known and loved through a Saviour whose biography is well authenticated. The facts of a man's life are always less than certain, particularly if he lived long ago and excited men's imagination by his spiritual qualities. The depth of meaning contained in the figure in which they devotedly recreated his human form is what matters, even if the records of his life are contradictory or dubious. It is this image of the 'human form divine,' which love can contemplate inexhaustibly and through which a light and power beyond our ordinary consciousness can flow.

The God with whom we seek union is neither personal, in our limited human conception of a person, which at best is tainted by our wants and attachments, nor the impersonal Absolute which remains when we strive consciously to eliminate subjective feeling

So long as these two approaches to truth are separate, as they are, for example, in sentimental religion or objective science, reality cannot be fully known and lived. That is only possible through the pure contemplation, in which feeling and thought correct and complete each other. To purify the feeling implicit in personal devotion, with its ardent impulse of self-giving, requires a continuous effort in re-collective thought, while recollection demands sustained faith and love.

'Love for what or whom?' it may be asked by those who require a well-defined personal God to receive and return their devotion. 'Love for the Light,' I would answer, for the ineffable truth, the transfiguring beauty, the unwilled goodness which unfold in the mysterious depths of the soul as it opens in pure submission to the Spirit that is all, and, through the awakened soul, in all the soul contemplates within and around it.

This is the Light of which St. Augustine wrote,

> *I entered, and beheld with the mysterious eye of my soul the light that never changes, above the eye of my soul, above my intelligence. It was something altogether different from an earthly illumination. It was higher than my intelligence because it made me, and I was lower because made by it. He who knows the truth knows that light, and he who knows that light knows eternity. Love knows that light.*

This submission of the soul to the Light of its being is imaged in Hindu mythology in the figure of Radha as she awaits the coming of her lover, Krishna, even as Mary received the angel of the Annunciation. For the Light loves the soul that is open to it, and our human love, even for the Master most dear to us, is partial and possessive until it is wholly infused with this Light of Wisdom. A Divinity which did not evoke love from us, and not merely as a spiritual hunger for some formless universal, but by Its adorable presence in the minute and concrete particulars of our daily life, would, indeed, be unreal. But equally unreal is the love which seizes on the particular and, in whatever degree, wrests it out of the keeping of the universal to cherish and cage it in its own private hands.

Down the ages the Great Masters have revealed to men what it is to be a Son of God, a being who radiates the Light of wisdom and the power of love with a redeeming intensity. Each of them reveals to mankind a new dimension of human experience, a new possibility of integrating being and awareness.

In the integrity of each of these Masters certain aspects of the Divine Nature have predominated and each, according to the cycle of time in which he lived, has quickened awareness on a new level, by which man has come to understand himself better and all that is involved in the task of being a man.

As Jesus opened men's eyes especially to the dark depths in themselves and the need of redeeming, through sacrificial love, the abysmal forces of the unconscious, Krishna, and after him, with a difference, the Buddha, showed how the cage of self-consciousness, in which the ego was torn between the opposites, might open and become a home for the super-conscious Light. According to our natures and our need we will be the more drawn to one or the other, or, it may be, to some guide less supreme and luminous than they, who is yet our destined teacher.

But every true Master, whatever the particular emphasis of his life and teaching and of the initiation which he can give, embodies that condition of pure consciousness and abounding life which we call divine. It is this which each of them bids us love and not his person. If we love the Master who speaks most intimately to our condition and our need in this way, feeling that through our devotion to the Creative spirit in him and our efforts to realize life as he did, we are enabled to share in that spirit, then we love God personally without false attachment and the path of devotion can lead more directly than any other to the goal of realization.

It is because the divine teacher of the *Bhagavad-Gita* never binds His devotee to Himself, but, like a sun of whom we are rays, invites us through faith in Him and by practising the Yoga which He teaches, to come into union with all life through That of Which all life is an expression, that for me He is truly one of the supreme Masters of them that know.

CHAPTER SEVEN

Doing and Knowing

I

IN THE *Bhagavad-Gita*, the Lord's Song, we come down to the psychological and practical problems which face us when we set out to realize in our lives the great affirmation of the *Upanishads*, 'That you are.'

'The whole universe,' declares the *Isha Upanishad*, 'and all that lives and moves on earth is clothed in the glory of the Lord. Renounce then the transient and enjoy the eternal.' Krishna, as he begins to instruct the dejected Arjuna on the field of Kurukshetra reaffirms in less ecstatic words this fundamental truth.

But that is just what Arjuna cannot do, placed as he is between warring opponents on a battlefield which represents essentially the conflict in his own soul. Thus the basic affirmation of the *Upanishads* is here put to the test of the stultifying dualism in human nature which seems to contradict it. The *Gita* begins by picturing this dualism in a dramatic scene and when it has reduced a heroic spirit to utter impotence.

It is a situation with which those of us who have lived during the last forty years through the hours preceding the outbreak of two appalling wars are painfully familiar. Yet to regard the *Gita*, on the grounds of its opening scene, as justifying the kind of warfare by which, throughout its history, mankind has only temporarily eased its most violent tensions is surely mistaken.

The *Gita* is part of the ancient Indian epic, the *Mahabharata*, and may well have been, in the form in which it has come down to us, a later interpolation. Its author or authors are unknown but it seems to have assumed its final form, shortly before the birth of Christ, over many centuries, in which it came to combine harmoniously the teaching of different schools of Yoga, notably those based on the non-dualism of the *Upanishads*, on the teaching of the great sage, *Kapila*, who lived, it is conjectured, a century or so before Gautama Buddha and originated the system of thought known as the *Samkhya*, and on such later teachers as Patanjali, whose 'Yoga aphorisms' became a classic of Yogic method.

I am not, however, concerned with the history, largely speculative of the *Gita*. But something needs to be said about the telling drama with which it opens. This links it closely with the great epic of which the divinely-born Arjuna is the chief hero. He is, be it noted, a man of action, who had declared earlier in the epic that 'he who possesses courage, though devoid of other merits, will overcome.' He is not a Brahmin, whose vocation it is to cherish and transmit wisdom. 'The Kshatriya's power,' (the caste to which Arjuna belongs), 'lies,' it is said, 'in physical strength, a Brahmana's in forgiveness.' The epic provides the immediate situation in which Krishna begins to teach. But though the *Mahabharata*, like the *Iliad*, has probably a background of actual events, its endduring meaning is mythical and the battlefield of Kurukshetra is a symbol, not only of man's spiritual situation on earth, but of the perennial conflict in the heart.

In prehistoric times, when man lived close to the natural world, war was a primitive activity in which it was more possible to engage than it is to-day without pangs of conscience and without threatening the destruction of mankind. Doubtless unthinking men in every age have engaged in it without scruple and such scruples as they might have had have been silenced by sheer necessity or by the sanctification of war by their religious and secular leaders. Admittedly, too, brutal physical warfare, even when bound by certain conventions which preserve some sense of man's dignity as a human being, is an elementary clash of the opposites, characteristic of unregenerate life. As such it provides, on the lowest spiritual level, an apt enough setting for the dilemma in which Arjuna finds himself. But to accept it literally rather than symbolically and to interpret Krishna's advice to him as justifying the bloody violence of war is hard to reconcile with the teaching which follows.

For what Krishna teaches Arjuna, as we shall see, and what he teaches us to-day is how we may learn to transcend the inward conflict of which warfare is a crude outward showing. The alternative which he puts to him is not between violence and recoil from violence. That is the alternative to which Arjuna has succumbed. And so far as to act with courage is better than to wring one's hands, Arjuna has made the worse choice on that level.

But the whole of Krishna's teaching is intended to show that this choice between two evils is enforced on man only so long as he is under fate and has yet to fulfil his true destiny as the spiritual man, who mediates creatively between the temporal and the eternal; that the problem which seems insoluble on the level of the divided self can be resolved at a higher level, and that though the conflict of life must not be evaded and on a primitive level involves a blind battle for survival, yet a man who is spiritually awakened can no longer identify himself with physical and mental warfare in any of its forms or under any of its plausible disguises.

So far as he enters into this warfare, it is by the redemptive power of love and light released within him. This may necessitate his consenting to martyrdom. But to kill with violence, however dispassionately, to enforce his will to the death upon another, would, for such a man, tear heaven and earth apart and shatter his integrity. Indeed, as Joseph Chiari has written[1] 'violence in all its forms can only be upheld in the name of philosophies which, whatever their denials, limit man's life to time.'

On these grounds alone I have always agreed with Gandhi that, for anyone striving to-day to live up to what Krishna teaches, the fight which he enjoins upon Arjuna throughout his discourse is, essentially, a fight against the ignorance in himself, though in the actual epic Arjuna, the warrior, takes up arms again.

This is not, of course, to argue that Krishna condemns all action which results in the destruction of physical life. Creation and destruction are the two modes through which the Divine manifests, as He will awesomely reveal to his disciple in due course. To deny one of them is to deny the other. But only the destruction which is truly a mode of creation and not a violent violation of life's inherent unity can be approved or participated in by an enlightened man.

Doubtless in ages when warfare seemed a legitimate expression of biological law, with which men instinctively conformed, its contradiction of a higher law was less apparent and it could be accepted as a necessary instrument of justice when every peaceful means had failed. But to-day, when 'total' war has become a mechanical outrage even upon biological law, the contradiction is inescapable.

[1] In *Symbolism from Poe to Mallarme*.

Nor can it be evaded by belittling physical destruction on the ground that 'he who thinks that the Atman kills or is killed is without discernment. It neither kills nor is killed.'

War is a stark display of the disease from which man is suffering, but to condone it by denying the responsibility of spirit to body is only to widen and perpetuate the split from which it springs. In any case Krishna is not speaking in the *Gita* to nations in arms. He is speaking to that single person everywhere who, like Arjuna, has come to a crucial turning-point in self-awareness at which, at whatever cost, he must embrace a new dimension of experience and a new mode of action or disintegrate.

The setting, then, of the *Gita* on a battlefield dovetails it into the epic story, but need not to be taken literally. The real battlefield is in the human soul at the point when self-consciousness reduces us to impotence. The conflict is the more intense because Arjuna is a man of truly heroic nature who can no longer play the unthinking heroic part. But Arjuna is more than a man or even an epic hero. So are all the chief characters present on the field of Kurukshetra when the stage is set for the dialogue with Krishna. The field, too, is more than a field. Outwardly the conflict in which Arjuna is so fatally involved is a family quarrel between cousins, the five Pandavas, of whom Arjuna is one, and the Kauravas, whose father had illegally seized the throne to which the Pandavas were entitled. Through trickery, too, the Pandavas had been deprived even of their one share of the kingdom.

Ultimately, despite all efforts at reconciliation, it seems that only war can decide the issue. The rival hosts are drawn up on the battlefield and it is then that Arjuna, the chief, though not the eldest, of the Pandava brothers, horrified by the prospect of a slaughter of close relatives and the destruction of the social order and its ancient laws, recoils from the battle. Throwing aside his bow and arrows, he sits down in his chariot, his heart heavy with sorrow. Krishna, who is acting as his charioteer, reproves him for his unmanliness without effect. But as he sits despairing between the two hosts, he begs Krishna to tell him clearly what he ought to do. 'I am your disciple,' he says. 'Teach me. I come to you for enlightenment.'

So the great dialogue begins. It is a dialogue, to quote Sri Krishna Prem,[1] 'between the human soul and the Divine Soul,'

[1] In *The Yoga of the Bhagavad-Gita.*

between the individual self and the Great Self, Whom it has yet
to know as its true Being. The contestants, the Pandavas and the
Kauravas, represent the opposites, with which we are now familiar. Though fallen into what seems irremediable antagonism, they
have the same primal sire, the 'One without a second,' in Whom
their ultimate destiny is to be reconciled.

It is in Arjuna, who represents the positive force in creation,
that this reconciliation must be effected. For his is the self-consciousness necessary to initiate the process by which the forces of
the unconscious may become conscious and thus cease to be alien
invaders. As yet, however, Arjuna is unequal to the task. Though
he sits between the two hosts on the battlefield, he is too self-
interested to mediate creatively between them. His apparent concern for his opponents, his horror at the prospect of destroying
them, does not open the way to fruitful relationship with them. It
merely paralyses his capacity for relationship. Antagonism itself
is to be preferred to this. For it does compel a vital recognition
of the other. Even his sense of family ties is only an extension of
the kind of self-attachment, which Jesus so sternly reproved when
he said, 'he that hateth not his father and mother is unworthy of
the Kingdom of Heaven.'

Yet his scruples are delusively human and reasonable. The divine
Lord admits as much when he begins his instruction by saying
'Your words are understandable, but your grief is misplaced.' It
is a self-centred grief, a shrinking of the sensibility, and Krishna
seeks first to recall Arjuna from attachment to the physical aspect
of things by reminding him that birth and death succeed each
other in the endless movement of life in time, and that the meaning of this movement is only to be found in the realm of unchanging values which enfolds and penetrates it. Arjuna is in no condition as yet to love and honour the body as the vehicle and crucible
of spirit. To love it so, without clinging to it, is, indeed, to be incapable of doing violence to it, not, however, through loss of nerve,
but through wholeness of spirit.

Arjuna's anguish is essentially a recoil from death. Indeed all
anguish, if we look deeply into it, has its roots in that. He rational-
izes this as a rejection of action which will shatter the existing
order. But what he really fears is the loss of the balance in himself
between chaos and order, which, as a half-conscious individual,
he precariously maintains. This is the order of existence of which

he fears the overthrow, if the battle is joined. And truly, through the violence of war, chaos does come again and the individual is engulfed, but not delivered or re-integrated in a greater consciousness.

The bond of kinsmen, so far as it is an extension of this individuality, belongs to the same order of existence. To break it, he says, is to live in hell, or, in other words, in the lonely void which underlies the domesticated surface of life with its racial or tribal leagues of offence and defence, its family ties and comforts, its biological bonds. From this hell, from the dark unfathomed part of his nature, he recoils, but unavailingly. For the bond is already broken or the hosts would not be facing each other on the battlefield, as they are in his own soul. They are there because the organic relationship between life and death, light and darkness, symbolized in the Pandavas and the Kauravas, has broken down. Evasion or kindly compromise is no longer possible. An impotent neutrality can only betray the light of consciousness which has begun to shine in his soul. The time has come for Arjuna, the man of light, to face and accept his shadow, that part of himself which he has repudiated either positively or negatively.

In other words Arjuna has entered what the mystics call 'the dark night of the soul.' His spirit must pass through it, if the bond he fears to break, but which in fact is already broken, is to be renewed in a new order of relationship. How this difficult journey may be accomplished and how the whole nature may be committed to it, Krishna proceeds to instruct him.

II

Like most of the scriptures of the world, the *Gita* has been a bone of contention between rival interpreters and particularly between those who have insisted that it teaches that, in the final release from the ego, all action must be renounced, and those who deny this. The former view drew strength from Shankara's commentary, in which he argued that since there is 'mutual opposition between performance of action and renunciation of it, as between motion and rest, the two cannot be accomplished by an individual at one and the same time.'

Self-interested action and the knowledge born of renunciation

cannot, indeed, be reconciled. But pre-eminent among all the
themes of the *Gita* is that which reveals the nature of the Self
which acts without acting, which is not 'the doer of actions' but,
in the purest sense, the supreme 'Actor' who plays creatively a
million parts. Different men at different stages of growth between
ignorance and illumination will incline more or less to outward
as distinct from inward action, to 'works' as distinct from 'knowledge.' But in the measure of their devotion the outward doers will
gradually learn, as the *Gita* puts it, to 'renounce all actions by
thought,' or, as we might say, to live more and more in the thought
or meaning of their acts, until 'works' express 'knowledge' and
knowledge culminates in enlightenment.

This theme and its implications in thought and practice, however, we shall explore more fully. I have only mentioned it here
as an outstanding example of the kind of controversy in which
generations of commentators have indulged. Similarly their coun-
terparts in the West, the Schoolmen and their successors, have
fought each other in the field of theological rationalism. Such dis-
putes once had meaning, a meaning so compulsive for those engaged in them that they led, in the West, to the same kind of
heartless brutality as the ideological conflicts of our own day. In
the East they were conducted in a more civilized way, but they
degenerated into endless wastes of abstract argument and counter-
argument, which were a substitute for the task of realization.

To that extent the 'existentialist' emphasis of to-day is sound.
But the human and psychological meaning of the *Gita* is inseparable from its spiritual meaning. From first to last it emphasizes the
eternal context of our existence, without a recognition of which
none of our human and temporal problems can be solved.

The main themes of Krishna's teaching recur throughout the
eighteen chapters. At first sight this reiteration may seem redun-
dant. But it is, in fact, essential to the gradual unfolding in the
reader's, as in Arjuna's, mind and soul, on different levels, of the
reality to which he is invited to conform.

As I have already said, the goal to which Krishna directs Arjuna is the realization of the Atman by which the errors of egotism
are finally dissolved. But herein lies the paradox. To him who has
not realized the Atman this Presence evades every conscious effort
he may make to realize it.

'Unshown, beyond thought and change, is This,' says Krishna.

'It comes to one as a vision of wonder; as a wonder another speaks of It. And as a wonder another hears of It. But though hearing of This, he knows It not.'

Since then It is closed to the kind of consciousness which we ordinarily exercise, however disciplined or refined that consciousness may become, we are required to cultivate a kind of unconsciousness as a precondition of realizing it. To seek to know It directly is to remain ignorant of It, however earnest our efforts or persistent our self-discipline may be. For the self which dictates such efforts will continue to stultify them. It is upon the right means, not the end, that we must concentrate our attentions. If these conform to the nature of Reality, we shall build up the conditions under which It manifests, as surely as the sun rises and sets on this planet, sustaining its life, because the earth circles round it.

These right means are laid down by Krishna in relation to the needs of different temperaments. Each of the different, yet congruent paths which he commends have been defined in more detail by other teachers. But their basic meaning is set forth in the *Gita* with a penetrating simplicity.

Arjuna is not a sage or the disciple of a sage who, remote from external stresses, can reason his way into truth. He is a man who has fought and thought his way to a standstill and who needs not only to know, so that he may regain his power to act, but also to act under enlightened direction so that he may learn to know. Yoga, as Krishna soon tells him, is both wisdom and skill in action. To seek wisdom, without learning to act it, will never unravel his bewilderment. A divided mind is only more distracted by the apparent contradictions of different scriptures or philosophies. Reasoning about these contradictions will not resolve them, and to such a mind true meditation is impossible.

'When your mind,' says Krishna, 'leaves behind the tangle of delusions in which it is caught, you will go beyond past and future scriptures. . . . When your mind, perplexed by what it has heard, rests unshaken in the Self, then the goal of Yoga will be yours.'

The mind which is subject to delusions and desires is that sixth sense, which, through countless separative acts, has spun round itself a dualistic web, in which, like a swollen spider, it catches the objects of its experience to feed itself. What enlarges this mind's self-esteem affords it pleasure. What reduces this sense gives it pain. It therefore longs for the one and recoils from the other.

The first fundamental step, then, towards liberation, Krishna declares, is to practise dispassion, to root out the habitual preference that we have formed for everything that gratifies and enlarges, even, it may be, by wounding our ego. Joy and sorrow, gain and loss, pain and pleasure will continue to come to us, but we shall cease to take sides for or against them, to measure their value by the degree to which they enhance our self-importance and conceal from us how delusive that kind of self-importance is.

There is, indeed, a Self-importance which is entirely valid, the importance of That which we truly are. For this the ego, with its continual need to assert and reinforce itself and its horror of deflation, is a pitiful substitute. But until a man has had some conscious experience of the real Self, the hold which the false self has over him will not be relaxed. The practice of dispassion is not commended for itself, but as a first condition of coming to know the reality which the various passions, and particularly those of fear, anger and greed, distort.

Our attachment to objects, including the images or opinions which we cherish, is, as I have shown, basically an attachment to ourselves. We need a reserve of such thoughts and things, to enhance our belief in ourselves, and the more dubious that belief may be, the intenser is our need. Of these objects those which gratify us through our senses have, over most people, the strongest attractive power. It is for this reason that Krishna places addiction to the pleasure of the senses as the first obstacle to be overcome. The lower mind, reflecting only what it receives through the physical senses, can offer no resistence to the ego which exploits it, as it exploits all the senses, for its own satisfaction.

The lower mind is the animal mind, the mind of physical existence. In the animal it acts unconsciously to preserve and perpetuate life. But self-conscious man has, to a smaller or greater extent, bound it to his partial purposes. The detachment from the objects of the senses of which Krishna teaches the necessity is to enable him to increase his spiritual awareness by beginning to think through a mind which is not tied to the animal level.

This higher mind or *manas*, as Vedanta calls it, is not the immediate organ of the creative consciousness, the intuitive Buddhi, but only reflects it. But it is sufficiently withdrawn from physical life to enable us to regard with detachment our bodily sensations or the images, pleasurable or painful, which we associate with them. It is attachment which is the obstacle, not the senses themselves, the claim to satisfaction, not responsiveness to the flame of life, to that 'desire' which the great 'Creation Hymn' in the *Rig-Veda* calls 'the primal seed and germ of spirit.'

> *When a man dwells on the pleasures of sense,* Krishna declares, *he becomes attached to them. From attachment arises possessiveness; from possessiveness springs anger (or excitement).*
>
> *From anger comes confusion of mind, then loss of memory (or recollectedness). From this comes loss of conscience (or inward discrimination) and in this wreck of understanding a man is lost.*
>
> *But he who moves in the world of the senses, free from attraction and aversion, obedient to the Self and harmonizing all his faculties in the Self, comes to peace and clearness.*
>
> *In this peace there is an end of misery. For in those whose minds are clear the understanding it utterly steadfast . . .*
>
> *When a man's mind is swayed by the roving senses, passion carries away wisdom as a wind a ship on the waters . . .*
>
> *He whom all desires enter, as waters flow into the ocean which, though filled from all sides, never overflows, is infinitely at peace; not so the desirous man.*
>
> *For the man who forsakes all desires, with no thought of an I and a Mine, finds perfect peace.*
>
> *This it is to abide in the Eternal. In attaining this, all delusion is gone.*

Here, very near the beginning of the *Gita*, the final attainment is held before the inward eyes of Arjuna. Again and again throughout the dialogue he is bidden to contemplate it afresh. Like a basic theme, stated in the first movement of a symphony, it recurs, illumined and enhanced by all that has meanwhile deepened its meaning and related it to the creative pattern manifest in the cosmos.

It seems, in this first statement of it, to provide the sufficient key for opening the door to the new world for which the aspirant longs. And so, in fact, it does, since self-attachment is the only obstacle to the joy and peace of realization. But to demonstrate this, however convincingly, is to bring home to an honest mind how deep and involved is our entanglement in self-interest of one kind or another, on this or that level of our nature, how subtle are the refinements of self-love even in the pursuit of what Fénelon called, in one of his famous letters to Madame de Maintenon, 'a certain perfection of virtue that one would wish to find in oneself.'

The degree of our self-love is the measure of our incapacity. To try, for example, to control or detach ourselves from the flow of introverted thoughts and images, which through years of selfcentred tension have scored deep channels in the mind, is to discover how far we are from being able to sit, as Krishna advises, contemplating and living the truth that 'we are no other than He.' And this is only one special way of renouncing the self in what Fénelon called 'a perpetual subjection to the signs of the will of God which is declared at every moment.'

Before commending the condition of unattachment to his pupil as the key to all else Krishna had, indeed, spoken briefly of methods for attaining it. He had dismissed as valueless the mere letter of scripture-reading or conventional religious rites. These, he declared, were as profitless for a truly discerning man as a tank in a place overflowing with water on all sides. Instead he had commended two ways of healing the sick psyche. He now enlarges upon the nature of these two paths, that of Karma Yoga or disinterested devotion in the ordinary work of life, and that of Jnana Yoga, of patiently practised discrimination between the real and the unreal.

These two paths are associated with two traditional schools of thought, those of the *Yoga* and *Samkhya* systems of philosophy. The advocates of the path of knowledge claimed that theirs was the superior path and that the man of true knowledge inevitably ceases to act. For he knows himself to be 'that Self who, as devoid of birth or any other change of condition, is immutable; he renounces all action in thought; he remains without acting or causing to act; he attains devotion in wisdom.'

So wrote Shankara in his commentary on the *Gita* and his words started a controversy which distracted countless minds from the

real meaning of Krishna's words and of the ancient Vedantic conception of the Self. As Brahman, that unborn and undying Self is,
indeed, declared to be pure consciousness beyond both action and
inaction. But, as Brahma, this Self creates and sustains the worlds
of manifestation by acts which are a perfect expression of knowledge. There is, therefore, no contradiction in the true nature of
things between knowing and acting for the man who has come
to live wholly in the presence of 'that Self.'

The quality and motive of his activity will, indeed be profoundly different from what they were before this realization. In
this sense it may truly be said that he no longer acts. For it is
creation itself that acts in and through him. This is the real meaning behind all the fruitless controversy concerning the respective
merits of the two kinds of Yoga. And it is this real meaning which
Krishna communicates to his pupil.

He begins by emphasizing anew the ingrained necessity of
action. But a man need not be inwardly bound by the energies
which bid him to act, provided he is personally unconcerned with
the fruits of his action. Such disinterestedness ensures a total
involvement in the service of life. It is the first step on the path for
the un-recollected and it completes and proves, as nothing else
can, any claim to enlightenment based upon interior methods of
contemplation. Self-love may lurk within sublime meditations and
be overlooked. But it is exposed plainly enough by our reactions to
success or failure in our acts. If we are selfishly elated by the one
or depressed by the other or in any way excited or disturbed by
either, we are still clinging to the fruits of action, as if they were
our own.

This is the sacrifice which the Self eternally asks of the self, because it is the law of Its own nature. 'I have nothing to achieve in
the two worlds,' declares Krishna,

> *nothing to attain which is unattained; yet I engage*
> *in action.*
>
> *For if I should tire of action, men would do the*
> *same. These worlds would perish in confusion, if I*
> *ceased to act.*

The acts of the Divine Actor are pure and total acts of being.
In that sense He may be said to do nothing. It is the same with
the man who offers all he does to the Self. 'Rejoicing and content

in the Self,' for him, too, 'there is nothing to do.' For having no selfish end in view, he is freed from all the nervous strain and waste of energy which self-centred acts involve.

Essentially Krishna declares, it is 'the fire of self-knowledge which reduces all self-determined actions to ashes.' There is, He says, 'no purifiers equal to this wisdom.' In such wisdom all wilful beliefs and opinions are, also, reduced to ashes. For just as all self-regarding hopes are but compensation for a lack of real hope, so do all such beliefs betray a lack of faith. 'Neither this world,' says Krishna, 'nor the worlds beyond nor happiness are for the faithless.' And by the faithless he does not mean unbelievers in religious doctrine, but those who do not commit themselves to the Atman.

Doubt of the Self necessarily goes with an illusory belief in the self. It is this doubt which 'the fire of self-knowledge' consumes. In consuming the doubt it destroys, also, the belief, whether in himself or in a doctrine, which divides a man inwardly, however forcefully he may affirm it.

For the purpose of the ego is always the same, whether masked by belief or unbelief. It is to perpetuate the delusion of separateness and to maintain its specious claim to determine what we do. 'Knowing the Truth,' says Krishna, 'we know that we do nothing at all, though we see, hear, touch, smell, eat, walk, sleep, and breathe.' It is 'the Great Lord of all worlds, the Friend of all beings' who acts in every faculty we possess and every breath we draw. To awake to the peace of His Presence is to 'rest happily in the nine-gated City of the body,' free from anxiety, vanity, and resentment; to be unperturbed in any situation, resourceful and expert; to injure no-one and to be beyond the injury of the world; to welcome whatever comes and to be at home wherever we are. 'Such a one,' Krishna declares, 'is exceedingly dear to me.'

III

Renunciation, then, of self-will, an abandonment of what the late Mathias Alexander called 'end-seeking,' in all our activities and in thought as in act, is the ground in which enlightenment can grow. But the ego cannot renounce itself, cannot rise above the flux of the separative life, which it has imposed upon the continuous movement in Nature from non-being to being in the process of becoming conscious. To act without desire for the rewards of action is at first no more than a method by which a man reduces the illusion, so powerful while he pursues his own interests, that he is the actor. It enables him gradually to realize that neither the energy nor the directing will behind what he does is his own. Thus he begins to become conscious of what Vedanta calls the Self, the Atman. He begins to understand, in Krishna's words, that he has 'no friend but Self, no foe but Self.'

The Self is friend to the self of him in whom self is con-. quered by the Self; but Self will war against him whose self is unsubdued.

Krishna does not mean to suggest by this that the Atman Itself is 'a jealous God.' It is we who, in denying the unity of Being, inevitably find life hostile to our claims.

But the more a man abandons self-interest in what he does, the less is he subject to the dualism by which the self exists. Discerning that life is a whole, in which all apparent opposites can fruitfully combine, he ceases to be the slave of his preferences and prejudices. He accepts what comes to him with an unshaken serenity. He no longer hates and loves according as a person or an object gratifies or offends his self-love. He sheds the bias of passion and from a new centre, that is forming within the void he thus accepts, he begins to experience life with love and equal-mindedness. The tranquility of such a man may seem to those who live by the passions a kind of indifference. And certainly in the transition from self to Self there will be phases when life's zest seems to fail. But what is dying in him is a specious vitalism which divides, even when it seems to unite. It must die, if he is truly to live.

Such equanimity, then, and the habits of conduct which lead to it, are a pre-condition of any more interior and intensive realization. But now Krishna begins to teach how the mind may be brought through meditation into union with its higher Principle so that it, too, like the body, may be freed from the thraldom which the ego has imposed upon it.

In meditation contact is sought with the creative consciousness of the Atman, which is Intelligence itself, pure and whole. Our real mind is no other than this. But except perhaps in flashes of illumination we are unaware of it. The mirror in us which should reflect the light of the Atman is thickly coated with a film of images, ideas, notions and opinions generated by the self from the time when it first began to manifest in our lives. This film is formed by the continued action of thought-waves, which in turn generate new thought-waves. Our sense-bound mind gives form to these thoughts, but it is feeling which excites them. And this feeling emerges from subconscious or unconscious depths and becomes active whenever the self makes contact with that which it regards as other than itself.

It would seem that in the hidden parts of our nature each one of us has a distinctive pattern of emotional tendencies and it is this latent predisposition and not the film of our habitual thoughts which Vedanta calls the *Samskaras*. They are the potentialities which determine our character for good or ill, though circumstances may modify them, and the Vedantist ascribes them, not merely to heredity, but to the impress of our own thoughts and actions in past lives..

But to extend the history of the self in time does not help to explain how and why this process of hidden feeling, exciting unreal thought, begins and continues. And since all meditation aims at reversing this process, it will be well to examine briefly its nature.

A good moment for observing the process is when we wake in the morning from a deep sleep. In those first moments of returning consciousness we are blissfully aware that our body is at peace, immersed in an ocean of unconsciousness of which it is still a part. Above it the mind floats in a dimension of its own, an airy realm spaciously empty of the forms which incessantly disturb it throughout the day. But though formless, this presence of mind is not meaningless. It seems momentarily to comprehend everything, to accept it and to love it, corresponding in this with the body's passive and unconscious acceptance of life.

But this condition is very transient. Almost at once another condition, with which we are far more familiar, supervenes. It is as if the mind resumed its hold over the body and at the same time became itself a thoroughfare for a stream of thoughts and images, following each other with an automatism which we can at best very imperfectly control. This transition from deep sleep to wakefulness is accompanied, if we observe ourselves closely, by a return of tension. We take a grip on ourselves. Our relaxed muscles imperceptibly contract, though we still lie passively in bed, and this physical contraction is only a reflex of a contraction in our mind.

We are resuming, in fact, the normal habit of our life in which we fight, however unconsciously, for life against death, for our own survival against all that threatens or seems to threaten it. Deep within us we feel insecure. The peace which came to us in body and mind when we committed ourselves to sleep is no more. Our faith is incomplete. Though apparently we may be happy in the prospects of the coming day, we are on guard once more.

Ordinarily we are unconscious or only obscurely conscious of this tension. But in periods of difficulty or moments of crisis our real condition becomes apparent and we may even, if what is testing us continues long, reach a breaking point. For however pacific our intentions, we are at war.

This may seem to be less a fact in more placid people than in the restless or ambitious or aggressive. But placidity may be due to easy circumstances and a temperament which has not yet exposed itself to the stress of consciousness. And different as are the relative degrees of strain in mind and circumstance, from the apparently calm and unruffled to the constantly agitated, it remains true that until consciousness has fully awakened, we are all necessarily at war.

When in the morning we wake from sleep, we do, in fact, fall asleep to the experience of unity which we unconsciously had while we slumbered. In this we are repeating daily the experience of which Wordsworth wrote in his famous ode and which, as self-consciousness tightens its hold upon us, dims or even closes the Eye through which 'the eternal mind' is meant to see.

Until that Eye is opened, we cannot reconcile ourselves to life or shed our fear of it. Between our need to *be*, as unique individuals, and the abyss of non-being which we feel to be waiting to engulf us, if we abandon the struggle to maintain our private claim on life, we can find no real peace.

This claim of the ego to be absolute in its own right is, like all the errors of the ego, the perversion of a truth. For in so far as we live in the Atman, we partake of its absolute and undying truth. We belong to the timeless and that is our reality. But it is a reality on which we have no claim. To claim it and to give preference to ourselves over the rest of life in our claim, is to lose it, to fall into unreality.

In the Atman, as we have shown, non-being subsists in harmony with being. There is no warfare, therefore, between existence and true Selfhood. The feud began when we became conscious of ourselves as distinct entities, struggling for survival in a world of rival entities asserting their claims at our expense. To survive and develop our own potentialities, above all the potentiality of a distinctive consciousness, we were compelled, it seemed, to range ourselves against the whole, of which each of us was a part, to fight for our entity not only against other entities, but against nonentity itself.

So the unity was broken; the true centre within us, in and through which the contraries are reconciled, was lost. In its place a knot was tied, eccentric to reality. It is to the untying of this knot that all forms of meditation are directed.

This knot within ties us fast to the outerworld, not in creative relationship but in a bondage against which we are always secretly rebelling. Yet so far as we see things as homogeneous and interrelated, we acknowledge the affinity which exists, in different degrees, between all objects. But we do this very imperfectly because we have moved away from our inner centre and so our vision of the circumference, of the world around us, is distorted. This leads us to strive to regain the unity for which we inwardly hunger by imposing our will subtly or crudely upon all that seems to oppose us, in an impossible attempt to swallow up an alien 'not-self' in the self.

This is the situation which meditation is meant to resolve, the prison from which it can be a means of release. Fundamentally every kind of meditation is intended to recall the consciousness and thereby the whole being to its true centre. Through losing this centre our experience has been vitiated and we are so habituated to the false vision and the self-centred reaction, that it is the way of wisdom and love which seems, if not eccentric, at least unrealistic, an evasion of a warfare which is basic to life.

Such a view of things, when it has become deeply ingrained, cannot be quickly dissolved. It may be necessary to begin the process by applying the acids of rational analysis to mental prejudices. This is a kind of meditation, though it be only on its rational fringe. Or again attention may be directed to some object with which we are familiar but which we have never observed for it-self. The more nearly we succeed in observing it for itself and identifying ourselves with it, the more, we discover, it ceases to be a mere object and becomes a living image, joining itself to an idea in our own mind. We may thus begin to recognize how self-enclosed we ordinarily are and how disinterested contemplation of a person or an object can give us a glimpse of an altogether new relationship. We begin to participate consciously in the creative mystery.

But even to achieve a momentary deepening and enlargement of vision, the mind with its incessant monkey activities, must be calmed. For this reason the tranquillising of the mind is as much a preliminary condition of all fruitful meditation, as acting without concern for reward and obeying the basic moral precepts. Never-theless the practice of mental tranquillity is only a means to the attainment of a new kind of knowledge.

'To him,' says Krishna, 'who sees Me in all things and all things in Me, I am ever present and he is present in Me.' Through medi-tation the mind grows into the knowledge of this Presence and, by ceasing to be self-centred in feeling and thought, re-enters the heart and learns to be imaginative and loving.

But truly to love, the ingrained habits of the mind have to be changed. And for those at least whose minds are restlessly active this involves a regular rule of practice. In theory all the ordinary activities of our daily life would be sufficient, if we could con-tinually and consciously employ them as means to union with the Self. In recognizing that we are not the doers, we can in fact, as Krishna has shown, live actively in some degree of union. Medita-tion of a more concentrated and interior kind in no way super-sedes such a habit of recollection.

But for the mind to be fully awakened to its higher nature, a special discipline is necessary. Krishna instructs Arjuna in the simple essentials of such a discipline, practised alone and free from interruptions. The kind of posture he enjoins is only important so far as it ensures against physical cramp and restlessness, which are themselves mental states. To sit erect and still, but without any strain, frees the mind from attachment to the body. Even to do this represents a real step in Yoga. Indeed it contains, on the level of the body, the whole of Yoga, when it is perfectly done. But it can only be perfectly done, when the other levels of the being are also brought to rest. Our bodies have acquired such a habit of restlessness that consciously to let them go is no easy task.

The important thing is to ensure, in a way most suitable to each person, a quiescence of the body and of that part of the mind which controls and, by reflex action, is controlled by the body. This is what Krishna intends by his brief instruction on posture and also on avoiding indulgence or undue abstinence in sleep and in food. For feats of bodily control can be achieved by the self and can feed its pride and ignorance. So can denial of the appetites. Only when peace and moderation grow out of unpossessiveness do they reflect a growing awareness of the reality of the Atman. To 'hold the body, head and neck erect and still, and to turn the vision inward,' as Krishna advises, is but the frame within which the new image of Being can begin to form, as He describes it in the following verses,

> *Serene-minded, fearless, constant in his abandonment of selfish desire, with mind restrained from wandering, let him sit, looking up to Me as the Supreme.*
>
> *Thus always, keeping the mind balanced, he who practises a true Yoga comes to the peace that ends in the extinction of the ego, the peace of my nature, of Nirvana ...*
>
> *As a lamp in a windless spot does not flicker, so is the man of subdued thought who practises union in the Self.*
>
> *When the mind is disciplined and becomes still, and when the Self is Self-perceived with inward delight,*
>
> *And when he knows the infinite joy, which is beyond the grasp of the senses and can only be experienced by the understanding heart, and is established in his spiritual truth, the innermost truth of his being,*
>
> *Then has he found the treasure incomparably greater than any other. Possessing and possessed by it, he is not shaken even by the assaults of grief.*

*Dissociation from pain is part of the bliss of
union, for which a man should resolutely work,
undiscouraged by difficulty or failure.*

*Putting away all wilful desires, restraining the
restless senses with discrimination, little by little
let him open himself to the Buddhi and having
centred his mind in the Atman, let him cease to
think of anything else.*

*Whenever the wavering mind wanders, it should
be brought back to communion with the Self . . .*

*The man who lives in union with the Self, whose
vision is disinterested, sees the Self in all beings and
all beings in the Self.*

*Such a man, who sees everything imaginatively,
(e.g. as imaging the Self), suffering equally the joy
and sorrow of every creature, him I hold to have
attained the highest Yoga.*

IV

This rather free rendering of Krishna's words embodies the basic
principles of his teaching on meditation. On this foundation
specialists in its art and practice have established methods in ac-
cordance with their own particular insights. It would be inap-
propriate to discuss these here. But there are two aspects of the
teaching which must be briefly considered, because they are easily
misunderstood.

Arjuna interrupts Krishna's discourse with the complaint that,
much as he wishes to attain the equanimity of union, the fickleness
of the mind, which is as wild and tameless as the wind, seems to
present an insuperable obstacle. Krishna admits that the mind is
restless and hard to subdue, but by constant practice and the exercise of dispassion, He says, it can be stilled, at least by one who is
obedient to the Self and uses the right means.

More important than any particular method is disinterested
motive. For the purpose of all true meditation, whether in act or
thought, is to approach nearer to a motiveless condition. Any

meditation, therefore, in which we consciously strive to control and purify the mind, and in which we cherish the idea of such control and purity, cannot release us from self-centredness. We may, indeed, succeed in disciplining the mind's turbulence. We may even in time achieve a static calm, which encloses us, like a protective shell, against the waves that beat without and the agitation which such waves ordinarily set up within. But we shall be no nearer union with the unmoved Mover.

The tranquillity steeped in wisdom, to which true meditation leads, which, indeed, it inherently is, can never flower in the barren soil of such purposeful control. It may be necessary to control the mind consciously for a time until, by reducing its restlessness, we can begin to hand over its control to the Atman. But so long as we conceive of our mind as an object within our grasp or of an enlightened mind as a mental form which it is within our power to fashion, we shall remain tied to our false centre.

It is not control, but disengagement of the mind from the habitual grasp of the self which is required and for which meditation is the means. Only when our mind is thus released can it come into union with pure Mind, the formless, forming Principle which the later Zen Masters, as we shall see, called 'No-Mind.' Hence the basic tenet of Krishna's, as of all the traditional, teaching is that we should cease to attach ourselves to what we think and feel (and feeling is thought on the unconscious levels of the mind). Modern psychology teaches the same truth when it argues that, to become adult, we must be weaned from dependence on 'the Mother.'

The Cosmos of which we are a part may be imaged as a calm sky of pure consciousness above us and a still ocean, equally vast and infinite, of pure unconsciousness beneath us. This is the sky and ocean which meet and interpenetrate in our true Centre and through which we are meant to think and feel. But in us, more often than not, thought and feeling, sky and sea are in conflict. There is storm and agitation or at least an uneasy tension. In some degree at least, this is our habitual state.

By ceasing to grasp at life, we regain our true relation to our creative Principle and to the Cosmos which embodies It as we do. We are reconciled, if only momentarily, with our Father-Mother, that dual Unity of Being and non-being, in and through which we think and feel as one. This unified consciousness is what Krishna tells Arjuna he will experience, when he has put away all wilful desires.

There is then nothing static or negative in Krishna's instruction to Arjuna that 'sitting firmly in a clean spot, neither too high nor too low,' he should control his senses and imagination and concentrate his mind, that by these means his heart may become pure. This control is only a way of preparing the conditions through which the miracle of union may occur. This miracle may be a long or a short time in coming. But to realize its inevitability, since it is in accord with the basic nature of things, is the sustaining faith of all true meditation.

The other aspect of Krishna's teaching in this chapter which may be touched on more briefly is that in which he declares that 'severance from union with pain is called Yoga.' This was to be the basis of the Buddha's teaching and I shall consider it fully later when I come to treat of that.

Here it is enough to say that those who are still tied to sensation by craving cannot truly suffer. They grasp positively at joy and negatively at sorrow, as they do, on a more elementary level, at pleasure and pain, because the one enhances, the other deflates their self assurance. It is the same whether it be their own joy and grief or the joys and sorrows of others, which they make their own or, by a necessary self-protective reaction, refuse to experience. In most of us there is a strong infusion of sympathy which carries us out of ourselves to share positively and helpfully in the sorrows and joys of others. Yet our ability to do so is limited by the fact that we are still, through our divided nature, 'in union with pain.' For self-attachment *is* pain and essentially there is no other pain.

What Krishna means by 'severance' from such union is severance from that which makes us greedy for joy and resentful of sorrow. It is when they are separated by our dualistic preference that joy is tainted with a false elation and grief overwhelms. Those who are blessed when they mourn, as Jesus declared, are those whom sorrow teaches this deeper acceptance of the mysterious oneness of life in death, chastening the vitalistic urge of the ego and slowly dissolving it in grief's dark waters.

'Severance from union with pain' does not make us insensitive to what is tragic in life or immune from grief when we experience it. But it enables us to participate in the conflict of self-centred existence, from which all tragedy stems, from a purer reconciling centre. What may seem unforgivable to the self that wishes existence to conform with its one-sided desire for happiness, can be accepted, even if it be hard to understand, when it is truly suffered.

Generally, in fact, the person who is most conscious of suffering is failing to suffer deeply enough. That is true even of physical ills when we meet them nervously and so become excessively conscious of them. Just as deep relaxation, in which we cease to grasp at ease or to react against discomfort, can reduce and even, at its deepest, almost eliminate pain, so in true Yoga we learn to suffer life in all its modes and movements without false preference. The tears of things are still as poignantly present to us as the joy and laughter. But they are not ranged against each other. We feel the pulse of sorrow in the heart of joy and joy unborn in the womb of grief. For they are the night and day through which the supreme bliss of the Atman shines in this dual existence. And, as Krishna declares, 'to him whose mind is tranquil, who has stilled passion and been cleansed of the taint of self in union with Brahman, there comes exceeding joy.'

Arjuna, however, is still at the stage on the spiritual path when he looks behind and before and measures risks. What, he asks, of the man who fails to win perfection in Yoga but loses, in striving after it, the zest present in the ordinary partial life of the ego. May he not lose one world without gaining another and find no support anywhere?

Krishna reassures him. 'Neither in this world nor in the next,' he tells him, 'is a man lost or comes to grief, who does good or aspires to it.' Nothing truly won by spiritual effort and discernment is thrown away. It leads inevitably, however long the journey, to the union with Brahman which is his true state.

> *Great is he who seeks to be at one with Brahman, greater* | *than those who mortify the body, than the learned, than the men of action. But of all devotees I call him my very own who loves Me in faith and inwardly abides in Me.*

This is what meditation essentially means. This is its ultimate nature and purpose, not knowledge or liberation for their own sake, but a consciousness suffused with and completed in love for the Beloved, whether we name Him Krishna or another. To meditate perfectly is to hear the voice of the Creator speaking to the soul, in the silence and through the many voices which become audible when that inner silence is found, voices of angels and of the unseen Master who guides, of men and animals, flowers and stones, of the sky or the sea, of wood and fields, hedgerows and gardens. All have a word to speak to the soul which has learnt to listen.

It is this listening above all which meditation teaches, silencing the anxious argumentative mind, hot for certainty and getting but dusty answers to its questions, but unsealing to the inner ear a reason untainted by fear. For this is the reason of our being in which faith is one with knowledge and to love is truly to know.

CHAPTER EIGHT

Beyond the Moods

I

Up to this point in the *Gita* Khrishna had laid down the basic conditions of a knowledge of Himself. But there are different grades of awareness, different levels of being which have successively to be committed to the Light of His presence. In the following chapters He describes, so far as it can be described, the essential nature of that Light and the manner in which It manifests, and this as a prelude to a revelation, for which Arjuna pleads, of His Cosmic form.

There are few, as He warns His disciple, who will strive to realize this Truth, though all else is contained in It. And of those who do so strive few wholly attain. Yet the striving is no less necessary. For without the leaven of those who seek, yet only partially or intermittently find, and of the rare few who do attain, the world would slip back into darkness. The bridge of consciousness which links man's vital and animal self with his spiritual being would be engulfed in the torrent of life and the possibility of creative freedom would be engulfed with it.

Of creation itself Krishna declares Himself to be the unseen principle and essence,

> *I am the source of the whole universe and its dissolution. There is nothing higher than I: upon Me the worlds are held like pearls on a string.*
>
> *I am the taste of water, the light of the sun and moon, AUM in the Vedas, sound in the ether, humanity in men.*
>
> *I am the pure smell of the earth, the gleam of the fire, the Life of all that lives, the death that purifies life.*

> *Know me to be the eternal seed of all that grows,*
> *the intelligence of those who understand, the valour*
> *of the brave . . .*
>
> *And whatever beings are predominantly of light*
> *or of fire or of earth, they proceed from Me. They*
> *are in Me, but I am not contained in them. It is be-*
> *cause the whole world is deluded by these Moods of*
> *Nature that it fails to see Me as I really am, distinct*
> *from the Moods and changeless.*
>
> *Truly it is hard to penetrate My veil of magic, but*
> *they who seek Me alone are freed from illusion.*

In these last verses Krishna refers to what are known in Vedanta as the three *gunas*. He will later devote a whole lesson to them. But their meaning must be briefly outlined here. The cosmology of the *Gita* is essentially that of the *Upanishads*. 'Behind the manifest and the unmanifest,' says Krishna, 'there is another existence, which is in all beings and dies not with them.' This is the Para-Brahman of the *Upanishads*, conceivable only as a total consciousness of Being, without distinction of subject and object.

But within Its unity there is an implicit principle of duality, which becomes explicit in creation. In becoming explicit the Supreme Consciousness and Its creation in form seem to divide. In Krishna's words 'the Knower,' which He declares Himself to be, appears distinct from 'the Field,' from the body of Nature, of which all bodies, physical, vital, mental or ideal, are a part.

As 'the Knower,' Krishna is the unchanging consciousness That watches the creative drama within the Field of His being, and He declares that the power to discriminate between 'the Field' and its 'Knower' is the essential condition of wisdom.

But the underlying substance of 'the Field' is as eternal in its own mode as its in-dwelling Consciousness. This formless substance in which 'the Knower' reflects and contemplates His image with such inexhaustible diversity, this womb of darkness in which the Creative Light quickens innumerable seeds of life, Vedanta names *Mula-prakriti*.

This is the dark ocean, which is also a mirror of the sky, in and through which the infinite nature of the One is mediated to our human senses. In the Supreme Brahman eternal mind and eternal substance brood in sublime communion. Infinite thought is at one with infinite potentiality. Within this Self-existent harmony the mystery of creative love is enacted and the marriage of the Light and the Darkness consummated, of which a universe of life is unceasingly born.

Manifested existence is inconceivable without non-being. Were it not latent in Being itself, such Being would be incapable of Self-expression. For creative expression consists in a perpetual transmutation of non-being into Being. In this transforming act non-being is not denied or repudiated. It is embraced and loved and so gathered into the heart of Being where it belongs.

Yet the manifested universe, as we know it, is born by a process of apparent division. The *Mula-prakriti* is a pure void. Only as such can it contain a pure fullness. But in the act of Creation in space and time IT becomes a matrix of forms, in which three qualities or tendencies manifest. In the void of *mula-prakriti* these qualities are not distinguishable, because they balance each other perfectly. It is only in the realm of visible Nature that this balance is no longer perfectly maintained.

Vedanta names these qualities the *gunas* and it is of them that Krishna speaks when He declares to Arjuna that whatever belongs to the states of *Sattva, Rajas,* and *Tamas* 'proceeds from Me. I am not in them, but they are contained in Me,' and adds that the whole world is distracted by these three moods and the mental states associated with them from seeing Him as He really is.

Sattva is the state of *Prakriti* which is most transparent to consciousness. It is that in us by which we can contemplate inwardly the light of our Being. *Rajas,* by contrast, is the state of *Prakriti* through which the light of pure consciousness becomes the dynamic fire of energy and action. All out-going movement belongs to it. Finally *Tamas* is nearest to the negative principle inherent in *Prakriti.* It is the state of Nature in which the light and the fire are absorbed and held captive, and idea and impulse harden into the apparently solid substance, of which, until recently, we supposed matter to consist.

These are the three moods or grades of consciousness which Krishna describes as proceeding from Him and as weaving together the texture of His *Maya.* They reflect in the realm of Nature the triune relationship of positive and negative and neutralizing principle which characterizes all creation. All of them exist in each of us. In the sub-human world they are equally present, as are the elements of earth, fire and air with which they correspond. They are not only psychological, but physical and, as such, are the ultimate stuff of the whole natural world. But it is in man as he becomes self-conscious that the unbalance between them is pronounced and we get the three different types which Krishna describes in detail in the fourteenth chapter of the *Gita*, the *sattvic*, the *rajasic* and the *tamasic* man.

Such are the modes of egoism. The man in whom *Sattva* predominates is least bound by his passions or by the weight of inertia, because he opens himself to the pure light of the Atman. But so far as he clings in the slightest degree to the serenity which the *sattvic* state ensures, he, too, lives but partially.

The man in whom *Rajas* predominates is more obviously bound by his hunger for action and sensation. Tied to his passions, he is consumed, swiftly or slowly, in their fire. But it is or can be a 'refiner's fire,' particularly in the heroic man of action who passes through it to the light of true being and bears the burden of the world in doing so. Consequently the *rajasic* man is more advanced on the road to self-emancipation than the *tamasic* man who staggers under the weight of negation and is stupified by ignorance. Yet *Tamas* is as necessary an element in our nature as *Rajas* and *Sattva*. Without *Tamas* there would be no condensation of spirit in matter, no gravitation to hold the planets in their places and our feet on the earth.

United and harmonized in the Creative Being of Krishna, each of the *Gunas* is faultless. In *Sattva* is the light of consciousness by which understanding shines through the mind and all the bodily senses. In *Rajas* is the divine power, which, informed by the light, energises every creative act. In *Tamas* is the void of non-being without which there would be no womb in which the seeds of life might grow and the idea evolve its perfect form.

But unbalanced, as they are in self-centred man, each *guna* shows a double face. The typical *sattvic* man is imperfectly committed to the life of action. High-minded, agreeable, refined, he is too much inclined to the light to draw sufficient power from the darkness. The *rajasic* man, through being insufficiently conscious of the force by which he is possessed, often acts unwisely even when his impulses are warm and generous. For he is impelled by desire, of which the inevitable fruit, for himself and for others, is pain. The *tamasic* man is the materialist, at his best doggedly faithful to the practical tasks which are laid upon him, patient, too, and humble in a negative way. But the more exclusively *tamasic* he is, the more sunk in sloth and even in squalor he tends to be.

In few, however, does one *guna* quite overpower the other two. Generally there is a relative balance, and spiritual growth depends on opening more and more to the light of the higher consciousness, implicit in the *sattvic* condition, without denying the fire of *rajas* or the formless depths of *tamas*. For the one-sidedly *sattvic* man is only relatively enlightened, and until the last hold of the ego on its psycho-physical components has been loosed, our integrity is incomplete.

Therefore Krishna declares again that the way to liberation is through discerning that the agent in all action is not the self, but Nature, working through her *gunas*, and that there is a Principle more essential than they and constant in all change in Which they come to rest beyond the unbalance that they manifest in ego-centric man. Thus, says Krishna, 'he will attain to My being.' For this Principle Krishna is.

And when Arjuna asks Him what are the characteristics of the man who has transcended the *gunas*, He replies that such a man accepts equally the manifestations of each of them when they prevail, and does not desire them when they are quiescent. He is undisturbed by their action, whether it exalts or depresses, since he knows that it belongs to them and not to him.

Poised and at peace in the Atman, he shows the same responsive face to friend and foe. Nor, when he acts, is he under any false compulsion to act, since he has ceased to want anything for himself and he knows that all true action depends on a complete renunciation of the delusion that he, as separate self, has any real power to do anything. As such he can only pervert a power that is not his own.

II

The middle part of the *Gita* is devoted to a revelation by Krishna of His own nature and of the means by which a man, by meditating on Him continuously, in act and thought, may at last be absorbed in and changed by the creative Truth Which he contemplates. All meditation culminates in the immediate experience of that Atman Which Krishna is. Only then is the bondage to birth and death broken, which is, also, a bondage to *Maya*, the magic power in Nature, of which Krishna proclaims Himself the master. Separated from Him, we are the slaves of *Maya* and its varying moods. But re-united with Him, Whose consciousness informs the whole world of manifestation without being attached to it, we, also, are masters of this *Maya*, this world of transient forms and energies which unfold and infold His meaning.

For, in truth, to the enlightened vision, existence is nothing, the divine genius in it is all.

> *I am the father of the world and its mother,* declares Krishna, *I dispense all things; I am the source of all knowledge and the purifier. . .*
>
> *I am the path, the sustainer, the Lord, the witness; the shelter, the friend, the origin of life and that in which it is dissolved, the treasure-house, the undying seed.*
>
> *I give heat, and withhold and release the rain. I am both immortality and death, Being and non-being, Arjuna.*
>
> *Even those who, devoted to other gods, worship them in faith, worship Me in ignorance. . . .*
>
> *Though a man has lived an evil life, let him but love Me with all his heart, and soon will he be cleansed. For be assured, Arjuna, that no true devotee of Mine is ever lost. . .*
>
> *Whatever is strong, beautiful and glorious springs from a part of My splendour.*
>
> *But it is needless to multiply details for this knowledge, Arjuna. Know only that I sustain the universe with a minute portion of Myself.*

Arjuna accepts the truth of all that his Master has told him. His ignorance, he says, has been dispelled. But now, greatly daring, he begs for more than description and instruction. He longs to behold the divine form of his teacher. If, he says, 'You think it possible for me to see it, then reveal to me, O Lord of Yogins, your changeless Self.'

He is asking for the impossible. But Krishna grants his request, so far as it can be granted, by endowing Arjuna with a super-natural vision, by which he beholds the divine act of creation in its overwhelming splendour and vastness. He sees 'the whole universe, in all its manifold diversity, lodged as one being in the body of the God of gods.' At that vision he is awestruck, his hair stands on end, and he bows low in adoration..

The vision is not only one of Glory, 'as if a thousand suns should of a sudden rise in the heavens,' but one also of dread and terror. For as the Lord answered Job out of the whirlwind and by a revelation of His infinite power silenced all his arguments and complaints and self-justification, so that he could only cry, 'I have heard of thee by the hearing of the ear: but now mine eye seeth thee. Wherefore I abhor myself, and repent in dust and ashes,' so Arjuna is shown the Universal Form of the Formless, in which the powers of light and of darkness, of creation and destruction, manifest equally in all their elemental power. In that supreme majesty death, with its relentless jaws and fangs, is as supernaturally present as Brahma, the Creator, throned upon the lotus.

Even the words of the *Gita* can only faintly convey this apocalyptic vision or the effect of it on Arjuna. And even to profit by the words it is necessary to have experienced in some degree that opening of the abyss of which I spoke earlier.

Theistic beliefs generally combine a God of anger, who punishes transgression, with a God of love and mercy who forgives the repentant sinner. But these two aspects of the Creative power, presented in this way, correspond so closely with our human temper and are, indeed, often so crudely anthropomorphic a caricature of the cosmic mystery, that instead of shattering self-complacency, they may even enhance it. How many tyrants has a 'God of judgment' bred.

The experience of the divine 'otherness' which Arjuna has and which awaits us all at a certain point in our journey is of another order. It compels acceptance of that in life which we prefer to exclude from our conception of the divine and to deny in relation to the self which we wish to preserve. It shows us our temporal nothingness and the nothingness of all that exists. It forces us to contemplate the gaping jaws, the 'fiery gullets,' into which all life, from the highest to the lowest, rushes, plunging back into its source. For Krishna, in His Cosmic Form, destroys as eternally as He creates. He is Time that makes worlds to perish. Each moment ripens in His hands to the ruin of some passing form. Its grace is inseparable from its transience, even while it reflects a beauty that can never pass away.

But we cannot wholly know this beauty, until we have wholly accepted what horrifies our tenacious ego, the phantasmal nature of everything to which we cling and which, in the guise of death, Krishna devours, 'licking with burning tongues,' probing 'with intolerable beams.'

We cannot but recognize in nature the ever-present necessity of death, but we are loth to admit it for our 'self.' It makes little difference whether we 'believe,' as people say, 'in personal survival.' For the materialist, who disbelieves in it, acts and thinks as if his ego were real and had survival value. If he did not, he would cease to view life and mind so one-sidedly as a mere product of physical nature. The idealist, also, who, in believing in his own survival of death, dreams of a future existence of the same order as his present one, is equally unaware of what he truly is. He, too, has yet to wake from the separative dream.

But the revelation which Krishna grants to His pupil loosens the last ties which hold him to himself. It is a revelation which is mercifully veiled from most of us until we are prepared for it. Arjuna has been carefully prepared, but even he is terrified to realize that the divine Power is as absolutely destructive of every limited form of life, including the spurious form of ourselves which we cherish, as It is creative of the undying reality which all such forms, in different degrees, obscure or express.

To know this, with every faculty of our being is, in the same moment, to abandon our last claim to be self-sufficient. The long struggle to build ourselves up as conscious entities against a nothingness that theatens to engulf us culminates, at this supreme instant of consciousness, in defeat. It is a defeat, not of Consciousness, not of real Being, but only of all that divides us from That in Which we truly are.

Compelled to surrender all our partial knowing, we discover that we have no existence and no awareness save in that Being Which destroys to create. From instant to instant, in death as in life, It makes and unmakes us. Our *Ahamkara*, as Vedanta names it, our 'I-am-ness,' finds its true form, changeless yet ever changing, in the unique imagining of this Cosmic poet, Whose love manifests equally in death and in life.

This is a rending of the tomb in which, as self-centred men and women, we lie. But the senses which we have taught to minister to our desires recoil in horror from the abyss which seems to open before them. So it is that Arjuna is utterly abased by the 'Form of fire, universal, boundless, primal,' in which Krishna clothes his Cosmic nature.

But purged by pity and terror, the doors of his perception are cleansed and the ineffable radiance of the Primal Cause, of Brahma, the Creator, floods into his mind. Clasping his hands and prostrating himself before his Master, he salutes and adores That which transcends all which he had ever conceived or imagined of power and majesty in heaven or in earth. 'Meet it is,' he cries,

> *that the world is moved by praise of you to delight and love, O Sovereign supreme. At sight of you the powers of darkness flee and the hosts of the perfected adore . . .*
>
> *O infinite Being, Primal Cause, Lord of Gods, Abode of the universe, deathless you are, the Truth that transcends what is and what is not . . .*
>
> *Rashly have I spoken of you, regarding you merely as 'Krishna,' 'friend' or 'comrade,' in heedless affection, blind to your surpassing greatness.*
>
> *Forgive, I pray, whatever I have done in disrespect or in jesting, whether alone or in company, at play, at rest or at mealtime, O immeasurable One.*
>
> *Father of this world, the unmoved and the moving, you only are worshipful, you the only true Teacher. There is none equal to you in the three worlds, O Being of incomparable might.*
>
> *Therefore I bow down, prostrate, and implore you, adorable Lord, to forgive, as father forgives his son, friend his comrade, and lover his beloved.*
>
> *Great is my joy at having seen what no one ever saw before me. But my mind is shaken. Show me your other Form, O God of Gods, Home of the universe, be gracious.*
>
> *Thousand-armed, myriad-bodied Being, let me see you as before in the form of Vishnu, crowned and bearing the mace and discus (symbols of the Lord of Time), but having four arms only.*

Being human, Arjuna cannot bear for long the vision of the divine in its naked power and splendour, its elemental otherness. But this vision has been necessary to rid his humanity of its habit of reducing the cosmic mystery to its own partial dimensions and so of clinging to itself in the very image of God before which it bows.

Krishna grants his disciple's prayer. He sheds the Cosmic form, blazing with light and primal energy, of 'the All, the Boundless.' Once more His majesty is veiled in the features of the wise teacher, the Father, Lover and Friend. But Arjuna now sees this familiar form differently, sees it truly as mediating between the super-human and the sub-human, and, though humanly dear and near to his heart and mind, veiled from any affection in which there lingers a trace of selfish want. Only to a love that nothing can affright, because it contains no desire for gain or fear of loss, does Krishna reveal Himself in a transfigured human form. For such a devotee God does truly take the form of Man, that man may know and live in his essential divinity.

III

Arjuna has been drawn back from the awesome vision of the cosmic form of Krishna to the intimate contemplation of Him as the One life in all and the cherisher of this One Life. The twelfth chapter of the *Gita* and indeed all but two of its remaining chapters are recapitulatory. They fill out what in essentials has already been taught. Alternatives, posited in earlier chapters, recur. But now they are centred in one act of the soul, that of devotion.

All the paths culminate and are eventually contained in the Path of *Bhakti*, as the Indians call it. But the word may easily be misunderstood. Devotion does not mean for the East what love often means for the West. Krishna does not ask to become the object of love in the sense in which Christians commonly speak of loving Christ. 'There is none,' He has declared, 'whom I hate, none whom I love. But they that worship me with devotion dwell in me and I in them.' He is 'beyond the pairs' and His true worshipper needs to be beyond them too.

He may begin to learn what this means equally by emptying his mind in meditation of all images so as to cleanse it in the formless fount from which all forms flow, or by concentrating it upon one form with an entirely disinterested love. To be 'beyond the pairs' is to have resolved, in this and other ways, the conflict which, for self-conscious man, exists, to a great or small degree, between subject and object.

To Western man this conflict has been the basis of all vital experience, as, indeed, it is at a certain stage of development. The forceful restless and experimental pattern of Western civilization expresses it and represents an attempt by the Western mind to master and reshape, according to its changing concepts, a phenomenal world viewed from outside. Eventually, as we now see, the objective world has, in consequence, tended more and more to swallow up or at least diminish the subject who confronts and experiments with it.

The teaching of the *Gita*, as of all the Eastern scriptures, regards such alienation between subject and object, even if it be only partial, as a reflection of the self's ignorance. True consciousness for the Eastern teacher embraces all divisions in its own unity. For it is based, as Krishna has shown, in an unconditioned Knower who reconciles the Field of Knowing with Himself, since there is nothing which is not a form of His Consciousness. Contained in this divine Knower, subject and object are linked to each other in a relationship, not of antagonism, but of reciprocity. Our human consciousness can enjoy this relationship in the field of its experience, when, by losing and finding ourselves in an object, we live in it imaginatively. This is what is meant by transcending 'the pairs.'

A Taoist Master, Chuang Tzŭ, describes it as 'placing oneself in subjective relation with externals, without consciousness of their objectivity,' or, in other words, 'transferring oneself into the position of the things viewed.' This, he declared, 'is Tao.' This, Krishna teaches, is to see as the divine Seer sees, to know as the unconditioned Knower knows, as distinct from what Chuang Tzŭ calls 'wearing out one's intellect in an obstinate adherence to the individuality of things, not recognizing the fact that all things are One.'[1]

Instead, therefore, of trying to master the phenomenal world by partial concepts and to subdue it to his own changing needs, it is man himself who must be changed. Only when he is Atman-

[1] See *Musings of a Chinese Mystic* by Lionel Giles.

conscious, will he comprehend both himself and the world and act creatively in it and upon it.

Such teaching is, of course, by no means foreign to the West. Platonic thought, before and after the Cartesian rift developed, has sympathized with it, and the poets and philosophers of the Romantic movement, in their cult of mystical and aesthetic 'participation,' have preached and practised it assiduously. Whether it is Blake losing himself in a knot in a piece of wood, Wordsworth in lines of curling mist or the figures of a shepherd and his dog, Shelley in the west wind, or Rilke in the bird flying through him and the tree growing within him—each and all of them were engaged in the task of reconciling the Knower and the Field, so that the perceiver and perception might be one.

But this inward re-orientation has been the goal only of exceptional men in the West. In general, Western man has poured his energies, not into changing himself, but into altering his surroundings, until to-day technology is his religion. There is, of course, nothing wrong in the impulse to make the outer world serve the truest needs of the inner. But unless these needs are understood, which is only possible through deepening Self-awareness, a technical mastery of the outer world, however expert, will be spiritually stultifying.

Admittedly the absorption of the religious man in the task of transforming himself may make him neglectful of material conditions. Essentially this should not be so, since real awareness, as it develops inwardly, creates a correspondingly finer awareness of outer things and a genius for co-operating with them fruitfully in the human interest. But this is obviously rated very differently by the man who believes that the chief obstacles to human happiness are wrong views and vain desires and by those who find them in a badly organized or insufficiently exploited environment.

A legal separation of self and not-self in active dualism is doubtless preferable to the divorce which occurs between them in a state of self-absorption, in which the conflict of existence is evaded. It is against this error that Krishna warns Arjuna in exhorting him to put aside his bewilderment and fight. Truly 'without the contraries there can be no progression.' But the contraries are essentially within us, and to redeem them we have to take, at some point in our development, the inward path. It is a hazardous path because it may either lead out of existence into a subjective limbo or to the centre, in which, by ceasing to be self-conscious, we experience existence as a distinctive part of our total being.

This experience is the goal which beckons those who choose the upward path, the path of responsible consciousness, and it is this choice and not the varying characteristics determined by the predominance of one or other of the *gunas* in a man that is all important. The *sattvic* man may be nearer to the goal than the *tamasic* man, because his nature is more transparent to the Light. But in all of us, whatever *guna* may distinguish our nature, the choice upon which all depends is between committing ourselves to the Light Which shines in darkness or turning away from it.

For in man self-consciousness has evolved to the point where it must rise to full Self-knowledge or, through failure to do so, sink into wilful self-destruction. The demonic tendencies, 'hypocrisy, arrogance, conceit, anger, cruelty and ignorance,' as Krishna names them, all lead to self-destruction. The divine tendencies, which He has already commended so fully to Arjuna, lead to re-creation.

By entrusting ourselves to the inward Light of the mind we gradually cease to exploit any of the *gunas*, to discriminate invidiously between them, or to claim as our own the action which they, as Nature's instruments, make possible. So is the intended harmony between them restored.

It is thus that a man, while living in the body of Nature and of her three Moods, is a free spirit. For, as Krishna says,

> *He who serves Me with unfailing love passes beyond the* gunas *and is fitted for union with Brahman.*
>
> *For Brahman, the imperishable life, abides in Me, the true inner Self. I am the Truth and the Joy that never fail.*

Jesus declared the same in like words. To enter into this joy, this *ananda*, this inexpressible oneness is, as Sri Aurobindo wrote, to experience 'an absolute delight beyond the *sattvic* happiness.' It is 'the completion of spiritual perfection.'

Yet to strive after such perfection as an end, in neglect of or impatience with the means, is to pursue a phantom. Only when each level of the being has been redeemed from ignorance will the Light flow purely through the cleansed window of *Sattva*, and the life-energy of *Rajas* obey the universal rhythm, and the passive depths of *Tamas* afford the stabilizing base without which both thought and act waste themselves in feverish striving.

Renunciation alone, Krishna has declared, 'brings instant peace.' And at the end of his discourse he returns to this theme, so central to all His teaching, and expounds it anew both in relation to the alternative of continuing to act in the world or withdrawing from it and to the kind of action which characterizes the three types of men, both personally and in the kind of service which they can best render to the community. Each man, He says, should devote himself to his own natural work, determined by the play of the *gunas* in him, and win perfection in and through it. All action in the unenlightened, is involved in imperfection as fire is in smoke. But to deny the law of one's own nature, Krishna repeats, is the cardinal sin. To obey that law perfectly is to sin no more.

This inner renunciation of all but the genius of Being, divinely present in our particular nature, is the true renunciation. If and when That is found, it matters not where we are outwardly, here in this existence or in some beyond. For the here and now are also the beyond. It is not a place to which we must escape for beatitude. We know then that when we are wholly here, we are everywhere. Otherwise we are, in reality, nowhere, though we cross far seas or travel, disembodied, to the farthest star.

As He concludes His discourse, Krishna concentrates into twenty-two verses the essence of His teaching as to how this inner renunciation may be attained and with it the experience of being at one with Brahman, which is the consummation of wisdom. The ideal of renunciation which, when fully realized, ensures a perfect inner quietness and so a mind transparent to the truth, is not peculiar to the *Gita*. It is found in all the ancient teachings. But the *Gita*, as Sri Aurobindo has said, gives us its psychological foundations with an unsurpassed completeness and clearness.

Brahman is the changeless Absolute of Being and of Knowing. But It is, also, without any conflict or contradiction, a Self of power and action present in all that lives and moves. In man these two aspects of One Being have separated into two natures at war with one another. Renunciation, by which this war may cease, is the beginning and the end of the art and the discipline of Yoga, into which Krishna has initiated Arjuna, a Yoga of different aspects but of a single intention, that of freeing mind, heart and will from self-stultifying ignorance.

Krishna's teaching culminates in a call to His pupil to devote His whole being to Him. To this extent the *Gita* is a handbook of *Bhakti* Yoga. But it teaches equally the Yoga of Self-knowledge and of skill and fidelity in action. To tread this threefold path to the end, through purgation and illumination to union, is to find that in the inmost heart of our being knowledge is love and love knowledge, while our true will is the creative power which springs from their union and which makes them one in action.

It is as the *cor cordium*, the great Heart of love in Which light and life meet and are wholly reconciled, that Krishna ends his discourse,

> *Hear again My supreme word, the most secret of all. For you are very dear to Me. Therefore will I tell you what is for your good.*
>
> *Commit your mind to Me and to the task of knowing Me. Devote all your heart to loving and worshipping Me. Serve Me in all your actions. Be as nothing before Me that I may be all of you. To Me you shall come. I pledge you My word. For I love you dearly.*
>
> *Make Me only your duty and your refuge. I will deliver you from all division and separation. Grieve no more . . .*
> *Have you heard this, O son of Pritha, with an attentive mind? Has your bewilderment been dispelled?*

To which Arjuna replies,

> *My delusion has vanished. By Your grace, O Infallible One, I am re-collected. I stand firm, freed from doubt. I will do Your Word.*

So ends what Sanjaya, the charioteer of the blind king, Dhritarashtra, calls, in a brief after-comment, this marvellous dialogue of Vasudeva and the great-souled son of Pritha. 'As often,' he says, 'as I remember the wonderful and sacred truths which Krishna confided to Arjuna, I rejoice again and again.'

Anyone who has lived long with these truths and plumbed the depths of their meaning will share Sanjaya's joy.

CHAPTER NINE

The Need to be Nothing

I

IN WHAT I have written of Vedanta I have tried to distil some of
the essence of its teaching and to expand some of the implications
of its basic themes. Vedanta comprises much more than this. Its
basic themes have been elaborated through the ages into a vast
system of ideas, have been interpreted variously by different
schools and teachers, have inspired what seem to be contradictory
forms of religious practice and run to seed in excesses of scholastic
and psychological subtlety. Yet these ancient insights have proved
their validity by sustaining the life and culture of a people of unusual spiritual sensitivity for nearly three thousand years.

With all this later superstructure I am not concerned. I did not
seek or find in Vedanta speculative adventures. What I sought and
from the first moment of contact with those ancient minds was
sure that I had found, was the wisdom which can ultimately dissolve the bondage and bias of the self-centred mind.

The disinterestedness which informs Vedanta at its source is
not that of intellectual curiosity, which has always an element in
it of self-seeking. It is rooted rather in the child's wonder before
the mystery of the universe, as immeasurable to the exploring
senses as it is unfathomable within the human heart. In such a wonder, combined as it was with a power of subtle reasoning which
has never been surpassed, there was no place for moral prejudice.
Yet it was intimately associated with a search for a conduct of life
which would accord with a reality intuitively perceived and with
its underlying Law.

In the poetic wisdom of the *Upanishads* and the *Bhagavad-Gita*
metaphysical and ethical insight combine. A divergence between
them came later in those who were intoxicated with ideas for their
own sake and so had diverged from the truth. These, with their
mental acrobatics, created what Gautama, the Buddha, called the

thicket of theorizing, the wilderness of theorizing, the tangle, the bondage and shackles of theorizing.' But in utterly disregarding that thicket Gautama did not deny the original metaphysic of Vedanta. It is implicit in his teaching. What he did do, more radically perhaps than any other, was to interpret and live its essential truth on a psychological level and devise a method for doing so which was uniquely his own and as such, 'a Way unheard before.'

Yet there can be no valid moral and psychological approach to life which is not based in a knowledge of the 'eternal order.' This knowledge may be implicit in our reading of the temporal order and of man's relation to it, as it was supremely in Gautama, who had no preconceived ideas, but was an artist in the kind of self-discovery which lays bare the hidden truth. But it is altogether misleading to suggest that he denied the validity of metaphysical thought, because he refused to discuss certain questions, such as whether the universe is eternal or finite, or whether a liberated person exists or does not exist after death or is neither existent nor non-existent. Pure thought is not concerned with such speculations which, as Gautama knew, merely tickle the mind and tend neither to tranquillity nor enlightenment.

Under his first two masters he steeped his mind in Vedantic thought, and in his enlightenment he only passed beyond metaphysical ideas because he had completely assimilated them. The fact that later, in the Mahayana or Nothern School of Buddhism, a subtle structure of imaginative and intellectual *gnosis* grew out of Gautama's teaching, enlarging, without transgressing, its essential truth and greatly illuminating it, proves that a metaphysical heart beat within the body of the original doctrine. Real metaphysical knowledge, being the fruit of pure intelligence, induces and involves a new disposition of mind. This was the knowledge which Gautama possessed and which, through being implicit in his ethical teaching, preserved it from any taint of moralism.

Nevertheless Gautama's repudiation of the artificial complexities and vested interests of an orthodox Brahminism grown decadent was very necessary, as also the antiseptic effect of his astringent mind upon the underworld of superstition and cruel custom which, in popular Hinduism, more than in other faiths, has lurked in the shadow cast by the Himalayan heights which its seers and sages scaled. More generally, his teaching is a corrective to dangers that are always implicit in the kind of speculation to which the Indian mind is particularly prone. For such speculation, in transcending the moral plane, is apt to weaken the foundations upon which a life, centred in reality, must rest.

Gautama's calm sanity, his unassuming, yet resolute moderation, his mind at once modest and most penetrating, his patient insistence on the 'here and now,' his rejection of all false abstraction are just what we need as we emerge from a prolonged study of the Vedantic themes. Here is a teacher who offers not only enlightenment, but an unshakable moral equilibrium.

II

Yet Gautama's wisdom was essentially Vedantic wisdom. He rediscovered for himself and re-stated a basic truth already enunciated in the *Brihadaranyaka Upanishad*. There Yajnavalkya declares that man, previous to his enlightenment, is formed of desire. As his desire, so is his will, and as is his will, so he acts. As he acts, so he reaps and becomes, and there is no end to this kind of compulsive action and the fruit it bears or to the cycle of birth and re-birth. 'But when all the desires that cling to the heart are let go, then a mortal becomes immortal and even here attains Liberation.'

This was the experience which Gautama had at the instant of his enlightenment. At that moment, too, it is said, when the self-conditioned thirst for existence died in him and an unconditioned love of all being was born, he described himself as Brahman.

We are reminded of Krishna's words in the *Gita*,

> *Such a Yogin, when his mind is perfectly stilled and all passion has died, knows the supreme bliss of being one with Brahman.*

The close kinship between Gautama's experience and Krishna's instruction is indeed, apparent. It explains why Gandhi once declared that to him Buddhism was a part of Hinduism and that Gautama 'did not give the world a new religion; he gave it a new interpretation.'

Yet the indisputable fact that he emerged from a background of Vedantic thought and practice and never contradicted its basic teaching diminishes in no way his spiritual genius. It is not knowledge of any scripture or philosophy that ultimately counts. What matters is that we feel in the person of Gautama and in the heart of his message to mankind something that no one else had experienced with such authenticity, so that what he gives to us is not more knowledge of something already known, but truth itself.

The particular truth which he gave and gives to mankind was not learnt by him from the *Upanishads*, though they may have directed his steps towards it. He learnt it by living it. No man can have felt the pain and the pity of the human condition more intensely than he. He felt it equally with his mind and his heart. And that is rare in itself. His genius for sympathy was matched with a genius for analysis, for breaking feeling up into its constituent parts, for dissecting it with the fine knife of discernment, for seeing in every effect its in-working cause.

The culmination of his search for this cause, after six years of wandering and of experiment in various extreme forms of self-discipline, is described in the *Lalita-vistara*. The knowledge of the world's wretchedness had oppressed him from the night on which he renounced his privileged home and embraced the life of a *sannyasin*. It was with this inescapable fact of existence that he grappled, a fact that was woven into its very texture and from which we all in some measure recoil, as he sat, at the age of thirty-five, so legend tells, under the Bo tree at Uruvela, when the moon was full in the month of May.

Link by link, in unflinching, yet compassionate thought, he traversed the chain by which he and all men were bound, from old age and death to birth which conditions them; from 'becoming' which conditions 'birth,' to 'grasping' which conditions 'becoming' and is conditioned by 'craving,' as 'craving' is by 'feeling' and 'feeling' by contact of the senses, and the 'senses' by 'mind and body,' and so to consciousness or mental activity, to the constituents of an illusory individuality and the 'ignorance' which leads us to suppose this illusion real.

This was the chain by which man in his 'selfhood' was bound. So long as we accept it as merely a piece of shrewd analysis, it offers little comfort to our minds and none at all to our hearts. But as, through that memorable night, Gautama unwound the chain of thought from effect to cause and from cause back to effect, suddenly in the third watch he saw, in a flash of absolute enlightenment, its meaning, a meaning which, divine paradox, transformed apparent bondage into perfect freedom.

The day broke and, in his own words, 'I duly knew: this is pain, this is the cause of pain, this is the cessation of pain, this is the Way.' Or, has the 'Song of Victory' over the false selfhood, which legend has attributed to him, declares,

> *Never again shalt thou fashion a house for me.*
> *Broken are all the beams,*
> *The king-post shattered.*
> *My mind has passed into the stillness of Nibbana,*
> *The ending of desire has been attained at last.*[1]

In him the wheel, set in motion by the first desire which transgressed the cosmic harmony, lay still and broken. With it the tyranny of pain was also broken. For desire and pain were but two aspects of one age-old error. And in the place of the broken wheel another wheel began to turn, the wheel of the *dharma*, of the true law of life and being, and of the true doctrine that enshrined it.

This crucial experience is one of the great moments of mankind's spiritual history. But inevitably it has been misread and always must be misread by those who feel their very roots in life, as they suppose, challenged and menaced by it.

In the context of Eastern belief re-birth, which Gautama claimed to have conquered, is associated with theories or doctrines of re-incarnation. To be delivered from the self was to cease to add to the actions done in ignorance, which, as *Karma*, bind men to the wheel of 'becoming.' It was, therefore, not only to enter into an entirely new relationship with existence on earth, but to be saved from returning to earth again, unless the released one consented to return to it as a saviour or teacher of mankind.

But Gautama was not primarily concerned with belief or disbelief in such doctrines. And the meaning for us of his experience does not depend on our acceptance of them. Deliverance, as he realized and taught it, meant ceasing to exist in the servitude of ignorance now and always, whatever conditions of existence might await us here or in another realm. In the course of the four meditations which are said to have preceded his final enlightenment he is credited with having remembered many former existences of

[1] As translated by Ananda Coomeraswamy in his *Buddha and the Gospel of Buddhism.*

himself and others. But he attached little importance to this possible extension of memory as the mind is purified. And this, like much else, may even have been a devout invention of those who, during the centuries after his death, curtained the man, his history and his teaching, in thick folds of myth and legend, much of it of a kind that he would have deplored.

Yet the profoundly human man, with his genius for sanity and for the unvarnished truth, survives unmistakably in the kernel of his experience and his teaching, above all in the first discourse which he gave, after his enlightenment, in the deer-park at Benares, to the five former disciples who had left him when he abandoned the negative austerity to which they clung.

Extremes of self-mortification, he declared at the beginning of his discourse, if not so vulgar as extremes of self-indulgence, are just as binding. Indeed a lust for pain hardly differs in its motive from a lust for pleasure. It was by avoiding both these extremes that he had found the Path which led to enlightenment.

This Path was Eightfold, because it contained within it eight characteristics and practices, 'right view, right resolve, right speech, right action, right livelihood, right effort, right mindfulness, right concentration.' Each of these virtues needed to be pondered, until their meaning in action was fully realized and by this path of moral effort, combined with meditation and constant reflection, others could come, as he had come, to full knowledge.

But this 'Noble Eightfold Path' was the last of 'Four Noble Truths,' which he enumerated, and it would not be trodden effectively unless the three preceding Truths were ever present in the mind, ensuring that resolve and effort and concentration and the rest were truly 'right' or, in other words, no longer self-centred. The three Truths were 'the Noble Truth of pain, the Noble Truth of the cause of pain and the Noble Truth of the cessation of pain.'[1] And here I will quote Gautama's words as recorded in the *Mahavasta,*

> *What is the Noble Truth of pain? It is, birth is pain, old age is pain, sickness is pain, death is pain, union with unplesant things*

[1] The word *dukkha* is better rendered 'pain' than 'suffering,' since to suffer in the true meaning of the word, a man must at least have begun to assimilate the lesson taught to him by pain, that he must take the woes and sorrows of existence into his heart if he is to redeem them. But pain must be understood to imply the condition of strain, discord, disease and anxiety with which human life is infected.

is pain, separation from pleasant things is pain, not getting what one wishes and pursues is pain; the body is pain, feeling is pain, perception is pain, the mental elements are pain, consciousness is pain, in short the five groups of grasping are pain. This, monks, is the Noble Truth of Pain.

What is the Noble Truth of the cause of pain? It is craving, tending to rebirth, combined with delight and passion, and finding delight here and there. This, monks, is the Noble Truth of the cause of pain.

What is the Noble Truth of the cessation of pain? It is the complete and trackless destruction, cessation, abandonment, relinquishment, and rejection of that craving which tends to rebirth and finds delight here and there. This, monks, is the Noble Truth of the cessation of pain.[1]

By reflecting in turn and repeatedly on each of these Truths, Gautama went on to say, knowledge arose, insight arose, intelligence arose, wisdom arose, light arose.' And it was only when he truly comprehended these three Truths and had trodden the Noble Eightfold Path which completed them, as true action issues from true understanding, that he was 'enlightened with full enlightenment,' that 'knowledge arose in me, and my steady release of mind and release of wisdom was realized.'

This was the rock upon which all the rest of Gautama's teaching and the great temple of Buddhist doctrine, meditation, devotion and metaphysics was founded. To many Westerners it has seemed a forbidding rock, hostile to life and refusing its joys in recoil from its pains. Is such a view justified or does it spring from wilful misunderstanding?

III

The prevailing ethos of the West, as of all people who are more active than contemplative, is to make light both of the pain they suffer and the pain they inflict. In respect of their own pain this is a healthy instinct, so far as it goes, an instinct which they share with the animals who suffer life with dignity because they are unthinkingly immersed in it. Such an attitude is obviously prefer-

[1] Translation by Dr. E. J. Thomas in *The Quest of Enlightenment.*

able to a morbid preoccupation with physical ills or a cowardly recoil from them. Those, too, who live with gusto are prepared to pay with the aches of the flesh and even with sorrow of mind and heart for the joys which compensate for them.

Gautama's teaching, however, is concerned with a stage of experience when such an instinctive balance between plus and minus in human existence is in course of breaking down or has actually done so, as it has, very generally, in most of the more civilized regions of the world to-day and in an increasing number of persons who live in them.

Far from being a coward in his approach to the problem of pain, Gautama had the rare courage to look pain fully in the face, not just physical pain, but the pain of heart and mind, the truth of which can only be learnt by a searching scrutiny of the inward man.

The real escapists are those who avoid this steady gaze into themselves, when such an inward looking has become necessary to growth. By so doing they remain spiritually adolescent, fated, at best, to exist on a shrinking capital of vitality, at worst to resort to artificial stimulants to mitigate a sense of emptiness and apathy. Such vitalism, modified though it may be by doubts and qualified by prudence, is still the creed of the unthinking world and of many who have begun to think, but feel they would be false to life if they carried their thought further and acted upon it. Until the sickness which underlies the apparent health of such an attitude has made itself much more felt, it will and does prevail.

But when a man begins to tire of grasping at a happiness which is always evading him, as it is evading countless others, despite their animated faces or gusts of laughter, and when his continued pursuit of it brings in diminishing returns even in transitory enjoyment, he will begin to ask himself whether all the time he has been pursuing a phantom, which, beneath a grinning mask, conceals a face whose lines betray a permanent ache of dissatisfaction, if nothing worse. Then, too, through his increased awareness of the truth of himself, he will begin to see the truth in the face of the world and will know that, so long as he remains what he is, he can do nothing to redeem the general pain, but only add his quota to it. Then and only then is he likely to be ready to listen to Gautama.

For he will have become sensitive to a new dimension of experience, the first effect of which is to make the world the ordin-

ary man accepts seem strangely unreal and quite unsatisfying. He
will have begun to awake from the long dream of spiritual childhood and adolescence and may well, as a result, be neurotic. For
he is face to face with the sickness which always underlay his apparent health.

The ordinary 'healthy' man, who boasts that he takes existence
as he finds it, does maintain a precarious balance between self and
not-self, though at the cost of remaining unawakened as a spiritually conscious person. But he who has partially awakened from
this sleep of the natural man is at home neither in himself nor in
that which is not himself. He is increasingly conscious of the pain
of his unrelated selfhood, bound to an existence which has less and
less meaning. He has not lost himself, but he has lost or is rapidly
losing all that made that self gratifying or even bearable.

He is, in fact, drawing near to the truth of Pain, which Gautama bid men contemplate. It is a truth from which the instinctive
part of us recoils. That is why morally muscular Christians, who
somehow succeed in regarding Jesus as the divine scoutmaster dear
to themselves, have always accused Buddhism of pessimism and of
life-denial. Doubtless Buddhism has, in some of its doctrine and
practice, perverted Gautama's teaching as Christianity has that
of Jesus. But we are not competent to judge how true this teaching
is until we have rid ourselves of certain illusions, to which we
tenaciously hold.

Above all, to understand it, we have to face the profound contradiction in ourselves which causes a basic sense of insecurity and
which betrays itself in our horror of nothingness. This horror is
in exact proportion to our lack of true being. We need to face this
lack fearlessly and determine its causes. Then we shall come to
realize that the nothingness which we fear, because, in becoming
self-conscious, we have had to fight against it, is in reality the
matrix of all creation and that, by resisting and rejecting it, we
make it destructive of the life and the being it would nourish.

The neurotic's recoil from non-existence implies attraction to
existence as his recoil from pain, even the pain of his own self,
necessarily implies attraction to the pleasures at which that self
delusively grasps. In this we are all neurotic, until we have disen-
gaged ourselves from the fatal embrace of these opposites. Until
we have achieved that release, our thought will make war on life
and also turn on itself for denying life.

This was the *impasse* which Gautama so clearly saw and for which he offered a solution. For in him thought confronts life only to release it on a new level by disproving the unreal notions which thwart its expression in consciousness, as in actual living. The thought he brought to bear on life thus restores to existence the depth and dignity of which the clutching ego has deprived it.

What is impermanent, the whole realm of Becoming, is only delusive so long as we greedily grasp at it. This prevents it from manifesting from instant to instant the reality within it. What Buddhism calls 'entering the Stream' is ceasing to resist the flow of the river of manifestation from the silted-up bank of countless selfish cravings and fears. To accept the flow and consciously participate in it, without imposing a self on it, is to learn the meaning of the Buddhist saying that there is neither existence nor non-existence. There is only a 'Suchness' or 'Thusness,' as the later *Mahayana* called it, the essential Nature of things, which is the reality in life's countless forms and is at once their fulness and their emptiness.

But this is to anticipate the metaphysic implicit in Gautama's 'Middle Path.' For though he eschewed metaphysical abstractions and was not a mystic in any emotional sense, his silence on abstract questions, as on matters of belief, was pregnant with the 'Divine Darkness' into which the mystics plunge to be continually reborn in that true Light, which is in existence but not of it. Attraction and revulsion, as felt by the ego, were immobilized on this 'Middle Path,' at first by the habitual exercise of detachment from instinctive feeling, but ultimately, and always in intention, by a radical surrender to That which reconciles opposing extremes in Itself.

In this, Gautama's teaching corresponds with that of Krishna concerning 'the pairs.' It differed only in his reluctance to give a positive name to the mysterious mediating Principle or to discuss Its transcendental nature. Instead, he laid all his emphasis on the ways by which men might get rid of the hindrances to a direct and calmly strenuous living of reality. But the moral effort and meditative practices, based upon the Noble Eightfold Path, depended, as I have said, on a profound acceptance of the three preceding Truths, of which the Truth of Pain was the first. Until these three Truths have utterly convinced and liberated the mind, all moral effort, the Buddhist insists, and any system of training, though both are necessary in advancing towards realization, will fail to dislodge the ego. Indeed they may even strengthen self-centredness by elevating it and so making it less crudely apparent and less obviously distressing to its victims.

I V

What, then, is the truth of Pain as Gautama experienced and taught it? It is not, except indirectly, 'old age, sickness, death, grief, depravities,' though these sad facts of existence may compel us, as they did Gautama himself, to search for a truth behind them. It is not physical torment or Hamlet's 'heart-break and the thousand ills the flesh is heir to.' The truth of Pain is the inescapable fact of the impermanence of all things which, being born, must die, because they are not single but compound, not Self-existent, but causally conditioned.

But why is the impermanence of things painful to us? It is not so to the rose that sheds its petals or to the rock that flakes away beneath wind and rain, cold and heat. Only as we ascend the scale of consciousness in life does pain begin to hurt creatures. Unconscious reflexes become sensations and thoughts, and as man grows increasingly aware of life's need to preserve and perpetuate itself, he associates himself with it. The more selfishly he makes this basic instinct his own, the more he perverts and at the worst contradicts it, so that, in seeking to preserve and enhance his own life, he destroys it. Yet consciousness itself it not at fault, is not opposed to life, to its abundance and its everlasting renewal. Pure Consciousness is not pain. It is, as all have testified who have entered even momentarily into Its presence, bliss and beatitude.

It is self-consciousness, then, which destroys the basic unity of life and consciousness and throws their purpose into apparent conflict. Pure Consciousness is timeless, but life, if endless, is transitory. And its impermanence is unforgivable to self-conscious man, because it seems to contradict something in him which demands to be eternal.

Man, at this stage, is only partially aware that he partakes of eternal Being. He feels life powerfully, but the Consciousness which outlives and outdies life is clouded in him. The impermanence of things and more particularly of his body and the desires, emotions and thoughts into which he has translated its basic instincts, affronts his eternal longings.

This compels him to defy the law of change and retard its processes for as long as he can. The obscure sense he has of his own nothingness as an 'I' only intensifies his need to annexe and hold tight something other than himself, the whole world, if necessary and if he can master it, thereby to supply from outside what he lacks within.

This desire is the second of Gautama's four Truths, the Truth of craving and grasping, which is the cause of pain, since it defies the universal nature of things, is wrong-headed and for ever doomed to failure. A craving for endless non-existence is, of course, just as stultifying as a craving for endless existence. Both transgress reality, which combines constancy and change in a happy mutual relationship.

The partial self, misconceiving the real nature of being and dreading its own extinction, cannot love the transitory, cannot, indeed, truly love at all. The real anguish, said Dostoevsky's Father Zossima, is not being able to love. And we cannot love, though we may seem to, our illusory self and the illusory world that self fabricates. In trying to eternalize itself this self has denied the Creative Principle in Which we need continuously to die and be reborn. It was not from this rebirth that Gautama had obtained and taught release, but from the endless renascence of a self that refuses to die.

Since it refuses to die, it seeks to hold fast the world of things and of people about it, which help to buttress its illusion of permanence. And when they escape its clutches and pass away, pain ensues, the pain of its own impermanence of which the objects it grasps unavailingly warn it, offering it a lesson which it cannot learn.

Thus it is, as I have suggested in an earlier chapter, that the fire of life, the force of nature, which at an unconscious level is regulated from within, becomes in man a fevered flame, a conscious conflagration, in which intelligence perverts instinct and instinct inflames intelligence and he is endlessly hungry for life and for ever unsatisfied.

This was the flame of insatiable desire in which writhed the damned of Dante's Hell, and of which Gautama spoke so memor-

ably on the night when he and some of his monks are said to have
seen from afar a forest fire.

> *For everything*, he declared, *O monks, is in flames. And what
> everything is in flames? The eye is in flames. The visible is in
> flames, the knowledge of the visible is in flames; the feeling
> which arises from contact with the visible, be it pleasure, be it
> pain, be it neither pleasure nor pain, this also is in flames. By
> what fire is it kindled? by the fire of desire, by the fire of hate,
> by the fire of fascination, it is kindled; by birth, old age, death,
> pain, lamentation, sorrow, grief, distress, it is kindled. . . .*

> *Knowing this, O monks, one who is wise becomes weary of
> the eye, he becomes weary of the visible, he becomes weary of
> the feeling which arises from contact with the visible, be it
> pleasure, be it pain, be it neither pleasure nor pain.*

This weariness of all desire-conditioned experience is, of course,
or should be, only a prelude to something else. There is no lasting
virtue in disillusionment, as the author of *Ecclesiastes* tended to
forget. Still less is there virtue in that cruder form of disillusionment, disgust, except in so far as it may lead to dispassion and dispassion in its turn open the way to an acceptance of life, undistorted by greed.

If greed be strongly entrenched, it may require stern methods
for its uprooting. But Buddhists who later advocated persistent
contemplation of 'the ten kinds of repulsiveness as seen in the
corpses of men and animals,' or a 'tenfold contemplation of the
Foul' tended to forget that death and decay can exercise as sensory a fascination upon man as life. Much, indeed, of Western
misunderstanding of Gautama's teaching is due to monkish perversions of it. Alas, in what shadow do all organized religions lie!
Each and all have betrayed their Master Light.

Gautama, in what has been called his 'Fire Sermon,' did not in-
tend, we may be sure, to condemn the flame of life itself. To what
extent sub-human existence is tainted with 'craving' is one of those
questions which he would have considered it idle to ask. But the
pure flame that sustains all creation is not 'craving' and is as eternal as Consciousness itself, of which, indeed, it is the ardent principle.

Man longs at heart to tread the path by which the flame of life in him is progressively transmuted into the Light of divine Consciousness. And the pathos of his desire for existence lies in the fact that what he really seeks are not the things of time at which he clutches, but the spirit which sanctifies and beautifies them, but which he endlessly thwarts by his ignorant grasping. This misconceived impulse may seem, in most people, to be hardly comparable to a forest fire. Yet whether it smoulders or burns fiercely, its cause is the same and its consequence is pain and the waste of pain.

This pain will be mild or acute according to the intensity of our self-conscious life. But it ceases, as the Third Noble Truth declares, only when no residue of attachment remains in us. This is both release and attainment, the last death of the ego, the crown of Buddhahood. But short of this total resumption in That Which is everything and nothing, a qualified, yet very real release can be won.

The first essential is to take these Truths out of the arena of disputation and argument and to begin testing them in our own experience. One would think that no one could deny the first of them, that the world we live in is a world of pain and that this pain is an ever-present ache in our souls. Many people, if asked, might acknowledge this. Yet they would hardly thank us for drawing their attention to it, since all their efforts are directed to forgetting it.

We have seen why this is. For to remember it is to be reminded of the transitoriness of that in which we seek distraction. Yet until we have wholly accepted this truth, we can never be fully and deeply at peace and it is foolish to wait for some disaster of loss to lay bare the desolation within.

We cannot wholly experience the real movement and rhythm of becoming, until we have ceased to resist it. So long as we resist it, we dread it and this dread is a barrier between us and its truth. Though many of us think that we accept the transiency of things, we do so very imperfectly. The magic of the fleeting is seldom fully known to us and consequently the wonder and beauty of That Which ever abides in and blesses the fleeting is, also, veiled from us. In refusing or even in grudgingly admitting the sovereignty of change, we reject a 'great world of delight.'

To resent change and cling to certainty, not only in material things but in our thought and the whole potentially rich realm of our inner life, is to deny, the creative spirit itself and the possibilities of unforseeable growth. For these, as Karl Jaspers has written,[1] depend upon our readiness 'to endure ambiguity in the movement of truth and to make light shine through it: to stand fast in uncertainty: to be capable of unlimited love and hope.' This refusal is the characteristic sin of a bourgeois society.

Similarly the Truth of craving is one which most of us would acknowledge and many justify as a necessary stimulus to life. Yet of those who have recognized the bondage of it, few have begun to realize how subtly pervasive that bondage is, how it informs even those activities in which we think ourselves unselfish, elevated in mind and purpose, or socially laudable; how it taints our religious profession and devotions and our most intimate personal affections; how, too, it tenses the bodily habits and responses of which we are largely unconscious, disturbing the harmony of life in ourselves and others.

It is to bring all this home to us that Gautama himself never tired of commending Mindfulness and that Buddhism, as it elaborated the Master's original directives, developed a varied discipline, at once moral and mental, by which all such unconscious habits associated with the three fundamental tendencies of the self, sensual desire, desire for existence, and ignorance, might be brought into the light of Consciousness and eventually dissolved in it.

For some such method of mindfulness is the practical outworking of the fourth Truth, the truth of the cessation of pain, of which the Noble Eightfold Path lays down the moral foundation in its eight basic virtues. This is the Yoga of Buddhism and if more exclusively mental in its emphasis than the Yoga of Vedanta and so appealing especially to a reasoning type of person, it can be adapted to the needs and circumstances of anyone who believes that a new mind is essential to a new heart.

V

But at this point it may be asked, if these four Truths are valid and if craving does cease in him who makes them his own and,

[1] In *Tragedy is Not Enough.*

with its cessation, that repeatedly tied knot of craving, which is the self, disappears, what, if anything, remains to initiate and sustain action or to focus the faculties of sensation and perception? Does another and truer Self fill the void into which the illusory self has vanished? And if not, in what way does this mysterious void differ from sheer vacuity and the extinction of self in it from annihilation?

This question has troubled many, the more so because Gautama's doctrine of 'non-selfness' *(an-atman)* has been mis-stated again and again by those who cannot conceive any alternative to 'individuality' as they know it but a limp nonentity. Nor, indeed, is any other alternative conceivable so long as a man clings to what he is and thereby disqualifies himself from beginning to experience consciously what he is not.

Yet the description of Gautama's doctrine as 'nihilism' has a certain plausibility, in so far as he seems to differ from the sages of Vedanta in denying that there is any persistent individuality behind all the changing mental and psychological phenomena which compose the ever-fluctuating shadow of the self.

But the self of which Gautama denied any permanent existence in this life or in any other was not the Atman of the Vedantists. What, he insisted, was illusive, unreal, and essentially without substance, was an entity claiming to be individually separate from the whole and striving, always at bottom unhappily, to uphold that claim. Such individuality was no less an illusion when it assumed the disguise of an immortal soul.

The Brahman-Atman of Vedanta, as I hope I have clearly shown, is not an entity or a soul in any individual sense. Creatively it is consciousness manifesting in and through forms. But It is quite other than the self to which un-liberated man clings, demanding that it should persist, other, too, than any form of life which is subject to change, to growth and decay. Thus Gautama's doctrine of 'non-selfness' conflicts in no essential way with the teaching of the *Upanishads* concerning the nature of the supreme Selfhood, as those who in modern times have studied it most thoroughly have had no difficulty in showing.

Where Gautama differed from the Vedantic sages was in generally refusing to name the Spiritual Principle in Which and by Which the man released from self lives. He concentrated his acute intelligence, instead, on demonstrating that the physical, emotional and mental processes of the body, with which man identified himself and from the recurrence of which he derived the delusion of a persisting ego, were, in fact, devoid of selfhood.

In a discourse known as 'the Marks of non-self,' he declared,

> *Body, monks, is without self; feeling, perception, the other mental elements and consciousness are without self. If, monks, this body were the self, the body would not be liable to sickness and pain, and the . . . production of pleasure in the body would thrive (if I said) may my body be so, may it be not so; and because the body is not the self, therefore is it liable to sickness and pain, and the production of pleasure does not thrive in it (if I say) may my body be so, may it be not so.*

The same words are repeated concerning feeling, perception, and mental activity. This statement, of course, in no way contravenes the truth that a man, by committing body and mind to the mysterious Creative Presence which is not an individual self, can find healing, and to that extent, as one who recognizes that reality belongs only to the Atman, can be a free co-operating agent within the realm of bodily necessity.

Gautama continues,

> *Therefore, monks, thus you must learn: whatever body there is, internal or external, coarse or fine, base or lofty, far or near, past or present or future, all that body is not mine, I am not that, that is not the self; even so is it to be viewed with right wisdom. Whatever feeling, perception, mental elements, consciousness there is, whether internal or external, coarse or fine, base or lofty, far or near, past or present or future, all that is not mine, I am not that, that is not the self. Even so is it to be viewed in truth with right wisdom.*[1]

To know with an absolute clearness of vision that 'I am not the impermanent body' is, Gautama declares, to be freed for ever from the corruptions associated with it.

When, however, we consider how ancient this habit of identification with physical life is, how it originated in dim ages when man lived almost wholly as a body and how through countless centuries his sense of being his body has hardened and narrowed into self-consciousness, we can see what a formidable task Gaut-

---

[1] Translation by E. J. Thomas, M.A., D.Litt. in *The Quest of Enlightenment*.

ama, like all the Masters, bids us undertake. It is no wonder that many Buddhist sages of the gradualist school assume the necessity of innumerable lives, devoted to a disciplined reversal of habitual thinking, before this ancient ignorance can be annihilated.

The stronger our attachment is to the physical, the harder is the task of disengaging the mind and the more we are likely to be tempted to take a short cut by repudiating the body and the whole sensory realm. Yet, obviously, to reject the body is still to be tied to it, still to be unable to grant it an existence of its own upon which we make no claim. Though we may spurn it, we shall continue to be its captive-tyrant, until we have succeeded in relating ourselves to Something which is not tied to it, but which persists tranquilly in and beyond all the changes and chances, the moods and impulses of physical existence.

To commit ourselves to this Void, this *Sunya*, as the Buddhists call it, is not to deny to the body its own necessary life. It is, indeed, to consent to that life for the first time, and not only to consent to it, but to be in a condition to love it for itself. We cannot love the body for itself so long as we appropriate it and thereby distort its innocent instincts, until, through misuse, these instincts master us and we come to hate the servitude which they impose.

To love the body for itself, as to love the natural world, of which the body is a part, is to feel for it the same kind of attentive fondness as we feel for a house in which we have lived since childhood, which, by protecting us outwardly, while offering us doors through which to come and go, and windows through which to see, has enabled us to grow inwardly, but to which we are in no real sense tied, though we may well have for it much affection.

But so long as we regard this body as 'me' and 'mine,' we cannot enjoy this free relationship with it, whether we deny or indulge it. The negations of a false asceticism into which Buddhists like other aspirants after a new consciousness and life, have often fallen, betray a persisting bondage to that which Gautama declared to be unreal.

Such a bondage is particularly noticeable in a monkish fear of contact with women, as it is in any tendency to regard the feminine as a shadow between man and God instead of as an emblem of the divine darkness, the shadow without which the divine light would be unbearable and manifested life impossible and love unlearnable here on earth where, as William Blake sang, we are put 'a little space' that we may learn to bear its beams.

Doubtless monks and priests are specialists in the spiritual life, for whom exceptional conditions for intensive development may be appropriate. For this reason it may be wise for such an aspirant to abstract his mind for a time, as completely as he can, from the sensory world, the better to break a strong attachment to it. And since woman is more closely involved in the realm of primary instinct than man and exerts over him a powerful force of attraction, avoidance of possible occasions for this attraction is an understandable precaution for a man or a woman who have taken the vows of the religious life.

Yet to regard a woman or a man, on account of their sex, as a temptation is to betray our ignorance of what we really are and our persisting identification of self with body. When two people desire one another, each wants to possess in the other, by projection, the self which evades ther own grasp. Desire, therefore, is a continual struggle for momentary relief from that sense of separation, which is the characteristic illusion of the self and an attempt to assuage a common thirst for existence.

This thirst and the isolation underlying it can only be assuaged, as the *Upanishad* declares, when men and women love the eternal in each other and meet creatively in Its mysterious Heart. This is union: all else is division, though there are, of course, many degrees of it according as loves redeems desire. Ultimately, in the wholly enlightened, desire is extinguished in love and the self-perpetuating impulse becomes purely creative. The world of generation, of existence as we ordinarily know it, becomes for the regenerated a world of Being.

According to one school of Hinduism sexual relations of pure love untainted by any desire for private pleasure are possible between the highly evolved. In other words the gulf between *eros* and *agape* is not uncloseable, as St. Augustine held, even in the roots of bodily appetite.

But Gautama was too much of a realist to play with such ideal possibilities, For him sexual intercourse, though natural to the young husband and householder, was incompatible with the pursuit or attainment of Nirvana. For this reason the monk, intent on attaining the total enlightenment necessary to perfect union, chooses not to expose himself to relationships in which desire may prove stronger than love. But such withdrawal, if continued indefinitely, is more likely to result in a warped development than in the release which it is meant to expedite.

In any case we need to be very sure that we are truly called to renounce the normal testings of life, before we claim a right to do so. Such renunciation, as a character in one of Ronald Fraser's novels remarks, 'is only for those who are ready for it, and we shall only be ready for it when every debt to life has been paid. It is useless, dangerous to deny the world until the time comes.'

Certainly recoil of any kind is essentially a contradiction of the Middle Path. To tread it is to yield neither to desire nor aversion and thus, by gradually reversing the habit of swinging between extremes, to become centred, more and more, in what Vedanta calls 'the Self' and Buddhism 'the Void.' Admittedly for the Buddhist the conditioned world is not a manifestation of 'the Void,' the *Sunya*, as it is of the *Brahman-Atman* for the Vedantist. But these two names image the same unnameable Reality, 'clean, pure, eternal, calm' in Its absolute Nature.

Gautama's statement 'You are not that,' namely the body, the world of component changeable phenomena and the stream of sensations and thoughts, is only another was of saying by implication *TAT TVAM ASI,*—'That you are,' or, 'in your innermost being the Divine IS and you ARE by virtue of Its presence.'

In short Gautama's 'doctrine of not-selfness' is not, as I interpret it, a one-sided negation, an annihilation of human hope, a denial of the goodness of being, but a key to the resolving of the life-destroying conflict between the positive and negative forces in divided man.

VI

Almost from the beginning of his mission to the world, Gautama's denial that any constant entity underlay the kaleidoscopic forms of self-consciousness did not prevent him from naming That which eternally IS, 'the Self.' Quite early we hear of him replying to the young men who asked him whether he had seen a fugitive woman whom they were pursuing,—'What now, young men, do you think? Which were the better to you, to go tracking the woman, or to go tracking the Self?'

The Self which he suggested that they would be wiser to track was not a private possession of each of them, but common to them all, however distinctively each of them might reveal or conceal It. It was not the 'I' which we build up through the continual recurrence of similar thoughts and sensations and which we credit with permanence. It is That of Which we can only say I T IS or I A M, according as we try to convey the impersonal or the personal aspect of Its transpersonal essence.

In the entire realm of becoming, Gautama insists, there is no self. But reflected and active in this realm there is a spiritual Consciousness, Which reveals Its being and Its power through a million points of light that vary in the degree and the manner in which they manifest It. The more, by seeing through our empirical 'I,' we allow This, Which we truly are, to take possession of us, the more we realize what it is truly to Be in all our becoming and the less do we dread the necessity of change. For we feel increasingly that we belong to the Constant and rejoice in the continual newness and spontaneity of its expression.

The inward assurance of the man who has abandoned the demand for certainty which the empirical self must always make, does not rest on rational considerations. It is immediately given. Its quality is well suggested in one of the verses of the *Dhammapada*, which, if not composed of Gautama's own words (and lamentably few of his living words have probably escaped being reduced to verbal formulas by later recorders), reflects truly the temper of his mind and spirit. There we read,

> He who has perceived the goal of freedom by realizing that life is empty and transient, his path is hard to trace like the flight of birds through the sky.

To understand these words and the whole body of Buddhist teaching on 'the Void' it is essential to recognize that it is the emptiness of phenomenal life which is stressed again and again. For until a man has awoken to the truth of this, he cannot enter into the fullness of another kind of life. To realize this is not fatal to creativeness, but only to the conditioned tension which is generally mistaken for creativeness in the West. Certainly a spasmodic creativeness can be generated through the very anguish of unrest and dissatisfaction, inherent in our illusion of a separate selfhood. In suffering this anguish we may intermittently shed the illusion and, in inspired moments, be possessed by That Which we had ignorantly claimed as our own.

Such intermittent and partial creativeness is, indeed, preferable to any life-denying creed or ethic, preferable, I am inclined to think, to certain forms of ascetic life, as practised by Buddhist monks. But so long as we identify ourselves with the flux of conditioned existence, we are, as Gautama said, 'like fish in a stream that is almost dry.'

For we have substituted for the deep river of time which flows in eternity and in which eternity flows, a shallow torrent engendered by our own desires. Into this we run, as the *Dhammapada* says, 'as a spider runs into the web of his own spinning.' This, too, is one of the meanings of the fable of Narcissus, that pure personification of the ignorance of self-love, who, supposing the fluctuating reflection of himself in the phenomenal stream to be real, plunged in and was drowned. If less infatuated with self than he, most of us differ from him only in degree. But the wise, as Gautama taught in a parable, cross the rapids of *Samsara* on the raft of the doctrine and its practice. By this they reach the farther shore, but then the raft is left behind. 'Thus, brethren,' he declared, 'understanding the figure of the raft, you must leave righteous ways behind, not to speak of unrighteous ways.'

For 'the yonder shore,' which in reality is an illusion of our selfhood, as is the dividing stream, is beyond the opposites which the 'self' conceives. Did we but know, we stand upon it now. Indeed we stand upon nothing else. For it is the shore of our timeless being. Among the opposites, between which the self is divided by hopes and regrets, are the past and future. And so the aspirant who would 'cross to the farther shore' is bidden in the *Dhammapada*, as he was bidden by Jesus, 'to be free from the future, free of the past, free in the present.'

In one school of Buddhism it is, significantly, Nature herself, in her purest manifestation as 'Prajnaparamita,' Lotus-Sophia, goddess of wisdom, who leads the soul across the river of *Samsara* to the far shore of *Nirvana*. For Nature, on every level of her being, is wholly alive in the 'Now.'

The yonder shore is, thus, at once the point of escape from the false stream of our desires and the point of entry into the river of Being. When we enter this ageless river that flows freely in us and we in it, we do not measure its movement from past to future, as we used to do when we shivered on its bank, the bank of our own making, fearing to plunge in. Instead we experience time as an eternal Now, for ever moving and for ever still.

Wordsworth, for an entranced moment, glimpsed this river, as he exclaimed in his sonnet 'Composed upon Westminster Bridge,'

> *Ne'er saw I, never felt a calm so deep!*
> *The river glideth at his own sweet will.*

And William Blake, in his illustration, entitled 'The River of Life,' of a text from 'The Revelation,' wonderfully evoked the ease of those who, committing themselves to the flow of the 'pure river of water of life, clear as crystal,' are utterly at rest in their movement, clothed in its current as in a garment that both conceals and reveals the forms it enfolds.

To be in this river is to glide by its will and to find that will to be miraculously our own. It is to be in the stream and beyond it. For that is the nature of this river. Moving in time, it eternally is. The flux of *Samsara* is resumed in the flow of *Nirvana*. Thus, in the teaching of Buddhism, it is necessary to cross one stream to enter another. When that is achieved, the two streams, of conditioned existence and unconditioned being, are found to be one, and we no longer need to escape from the one to live in the peace of the other.

But this realization need not prevent us from conceiving the nature of Being, in which we lose and find ourselves, as a Selfhood of another order and kind. When Vachhagotta questioned Gautama about the Atman, his answer was Silence. And when his Silence was questioned, he pointed out that if he replied 'Yes' to those who asked if there was a Self, they would be strengthened in their assumption that the illusory self was eternal, while, if he replied 'No,' they would accuse him, as he remarked on another occasion, 'wrongly, baselessly, falsely, and groundlessly' of being a nihilist, one who preached 'the annihilation, destruction, and non-existence of existent being.'

Silence, therefore, was the true answer for one who trod the Middle Path which negatived such false alternatives. For the condition of the man who has experienced the Void and knows himself as nothing cannot be defined in the terms of attached individuality and its assumptions. Clearly the released man *has* no self, since he has ceased to possess anything. Thereby he has broken the

chain which binds him as an automaton to the cycle of birth,
death, and rebirth. But he has not 'returned God his ticket,' as
Ivan Karamazov wished to do. He still participates in the mystery
of birth and death, but freely. By consenting to die he has entered
into a fullness of being in which his previous thirst for self-sur-
vival can only seem a pitiful ignorance. To be thus at home in the
dual infinity of death and of life, to be inexhaustibly nourished
out of both, is, as Rilke put it, 'to achieve the greatest possible
consciousness of our existence.'

To 'comprehend that rebirth is destroyed' is not to repudiate
existence. Gautama's long life of compassionate service towards
those still immeshed in the ignorance he had outgrown proves
that he did not encourage us to turn our backs on the world, but
rather, as free agents, in whom creative light and love could manifest, unimpeded by ignorance of what we are, to work for the
eventual enlightenment of all.

> *And he lets the mind* (says a much-quoted Buddhist Scripture,
> which forms the basis of a devotional practice), *pervade one
> quarter of the world with thoughts of Love, and so the second,
> and the third, and so the fourth. And thus the whole wide world,
> above, below, around, and everywhere, does he continue to
> pervade with heart of Love, far-reaching, grown great, and
> beyond measure.*

> *Just as a mighty trumpeter makes himself heard—and that
> without difficulty—in all the four directions, even so of all
> things that have shape or life, there is not one that he passes by
> or leaves aside, but regards them all with mind set free, and
> deep-felt love.*

Such universal compassion, which at the same time reaches
down to all particulars, can only manifest in the truly wise who
see in all sentient beings their own Self. 'The man,' said Gautama,
'whose mind is thus released cannot be followed and tracked out
even by the gods . . . so that they could say, "There rests the consciousness of a released person." And why? Even in this actual life,
monks, I say that a released person is not to be thoroughly known.'
On another occasion he compared him to 'a flame blown out by
the wind, which disappears and cannot be named.'

The identity of the wise is so incomparably other than isolated
individuality that they may seem to be anonymous, manifesting

as they do that perfect Being in non-being, of which the unending conflict of self and not-self is the sick shadow in fallen man.

'How transient are all component things,' said Gautama on his death-bed. He had emphasized this truth so much that its corollary, the constancy of That which is not composite, has been overlooked. But assuredly it was not overlooked by him. These were the two sides of the One Truth, perceived by those who trod the Middle Path. Transiency was everywhere apparent; That which was constant and unchanging was hidden and was perceived by other faculties than the senses. Hence his silence about it. But the silence of one who, as Rilke put it,

> *Forgets what we experience—*
> *who experiences that which makes us forget,*

is supremely affirmative.

In fact a contrast is frequently drawn in the Buddhist canon, as in Vedanta, between self and Self. The *Upanishadic* sages, who viewed man from the standpoint of Reality, insisted that the Brahman-Atman cannot be positively described, that we can only hint at It by saying what It is not. Similarly Gautama who focussed his vision first and foremost on man, demonstrated that he was not, in his ignorance, real as he thought he was, and remained silent when asked to define positively what reality was.

Yet both the Vedantic sages and Gautama bid men take refuge in 'the Self that is Brahma—Brahma-become.' In the *Dhammapada* we read,

> *The Self is the Lord of self; what higher Lord could there be? When a man subdues well his self, he will find a Lord very difficult to find.*

Or again,

> *Rouse your self by Self, examine your self by Self. Thus Self-guided and mindful you will live happily.*

These texts have close parallels in the *Gita* and suggest that Gautama's doctrine of not-self is simply the converse of the Vedantic affirmation of the Atman. The one makes possible a true realization of the other. The belief in a private self is, of all beliefs, the hardest to overcome. Vedanta declares it to be an illusion no less than Buddhism.

But Vedanta can seem to offer a loophole to the tenacious ego by explicitly stating, 'That you are.' For the ego is diabolically clever at turning truth to its own uses. Instead of allowing itself to be extinguished in the Atman, it can assume the Atman as a mask. It can clothe its demonic nature in the vesture of divinity. It can worship a god which is a sublime, yet enslaving, image of itself.

This happens, of course, more easily to those who subscribe to monotheistic creeds and no one who had really understood Vedanta could ever fall into this error. Yet until we are enlightened on every level of our being, the lurking ego will be liable to seize upon any image of Selfhood to perpetuate its own phantom existence.

It was because Gautama knew this, as no one had so relentlessly and yet compassionately known it before, that his interpretation of the ancient wisdom of his race struck at the very roots of that attachment to existence, that thirst for separative living, which is the disease of which man longs, consciously or unconsciously, to be cured. He did not claim to be an innovator. 'Even so, brethren,' he declared, 'have I seen an ancient Path, an ancient track traversed by the Perfectly Enlightened Ones of former times.'

But because he refused to personalize That in which healing was to be found, knowing that, in a world imprisoned in names and forms, it could only be approached as nameless and formless, and because he directed his matchless powers of analysis to disproving the reality of what man deemed most real, it has often been said that he denied the Atman Which Vedanta affirmed.

The truth is succinctly stated by J. Evola in his *The Doctrine of Awakening*, when he writes, 'Buddhism does not say: the "I" does not exist—but rather: one thing only is certain that nothing belonging to *Samsaric* existence and personalities has the nature of "I." This is explicitly stated in the texts.'

No analytical demonstration of the unreality of the ego as part of the *Samsaric* flux will in itself cut the bonds of attachment. It can only help to remove hindrances to the release of a higher consciousness in which the truth is immediately known and detachment ceases to be a habit laboriously cultivated and becomes a spontaneous freedom. Living more and more in the disembodied essence of our being, we realize how meaningless is the automatism, how tedious and humiliating the incessant hunger of the life-force to which we had clung and to which we had attached the name of 'I.'

But out of this realization of hell there springs a creative vision of a heaven that continually redeems hell, of the awesome beauty and inexhaustible meaning of That Which manifests in the myriad forms of life, and Which, moment by moment, if we will let It, informs, destroys, and re-creates us in the image of Its blissful Being.

This, too, Gautama himself declared to be the reward of him who, having put away the stains and faults and vices that lead to states of misery and existences of suffering, discovers in himself a new Causal Law at work, not that of craving and pain, but of the happiness which nourishes concentration.

He reflects on himself as purified from all these bad and evil qualities, he reflects on himself as released. As he reflects on himself thus purified and released, exultation arises, as he exults, joy arises, with his mind full of joy his body is calmed: when his body is calmed he feels happiness, and being happy his mind is concentrated. Having his mind accompanied by love he abides . . . with abundant, great, immeasurable freedom from hatred and malice.[1]

Gautama went on to compare the doctrine and discipline he taught to a lotus pool of clear, sweet, cool water, limpid, with good steps down to it, at which a man, overcome with the heat, parched and exhausted, could quench his thirst with that same water of which another Master told a woman of Samaria that whoever drank of it should thirst no more.

This is the joy, peace and equanimity to which those attain who tread the Middle Way and pursue 'the proper path of self-discipline' with faith, knowledge and assiduity. He who so attains is, as the Buddhists say, 'de-spirited,' disintoxicated of self. And so for him joy, peace, love and mindfulness are utterly established in the Nothingness which ensures their constancy. The reality of such attainment cannot be conveyed in words. But P. D. Ouspensky's account of his experience in contemplating an image of the Buddha with sapphire eyes in a temple in Ceylon may help to communicate something of its essence to others, as it did, when I first read it, to me.

[1] Translated by Dr. E. J. Thomas in *Early Buddhist Scriptures.*

The face of the Buddha was quite calm but not expressionless, and full of deep thought and feeling. He was lying there deep in thought, and I had come, opened the doors and stood before him, and now he was involuntarily judging me. But there was no blame or reproach in his glance. His look was extraordinarily serious, calm and full of understanding. But when I attempted to ask myself what the face of the Buddha expressed, I realized that there could be no answer. His face was neither cold nor indifferent. On the other hand it would be quite wrong to say that it expressed warmth, sympathy or compassion. All this would be too small to ascribe to him. At the same time it would also be wrong to say that the face of the Buddha expressed unearthly grandeur or divine wisdom.

No, it was a human face, yet at the same time a face which men do not happen to have. I felt that all the words I could command would be wrong if applied to the expression of this face. I can only say that here was understanding.

Simultaneously I began to feel the strange effect which the Buddha's face produced in me. All the gloom that rose from the depths of my soul seemed to clear up. It was as if the Budha's face communicated its calm to me. Everything that up to now had troubled me and appeared so serious and important, now became so small, insignificant and unworthy of notice, that I only wondered how it could ever have affected me. And I felt that no matter how agitated, troubled, irritated and torn with contradictory thoughts and feelings a man might be when he came here, he would go away calm, quiet, enlightened, understanding. . .

All Buddhism was in this face, in this gaze. . .[1]

We are reminded by Ouspensky's account of his experience in a temple in Ceylon of the story, in the *Maha-Parinibbana-Sutra*, which is also a parable, and which tells how, in his last days, the Blessed One, when weary, rested at the foot of a tree, and how the faithful Ananda went to fetch water for him from a nearby stream, but found it stirred up and fouled by the wheels of carts that had passed through it. He wished to go instead to a river, not far off, that was flowing 'clear, pleasant and transparent.' But the Master bid him return to the muddied stream. Twice this happened

---

[1] From P. D. Ouspensky's *New Model of the Universe.*

and twice Ananda returned with the same complaint and the same request.

But on going a third time he found that the stream had begun to flow clear and bright. 'And taking water in the bowl he returned towards the Blessed One, and when he had come where the Blessed One was he said to him: "How wonderful, how marvellous is the great might and power of the Tathagata! For this stream which, stirred up by the wheels, was but just now become shallow and flowing foul and turbid, now, as I come up to it, is flowing clear and bright and free from all turbidity. Let the Blessed One drink the water! Let the Happy One drink the water!"

Then the Blessed One drank the Water'.[1]

Even so through the patience, non-attachment, mindfulness, and compassion, taught and lived by Gautama, does the turbid stream of *Samsara* become pure and limpid as *Nirvana's* water is. And when it does, we discover that it is not a senseless phenomenal flux and that we experience it as such only through the distracted superficiality of our response to the movement of life. 'All things flow,' as Heraclitus declared, but they flow within a rhythmic and persistent pattern or, as Walter Pater put it,[2] 'a continuance of orderly intelligible relationships, like the harmony of musical notes, wrought out in and through the series of their mutations.'

This plastic and harmonius order reflects in the stream of becoming the creative reason of that nameless Being in Whose art we are meant fully and freely to participate.

---

[1] From *Sacred Books of the East,* vol. XI. Translated by J. Rhys David.
[2] In *Marius the Epicurean.*

CHAPTER TEN

Faith's Awakening

I

WHAT GAUTAMA named *Nirvana*, Jesus called 'the Kingdom of Heaven.' Each had the same reality in mind, but each experienced it in his own way, the one realizing the transcendent peace at its heart that heals the pain of the world, the other knowing and living it as the outflowing love of a Father for a prodigal son, which reconciles all men in Himself. Yet essentially the two symbols represent the same state of wisdom, love and self-release, an inward condition, though of its nature it embraces and transforms everything without.

Both *Nirvana* and 'the Kingdom' are indescribable and, in one sense, unthinkable, since, in their essence, they transcend imagination and thought. But both Masters spoke freely about them, Jesus employing parables to suggest the reality which only awaited a radical change of heart to be experienced, Gautama occasionally speaking in parables too, but always declining, when asked, to describe *Nirvana* positively. Instead, he devoted all his skill as a teacher to plotting more precisely than Jesus did the path of mental and moral discipline which lead to its realization.

This difference between the Masters is more than a difference of method. It is a difference of emphasis, intrinsic to natures differently endowed. Each, by virtue of his spiritual genius, was established in the condition which he invited his disciples to attain. Each was in union with the real, but the Light of that Union manifested primarily in Jesus as redemptive love, in Gautama as releasing wisdom.

The love which Jesus gave and taught to mankind was steeped in wisdom. The wisdom which releases the human mind from ignorance through Gautama quickens a new and true love in the no longer hungering human heart. Yet the difference in emphasis is basic. The qualities of wisdom and love are blended in every liberated soul, yet they blend distinctively according to the path chosen. The devotion and charity which animate ardent Christians and mould their very features are akin to and yet distinguishable from the serenity and compassion that tranquillize the face and the movements of a true follower of Gautama.

But the difference is more clearly displayed in the defects than in the virtues of the two religions, which grew out of these Masters' teachings and, at a deeper level, out of the particular ray of redemptive light which shone through them into the world; the defects of emotionalism, obscurantism and passionate attachment in historical Christianity, and those of mental aridity, life-denial, and a recoil from the realm of feeling, which have tended to characterize monastic Buddhism.

The truth of a Master's teaching, however, is not to be estimated by the perversions of his faulty followers. A Master of love will evoke in some the shadows of love rather than its light. It is the same with a Master of Wisdom. We need to-day, more than ever, to go to the fountain-head and draw the water of truth from its pure source in the inspired teacher or from those who in spirit have been nearest to him and so best qualified to transmit without distortion his original insight. Time has not sullied the truth of such insight, though the historic religions, which strove to enshrine and popularize it, have often done so.

For Gautama and his followers reality is not a God to be worshipped, not a theistic quest, as for the Semitic people and those who have come under their intensely personal sway, but a Consciousness to be known and lived. To experience *Nirvana*, which is without beginning and end, is as *The Tibetan Book of the Great Liberation*[1] declares, to seek and find one's mind in its true state and original nature and, as such, 'not realizable as a separate thing, but as the unity of all things, yet not composed of them.'

It is in truly knowing the Mind that final liberation is to be found. This is the key-note of Gautama's teaching and of Buddhism. For within one's own mind is Mind Itself, the native resting-place of everything that is, Whose nature it is to know and not to be known, to be all meaning and all mystery. Only by relating our own mind to this Consciousness Which is, in Its original state, as the Buddhist sage taught, transcendent over creation, can we destroy the illusion of possessing and being imprisoned in a finite mind

[1] *Introduced, Annotated and Edited by W. Y. Evans-Wentz*

and all the false and imperfect notions of a finite world which spring from that illusion.

It was in the sages of the Mahayana School that the meaning of the doctrine that the only reality is Mind, pure and perfect in It-self, ever clear and ever existing, yet invisible, the source equally of the bliss of *Nirvana* and the sorrow of *Samsara*, was fully de-veloped. But all that the Mahayana divined of the nature of this primordial Mind Which, possessing not conditioned existence, dwells freely and untainted in the hearts of all, derives from such sayings of Gautama as, 'Be mindful, and seek the state of nothing-ness; resting upon "nought is," cross through the flood.'

For the true Mind and the true Void are names for the same nameless mystery.

Mindfulness is the heart of Buddhism. Essentially its wisdom consists in participating in the Consciousness Which pre-exists and underlies all division and, by the light It sheds, to discern a new world, not of disparate things, misconceived through subjective ignorance, but of 'Suchness,' of a Reality that recreates Itself in every instant.

Nirvana and *Samsara* correspond mentally with two levels of Mind, one which is still, deep and central, the other which is a continually agitated surface. The early practice of 'mindfulness,' as we shall see, is an exercise in concentration and watchfulness. Such an exercise is only of real value or likely even to be success-ful in its more limited aim, if it is related to the deep centre of which we are meant, through it, to be increasingly aware. As Dr. Conze has written,[1] 'however diverse, such exercises all aim at guarding the incipient and growing calm in our hearts, that patch of inner calm which may at first not seem very large. A line is, as it were, drawn round this domain, and we keep watch on trespassers at its boundaries.'

But this defensive technique, though in most of us it may have to be maintained indefinitely, is meant only to establish on the surface of the mind an undistracted condition which will enable us to descend progressively into the depths. Indeed, from the be-ginning, all mindfulness should be viewed as an experiment in depth and inwardness. Our aim is to be full of Mind by emptying ourselves of mentality and its monkey-tricks. This implies a re-cognition that pure thought exists, a recognition which, though

[1] In *Buddhist Meditation* by Edward Conze.

inevitably provisional until the essence of the Supreme Wisdom is known by direct experience, is nevertheless sufficient to awaken and sustain faith in the transformation for which we are working.

The particular value of the Mahayana School of teachers lies in their insight, at once intuitive and subtly reasoned, into the nature of 'the invisible immaculate Mind,' the 'Self-Born Wisdom,' which 'has in reality been shining forever, like the Sun's essentiality, itself unborn' and which shines in a human mind become transparent to Its 'Clear Light.'[1]

The quality of this 'pure *dharma*' or 'Suchness' and Its relation to the ego-consciousness which both reflects and obscures It, have been nowhere set forth more persuasively than in Ashvaghosha's small, but intensely concentrated treatise, *The Awakening of Faith*.[2] Ashvaghosha lived and taught in eastern India in, it is thought, either the first century before or the first century after the birth of Jesus in Palestine. He was the author, too, of a famous poem on the life of the Buddha and his short treatise, distilling, as it does, the reasoned wisdom of a poetic mind, makes him, in Dr. Suzuki's words, both 'the first expounder of the Mahayanistic doctrine and one of the deepest thinkers among the Buddhist patriarchs.'

It is characteristic of all Buddhist teaching that the awakening of faith is for it neither an emotional conversion nor an intellectual assent to doctrine, but an awakening to Mind Itself. Previous to this awakening, faith, however vocal or active, is asleep and at the mercy of its dreams. At best it is an instinct which, until it is purified by consciousness, is tainted by self-centred fears and desires, of which the desire to dominate is one.

The awakening which Ashvaghosha, like his Master, advocates and expounds in his treatise is as direct an experience as any emotional convulsion that sweeps through a revivalist meeting. It differs in being an experience of incomparably greater truth and essentiality. It is an awakening to what the Mahayana calls 'Suchness,' and what Eckhart called 'Is-ness,' to the feel of Its presence in the mind, to the thought of It in the heart, to the light of It, cleansing and irradiating the windows of the senses. All mental and moral disciplines are practised as a means to this awakening. They are in-

---

[1] From *The Tibetan Book of the Great Liberation*.
[2] See Ashraghosha's *Discourse on the Awakening of Faith in the Mahayana*. Translated by Teitaro Suzuki.

tended to bring to a stand the habitual mental states, which prevent the experience of 'Suchness' by interposing a barrage of distracting sophistries and sensations.

What Ashvaghosha calls 'cessation' is the letting go of all this ingrown mental activity, in conformity with Gautama's third Noble Truth. This will lead to a first faint appreciation of the ever-present reality of 'Suchness,' a first happy and humbling experience of what 'presence of Mind' truly means. As this inner calm deepens and becomes more constant, we can begin to explore and examine the nature of that supreme Consciousness, with which we are in communion, until, eventually, intuitive insight will develop within the zone of stillness recovered from the world of noise.

It was of this stillness that Gautama himself spoke when he said to a disciple 'desert not the Ariyan silence! In the Ariyan silence establish your mind. In the Ariyan silence make your mind sole arbiter! In the Ariyan silence balance your mind.'

For a time, long or short according to the beginner's persistence and docility, Ashvaghosha says, the two exercises, that of relaxing and emptying the mind and that of pondering the nature of Mind Itself, thus gaining intellectual insight, will be practised separately. 'But when by degrees he obtains facility and finally attains to perfection, the two will naturally become harmonized.' In other words our thought will then be no longer at odds with the true Thinking Principle and 'Suchness' will manifest equally when we think actively and when we rest in the silence of Thought and pure attention.

The awakening of faith, then, consists for Ashvaghosha and for all the Mahayana teachers in the cleansing of the mind from subjective delusion, so that it ceases to be storm-tossed and becomes Mindful. This is possible, indeed inevitable, because the Mind, present in all things, is, in Its own nature, pure and utterly peaceful. The waves of agitated mentality that ignorance excites do not affect Its clear depths, even though It is the substance of all mentality, however shallow and disturbed, as water is the substance of the waves that fret its surface.

A main hindrance to becoming conscious of It and of the totality of things is what Ashvaghosha calls 'self-particularization.' We see everything through the distorting lens of self-interest, which destroys imaginative vision.

Particularizing, in the sense in which Ashvaghosha uses the word, is mental clinging. It exemplifies Gautama's second Noble Truth and is the cause, not only of pain, but of blindness to the true nature of things. Phenomena, stripped of our personal interest in them, are impersonal processes endlessly evolving from cause to effect in a regulated pattern. So long as we impose ourselves upon this pattern, we cannot understand it. Nor can we break it. On the contrary it will break us in the degree that we defy it.

We defy it by trying to make it serve our private interests, when it serves only the common and universal interest. For transitory as all phenomena are, they reflect a Mind that is eternally whole. Clinging mentally to phenomena, which thus become desired objects to our senses, is only a mode of clinging to the self. It is this which Ashvaghosha calls 'particularizing.' It prevents us from experiencing the universality of each minute particular, the unceasing crystallization of the 'Suchness,' as It manifests in form.

Partial seeing is not altogether illusory, because all seeing has its source in the all-seeing Mind, so that even our distorted vision contains some reflection of its origin. A partial vision may penetrate deep within its exclusive field, as the specialized sciences, based on a very partial view of nature, demonstrate. But even the practitioners of these sciences, despite all the safeguards they employ to ensure impartiality, are afflicted by what Blake called 'single vision and Newton's sleep.' The subjective bias remains. What they discover in part, transgresses the truth of the whole, with consequences that are apparent in a civilization which is the outcome of such discoveries and in which organic living is being destroyed by mechanic invention. At bottom the scientist sincerely disinterested as he means to be, sees only what his ignorance and his unconscious preferences allow him to see. He has not achieved the wisdom of non-particularization.

This is the sin of Blake's 'Ratio,' of all mental abstraction and exclusively intellectual knowledge. The real insights, as Mr. William S. Haas has written,[1] 'require, as a condition of their attainment, a state of mind other than an intellectual act. The higher we ascend the scale of insight, the more that state of mind loses the character of condition and merges with a means of knowledge. Finally . . . this state is itself knowledge. '*Being equals knowing*,' and '*no knowing without the corresponding adequate being*.'

[1] In *The Destiny of the Mind. East and West.*

Being only equals knowing when, in Ashvaghosha's words, 'Suchness perfumes ignorance, and, in consequence of this perfuming, the mind, involved in subjectivity, is caused to loathe the misery of birth and death and to seek after the blessing of Nirvana.' This loathing by the mind of its bondage to the phenomenal world and this seeking of a principle of freedom in which it may lose and find itself, indicate that we have begun to perceive within ourselves a Consciousness which is not bound or tainted, a Self which is reflected in us as a sun in a flowing stream.

It is this Consciousness which tells us, the more attentively we listen to it, that all phenomena, including that complex of changing phenomena we call the self, have no independent reality. Little by little, as the truth of this comes home to us, people and things will be seen and known for what they really are, not through an illusory veil of ideas and sensations, but as breathing images of a Consciousness that unveils Itself in myriad forms, each one of which contains 'an immense world of delight' and is of infinite value, by virtue of its informing spirit. It is by this cleansing vision that 'we attain to *Nirvana* and that various spontaneous displays of activity are accomplished.'

For *Nirvana*, so far from being a condition of tranced passivity, as is popularly supposed in the West, is one in which the spirit, released from the fetters of egoistic thought, can act in us with creative immediacy and sureness. This is the true nature of 'Suchness,' which is Itself always wholly present in us and 'perfumes' us all equally. Only we do not recognize It and our intellectual and emotional prejudices, our beliefs and scepticisms, are forms of this ignorance, which vary in each one of us according to the grade of our intelligence and sensibility, grades so manifold, as Ashvaghosha wrote, that they 'outnumber the sands of Ganges.'

But the universal Wisdom, working through a thousand channels and agents, makes its presence felt, even in those who in ignorance deny it. For the self of ignorance is always perishing and we have only to step out of its shadow to be clothed in the sun and in that 'Body of Bliss' which is wisdom's form and in which matter and meaning are wholly one.

It may be complained that Ashvaghosha and other Mahayana teachers, in their analysis of the indefinable, overstrain the mind by their subtleties and so fail in their aim which is to illuminate. There may be a certain truth in this. Yet to minds which are at home on this level the subtle reasoning of Ashvaghosha's discourse is a kind of music, comparable in its intensity to the pure spiritual counterpoint, at once intellectual and mystical, of a Mass by Byrd or Palestrina.

To me at least, as to so many in the past, it is full of luminous insight into the nature of that supreme Consciousness which, as the *Dhammapada* declares in its first two verses, underlies all our tendencies of character and determines all that we are. For essentially we are composed of Mind and of naught else. Our body is the activity of Mind and it is only when we see and feel the truth of this that we can be spiritually at home in the physical world. For we realize then that Mind, that 'Great Body of Radiance,' as It is called in the 'Tibetan Book of the Dead,' is in us, as in all else, undivided, and that consequently nothing in the universe is really outside us, but that in each moment of unself-conscious awareness we and the world are one, comprehended in That Which ensures our power to comprehend.

It is through this understanding that we awaken to the meaning of wholeness, of 'belonging,' and thereby experience the joy of release in and from ourselves and a corresponding compassion for all bound beings, which moves us to serve them, as Ashvaghosha wrote, with the dauntless energy natural to an enlightened vision. For the consciousness of faith awakened is not a reflective, but a creative faculty. What it sees and knows, it acts and is. This is the seeing and the knowing of imaginative love. Such love is only fully released in us when we simply and clearly know that we have no self of our own either to love or to hate. In this devoted awareness we truly are the 'Suchness,' Which is the mind and the heart of being.

II

But before we consider in conclusion the practice of Faith as Mindfulness and its methods in two schools of Buddhism, it will be well to try and meet a criticism that the apparent extremes, to which the Mahayana pushes the doctrine of 'no self,' can hardly fail to provoke. For to assent to this doctrine in its ultimate purity inevitably seems to an 'individualizing' mind to involve a kind of mental and spiritual suicide. The ego-centric will to live must resist to the last a doctrine which cuts through its very roots.

Many even of those, in whom this will has been chastened by experience, see in a Buddha or a Bodhisattva, as the Mahayana conceives them, subtle tempters, who would seduce man from his allegiance to earth and suck the life-blood from his humanity.

Visitants from some immaterial nowhere, they smile their enigmatic smile of escape. They contemplate our joys and sorrows and pity us for our addition to both. But since they know all such experience to be illusory, they cannot enter into our life, but only stretch out a hand from their ghostly void and try to draw us in.

Perhaps, such questioners will say, this is the inevitable end of life on the path of no-return. But we who have not reached that end, who still cling with all our imperfections, to what we like to regard as 'the safe foundations of human-heartedness' (to borrow Confucius's phrase) may well see in it an arbitrary curtailment of the potential strength and goodness in man, a death to what Wordsworth named with gratitude 'the human heart by which we live' rather than a life re-born and regenerated. Such humanists cannot but ask—'Did the Buddha, on the path he trod to enlightenment, leave something out? Did he achieve his super-human peace on the higher levels of his being by mentally anæsthetizing the lower? Was the body with its sensory and affectional faculties merely neutralized, its vital conflicts negatived rather than resolved? In short does Buddhism offer to its disciples a state of tranquil but inhuman spiritual celibacy or does it contain within it the wholeness of a true marriage of the depth with the height, of earth and heaven, of man and That Which, under so many different names, he feels to be Divine?'

We of the West, whose civilization has for centuries drawn its energy from individualism, can seldom be disinterested in asking or answering these questions. As Hermann Hesse has written, 'the illusion of personality that cost India the efforts of thousands of years to unmask is the same illusion that the West has laboured just as hard to maintain and strengthen.'

Admittedly, too, as I have said, the light of every Master evokes a distinctive shadow in the minds and hearts of those who respond to it. This shadow is as evident in historical Buddhism as its counterpart in historical Christianity. The temptation to deny the body and its vital instincts rather than to accept and cease to exploit them. is common to all religions. It is a particularly strong temptation to the Oriental, who tends to be as strongly drawn to the plane of impersonal spirit as the Occidental is to be immersed in the feeling moods of the personal soul.

But the teaching of Gautama, who accepted his status as a man without any divine privileges and urged his followers to do the same, is as little hostile to the humble faculties and organs of human nature as was the teaching of Jesus, who, also, in the record of the earliest gospel, made, it would seem, no claim to the deification thrust upon him by the later chroniclers.

The Middle Path is not for monks only to tread. It runs through the whole of life and though many worldly activities cannot be reconciled with the treading of it, because they bind men to self-interest, marriage and parenthood are not necessarily among them. The noble Eight-fold Path contains no injunction to celibacy, though in the distinction drawn from the beginning between a discipline appropriate to the many and to be practised by the chosen few, it was recognized that as a man or woman advanced on the path, they would outgrow the desires associated with propagation.

Certainly both Gautama and Jesus stressed the self-evident truth that in our efforts to spiritualize our humanity we shall find our body and its appetites and affections to be the seat of some of our strongest and most obstinate attachments, and that even our love of family and kind, of wife, husband or friend, can be a chain of self-love which must be broken. We remember Jesus's saying that he who hates not his father and mother cannot enter the Kingdom of heaven.

Gautama, who eschewed extreme statements, never spoke so challengingly of the bondage that lurks in many socially sanctified human relationships, as it generally does in the value which we attach to 'personality' in others, as in ourselves.

Mixed with all such impure affections is the distinction of mine and yours, which, so long as it divides our consciousness, prevents us from understanding, but not from misjudging, what the condition of 'no-self,' the "Buddha-state' essentially latent in all, truly is.

Admittedly some of the Buddhist *sutras* lend themselves easily to misunderstanding, few more so, perhaps, than one of the most famous of them, in which the consciousness of a *Tathagata*, of one who is at one with the essential Nature of things or, more briefly, a 'right-farer,' is explicitly set forth.

The *Diamond Sutra*, sometimes called 'The Diamond Cutter,' since it is meant to initiate its reader into the 'Union like to the Diamond' which no dualism can break through, is one of the most venerated books of devotion in the literature of the Mahayana. Yet to any Westerners who associate devotion with pious adoration of a personal God or Saviour, it will seem an oddly comfortless document. Its purpose, like that of all Buddhist teaching and practice, is to break the dualistic spell under which we live in our ignorance, so that Knowledge Itself, the Divine Word, can act in and through us. Two quotations from the *Sutra* will suggest how it does this. Of those who have been freed from this dualising habit the teacher declares,

> *There will not arise in them any idea of self, any idea of a being, of a living being, or a person, nor does there exist for them any idea or no-idea. And why? Because, O Bhagavat, the idea of a self is no-idea, and the idea of a being or a living being, or a person is no-idea. And Why? Because the blessed Buddhas are freed from all ideas.*

Again, the Buddha is credited with saying of an incident in one of his previous incarnations,

> *At the time when the king of Kalinga cut my flesh from every limb, I had no idea of self, of a being, of a living being, or of a person. I had neither an idea nor no-idea ... If I at that time had had an idea of a being or of a person, I should also have had an idea of malevolence.*[1]

The aim of the *Sutra* is to shock the mind of the reader out of its habitual separative notions. But if it fails to do this, it may well seem to be denying what is very real and very dear to most of us —living beings and the mystery of their uniqueness. But the *Sutra* does not deny these realities. 'No one,' it declares, 'is to be called a Bodhisattva for whom there should exist the *idea* of a being, the *idea* of a living being, or the *idea* of a person.'

I have italicized the word 'idea.' For it is not the reality of communion between beings and persons, which is repudiated. The communion of a Buddha with his fellow-beings and with all creatures is, by virtue of his spiritual insight, incomparably deeper

[1] As translated by F. Max Muller in *The Sacred Books of the East*. Vol. XLIX.

than that of the ordinary man who defends his attachments against rivals or even of those more enlightened people who make a self-conscious cult of 'personalism.' Moreover a Buddha is in conscious communion with beings in the unseen whose light and love can reach us through him, unobscured by the shadow of self-centred ignorance.

It is against this shadow that the words of the *Sutra* are directed, a shadow which manifests in a thousand illusory and partial ideas, all of which stem from the false idea of a self. In the true image of someone or something, idea and sensory perception coalesce. But the false 'idea' of a self shatters the true image of a fellow-being which is meant to form in the mind and does form in a mind enlightened by being freed from its separative illusion. Such a mind sees wholes, sees in men and women what Blake called 'the human form divine,' because it is at one with That Which, as Krishna taught, is the Eye of the eye, and the Mind of the mind, the universal Seer, whose qualities are 'Love, Mercy, Pity, Peace,' and Whose essence is Wisdom.

By the *idea* of a being the Sutra does not mean the creative idea inherent in a true image, but rather the mental film which dims the eyes of imagination, like a kind of cataract through which our ordinary vision peers. I am reminded of Keats's lines,

> "High Prophetess," said I, "purge off
> Benign, if so it please thee, my mind's film."

This film is a product of the disease of self-centredness. The blessed Buddhas who have stepped out of the shadows of self into the light of being 'are freed from any idea,' as from its opposite, 'no-idea.'

It may be hard for us to conceive the nature of a direct experience of reality, stripped of all the obscuring haze and fog of thought and feeling generated by the ego. Yet there are moments when the doors of perception are miraculously cleansed and the living truth of the unity which is pure relationship comes home to us, still but partially compared with the clear and constant Light in which a Buddha lives, but with sufficient power and beauty to reveal what a life no longer befogged by 'ideation' might be.

Nevertheless, it may be said, the awareness of a Buddha is so indescribably beyond the attainment of ordinary mortals that to invite us to emulate it is at best to tantalize, at worst to ensnare us in a dream of escape from the necessary battle of life and the world of educative suffering. It is senseless and demoralizing, so the argument runs, to aspire so utterly beyond our capacity, to seek to pass beyond life before we have even partially lived it.

Arjuna, it will be remembered, feared as much, when he asked Krishna what would be the end of a man who embraced His Yogic teachings, but failed to win to Union. A Buddha would give the same answer as Krishna did. In fact we need to aspire to that which seems unattainable, if we are to take one effective step on the Path.

A repudiation of life in the effort to naught the self is one of the chief dangers of the spiritual path, one of the subtler triumphs of the self. But Gautama's Middle Path involves no such repudiation and it can be trodden, faithfully and sensibly, by men and women who have still to find their true centre and gradually gravitate towards it by the act of walking steadfastly on, in this Middle Way in which the opposites meet.

The practice of Mindfulness, as I hope to show in a concluding chapter, begins on a humble human level within the capacity of anyone who is sincerely ready to devote himself to it. Nor does it ever cease to rest on this humble, actual basis even for those who approach or attain the ultimate goal of perfect detachment and insight. The goal does not tower above us, like a snow-capped peak that attracts from afar, but daunts the nearer we approach it. It is not an end at all, still less one that is remote and dizzying to contemplate. The goal is the Way Itself and Its inward deepening, as the habit of Its wisdom grows in us, until we come to the golden heart within the Mind, the heart that is neither of mind nor body, but of the 'Suchness' in which they meet.

There is no morbid hunger or starved searching for the infinite over far frontiers or horizons in Gautama's teaching. It rests all the time on an acceptance of the necessary bounds of human experience into which the infinite enters to inform and enlighten. In the middle of the Path which the mindful wayfarer treads the infinite meets the finite, and the unreal, self-conceived conflict between them is resolved. There, in the absence of self, the 'Suchness' is ever present, creating a whole cosmos in the minutest particular. It is to be found here and now, in that instant between the past and present which dissolves and unites them.

But to experience this instant we need to have our feet on the ground. The ground on which the Buddha rests in the traditional image of him is a lotus, but its roots are in the fathomless depths of water and earth. His posture is one of compact composure and awareness in marked contrast to the harrowed, ecstatic or passion-torn features of many Christian saints, as they are depicted, or the tortured body of the crucified Saviour.

Does, then, faith fully awakened into knowledge and comprehensive insight, as Buddhism conceives and expounds it, lose, not only militancy, but ardour and passion? So far as ardour and passion are a fire consuming the dross of a nature, still incompletely awakened from the dream of self, the answer can only be 'yes.' In the 'Suchness' the fire of life is continually transmuted into the light of understanding. Passion shines through dispassion as compassion. Emotion manifests as the warmth of wisdom, never as a hunger for love and truth still to be satisfied. For Gautama truth was a lamp that could be wholly trusted to dissipate darkness when its presence was known and accepted.

Ultimately the darkness would vanish in a flash of light, as it had done in his own experience. But this final enlightenment could be approached gradually by a patient adjustment of mental habits, until at last they wholly conformed to That Which truly and ever-lastingly is. Then the wonder of awakening occurred. Gautama did not talk grandiloquently about dying and death. He spoke out of a divine knowledge, but always as a man of sense and moderation, with a deep tenderness for life and for all that lives, whose right to life should never be violated. Yet his Middle Path involves a death, both gradual and sudden, and perhaps a more radical death than that of crucified passion, for being so unostentatious, so quiet, patient and impersonal.

One may sacrifice oneself to others for a life-time, as one may join fervently and prayerfully in the sacrifice of the Mass or the Eucharist, without fully awakening from the sleep of self. Gautama's teaching offers no humanistic or ritualistic substitute for this real death. Nor did he offer himself as a Saviour or vicarious Redeemer, though after his death his followers inevitably made him an object of devotion.

But that was not his wish. Among his last words were,—'Therefore be ye lamps (or islands) unto yourselves. Be ye a refuge to yourselves. Betake yourselves to no external refuge. Hold fast to the Truth as a lamp,' and 'work out your salvation with diligence.'

These were not the words merely of a moralist. Gautama had committed himself so completely to the mystery that it flowered in him as a divine common sense. Yet the combination of tenderness and transcendence which Indian art conjured into the faces of those who had learnt the lesson which he taught reveals a mystery of Union and a grace of being in which the moral, intellectual and emotional are fused and forgotten. M. René Grousset has memorably described the impression the face of such a being of perfect wisdom makes upon those who contemplate it.

> *Freed from the attachments of the ego, his transitory personality has been dissolved, or rather has become impersonalized, and the pure ideals into which it has melted have gone* *to join the ideality of the universe. His gaze, animated with such an intense interior life, is as though lost in the immensity of the aerial depths, and void of all material content. It is because, like the face of the world, the soul of the sage has emptied itself of all concrete reality.*
>
> *In the disappearance of the world and the ego, their appearance is suddenly found to cover a supernatural radiance.*[1]

For the man who champions, as a moralist or a materialist, attachment to this world and suspects all efforts to redeem its conflict by transcending it, this inward gaze of the released being is disconcerting and even reprehensible. To him it may well seem the gaze of someone who is no longer effectively here. To-day few believe that such beings have a part to play in the salvation of mankind or that it may be more dynamic in its utter stillness than the vociferous strivings of social and moral reform, which never change the quality of life radically, though they may ameliorate where they cannot transform.

Most of us have much to learn before we can enter fully into this life of inwardness in which the light of redeeming wisdom shines. But the task which these Masters of life have fulfilled is, at every stage of imperfection, our only task, the task through which mystery may unfold as mindfulness and faith awaken into knowledge.

It is in the darkness of faith that the work is done which culminates in the radiance of knowledge. We can observe and study objectively the changing complex of thought and mood, which

[1] From *In The Footsteps of the Buddha* by Réné Grousset.

we miscall self. But what we are and are not, the Atman, the 'Suchness,' we can never observe, because It is Its own object and, as such, mediates unseen, though not unfelt or unknown inwardly, between subject and object, in us and in all else, as a reconciling principle.

This is the Being of wisdom and love of which we need to become so inwardly conscious that we are conscious of nothing else. To achieve this we have to gravitate to a centre, where we no longer are, where self-consciousness disappears in an awareness that comprehends the without in the within and the within in the without. This centre which is everywhere and nowhere is the Void in which the delusion of self is swallowed up. We are poised above it as we tread the Middle Way between the opposites, and as it opens in our depths the comprehension dawns which we see in the serene, Truth-possessed, wholly attentive, benignant face and posture of the Buddha.

Here is the image of Faith truly awakened to knowledge, of mind and all the humbler senses gathered into the compassionate embrace of Mind, in which they rest beyond all craving, distraction or perturbation, organs of light, love and understanding.

CHAPTER ELEVEN

Mindfulness and No-Mind

I

GAUTAMA WAS neither a theist nor an atheist, though he is often named the latter by those who can see no alternative to being one or the other and who do not recognize that theism is as much the converse as a contradiction of atheism. His spiritual genius mediated between these opposites, as between all others, accepting and reconciling the truth which is in each of them.

No teaching makes more room for direct experience and first-hand knowledge than his. It empties our minds of all preconceptions and leads us to the very kernel of truth, to Mindfulness itself. We must go back to the beginning, strip ourselves bare of all subjective notions and emotions and consciously offer ourselves to the mysterious workings of the unconditioned Consciousness in Which we essentially live and of Which we essentially are. This surrender to That Which is not-self initiates an utterly new relation to life of both freedom and dependence.

When Gautama, at the end of his life, bid his followers to be 'islands' to themselves, he meant that they should be islands in this ocean of universal Mindfulness, washed by Its encircling waters, filled with the sound of Its rhythmic voice, anchored in the plumbless depths of Its peace. To become such an island is the purpose of all Buddhist meditation.

It is equally, of course, the purpose of the Christian practice of mental prayer or of the Taoist practice of the 'Circulation of the Light and Protection of the Centre,' of which it is written[1] that 'when one begins to apply this magic, it is as if, in the middle of one's being, there were a non-being. When in the course of time the work is finished, and beyond the body there is another body, it is as if, in the middle of the non-being, there were a being.'

---

[1] In *The Secret of the Golden Flower.* A Chinese Book of Life. Translated and explained by Richard Wilhelm.

There is nothing fanciful about this experience. It happens exactly as it is described here, as those who have persisted in true meditation can testify. The transference of will and attention from a false centre to a true one, from the eccentric to the concentric, is magical or, as a Christian would say, a gift of Grace, in so far as it is, like all creative acts, not our own doing. But it is also, the unfailing consequence of recognizing certain laws and learning to conform to them.

We are, in other words, required 'to work out our salvation with diligence,' as both Gautama and St. Paul declared, and with complete assurance that if our efforts are rightly directed, the promised liberation will ensue. There is no favouritism or caprice in the Divine, on whatever level It manifests, though Its gifts, because they issue from a pure giving beyond our limited human capacity, must always seem gratuitous.

Buddhist teaching and practice are particularly valuable for their clearness and simplicity, the absence from them of occult references, and their direct application to the conduct of ordinary life. They are based on the truth, enunciated in the first verse of the *Dhammapada*, which I have already quoted, and which declares that all we are is due to what we have thought, is founded on or composed of our thoughts. All life, indeed, is precipitated or embodied thought. As Gautama said, 'Whatsoever there is of evil, connected with evil, belonging to evil—all issues from mind.' So, he added, does the good and all that is connected with and belongs to it.

Feeling is, of course, a manifestation of Mind, though even more liable than intelligence to be an impure one. That is why the emphasis in Buddhism is so strongly upon Mindfulness. For until the heart, the senses, and the intelligence have become wholly Mindful, they are deceived by the unreal. To tread the Middle Path, to recollect continually and rest in the neutral point which is above as well as between the opposites, is to practice Mindfulness, a kind of awareness that is utterly other than 'knowingness.' This practice, by which eventually the whole nature may be conformed to the Real, is a necessary consequence of accepting the truth of Gautama's discovery of the cause of pain and the way that leads to its cessation through no longer associating a self with the world of change.

This truth has now to be realized in action, to be put to an inti-

mate and sustained testing. Only thus can we really know it to be
true. The practice of Mindfulness, as Gautama taught it, is simply
the method by which we can enact the third 'Noble Truth.' For
in pure Mind there is no craving, since It contains all within Itself.
That Mind we are. By learning to live in It we cease gradually
to cling to the world of things and names and notions which are
not Its true expression, but only reflections of our self-centred
minds, and which entangle us in a multiplicity of false discriminations that excite greed and anger, because we identify ourselves
with them. In Gautama's words, as recorded in the *Lankavatara
Sutra*,

> *The world as seen by discrimination is like seeing one's own
> image reflected in a mirror, or one's shadow, or the moon re-
> flected in water, or an echo heard in the valley. People grasp-
> ing their own shadows of discrimination become attached to
> this thing and that thing and failing to abandon dualism they
> go on for ever discriminating and thus never attain tranquillity.
> By tranquillity is meant Oneness and Oneness gives birth to the
> highest Samadhi which is gained by entering into the realm of
> Noble Wisdom that is realizable only within one's inmost con-
> sciousness.*

Through the steadfast practice of Mindfulness we may centre
ourselves in this Oneness in which the light of insight scatters the
shadows of external discrimination, and differences no longer
divide, but enrich and unite. 'This,' declared Gautama, 'is the only
way for the purification of beings, for the overcoming of sorrow
and lamentation, for the destruction of pain and grief, for reaching
the right path, for the attainment of Nirvana, namely the four
Foundations of Mindfulness.'

These four foundations consist in learning to contemplate disinterestedly our body, our feelings, our state of mind and the
contents of our mind. In the process of doing this we detach our
consciousness from the objects to which it habitually clings. As
the clinging ceases, the shadow of the self fades and illumination
comes, penetrating the body, the feelings, the states of mind and
its contents, all of which are now increasingly transparent to the
light of pure Consciousness.

In that light and by it the world of forms around us is, also, irradiated with meaning and beauty, even though they be tragic,

and assumes a relevance which it never possessed before. We may recall the two birds on the one tree of the *Upanishad*. Now no longer does the bird, which signifies the contemplating Mind, look sadly on, while his fellow obliviously devours the fruits of life. Now he who acts and he who contemplates are true friends. The unconscious soul is at one with Mindful Spirit.

Truly to attain this unity of contemplation and act requires long and intensive training. Yet from the first moment that we begin seriously and persistently to practice Mindfulness we are closing the gulf which exists between our acts and our consciousness.

The right Mindfulness, which is the heart of Gautama's teaching, begins and essentially continues in the simplest exercise, which is within the capacity of anyone who is seriously committed to the task of awakening to reality and will persist steadfastly in it. This exercise requires no elaborate conceptual knowledge which is, in fact, one of the hindrances to be overcome. Gautama did not, in his four Noble Truths, enunciate concepts. He distilled experience basic to every man and woman. The practice of Mindfulness which he taught is intended to liberate us from abstract thought into the immediacy of spiritual experience. We are unlikely to embrace the practice until we have understood and assented to the Truths. But such understanding and assent is more than intellectual. We recognize, however imperfectly, that the four Truths explain the pattern of our lives, as they are and as they might be.

In this concluding chapter I can only touch on certain salient parts of the practice of Mindfulness which I have tested myself, and I must begin with the exercise which is fundamental to every branch of Buddhist meditation and without which no advanced exercise would be possible.

II

All consciousness is a kind of attention. It begins the moment we awake from sleep, though it is partially present in our dreams. It began in our infancy when we first took notice of forms around us. At that time, though extremely limited, it was pure and uncomplicated by any self-conscious notions and associations. These associations were necessary to link up objects with one another and thus form relations in our mind between them. In this way we learnt to generalize and our first imaginative seeing was supplemented by abstract thinking. This, too was necessary to enable us to organize the world about us. But because, as our vision thus developed, we had succumbed to the illusion of a separate self, we had lost the capacity to be wholly attentive. The film of our self-interest interposed. We saw what this self-interest allowed us to see and we were continually distracted by the mental and emotional activities, the memories and anticipations in which self-centredness entangled us.

The basic purpose of the Buddhist practice of Mindfulness is to regain the true attentiveness which we have lost, or what Simone Weil rightly called 'l'attente de Dieu,' because it represents a gearing of all the faculties to the creative centre.

As our attention becomes more pure and single, we become detached from the self-generated whirlpool of ideas and images in which, before, we unconsciously or half-consciously revolved. By withdrawing from it, we not only discover clearly for the first time the mechanical wheel to which we have been tied, but the automatic movement of the wheel is arrested. It slows down and, so long as our attention holds, it ceases to turn.

The systematic practice of Mindfulness, then, begins for Buddhism in what is called 'Bare Attention' and to whatever heights and depths the consciousness eventually attains, it never ceases to depend on this simple, uncomplicated bending of the mind on the objects of its regard. I cannot do better, here, than quote the description of it given by the Venerable Nyanaponika Thera, in his *The Heart of Buddhist Meditation*. 'Bare Attention,' he writes,

> is the clear and single-minded awareness of what actually happens to us and in us, at the successive moments of perception. It is called 'bare' because it attends just to the bare facts of a perception as presented either through the five physical senses or through the mind which, for Buddhist thought, constitutes the sixth sense. When attending to that sixfold sense impression, attention or mindfulness is kept to a bare registering of the facts observed, without reacting to them by deed or speech or by mental comment which may be one of self-reference (like, dislike, etc.) of judgment or reflection. If during the time, short

or long, given to the practice of Bare Attention, any such comments arise in one's mind, they themselves are made objects of Bare Attention, and are neither rejected nor pursued.

Anyone who has begun to attempt this 'clear and single-minded awareness of what actually happens *to* us and *in* us' will discover in what a Nessus shirt of mental, visual and verbal illusion he has clothed himself. Yet though at first such pure attentiveness for even half a minute may seem beyond our powers, the practice in itself is exceedingly simple and is equally applicable to any of the four Foundations of Mindfulness, which Gautama denoted as the body and the feelings, the states and contents of the mind, and to every activity and interest of our daily life. Indeed it is essential that Mindfulness should be practised continuously, so far as possible, and not confined to periods of concentrated meditation. For this the exercise of Bare Attention is perfectly adapted.

That the effort to maintain it seems at first extremely difficult is due to the fact that we have habitually misused our mental muscles and continue to misuse them in striving to relax them. What Keats wrote of the genius of poetry that it 'must work out its own salvation in a man: it cannot be matured by law and precept, but by sensation and watchfulness in itself,' is true of the genius of life and of creative living.

Before, therefore, we can begin to be really Mindful our habitual mode of action has to be relaxed. We need to become quite passive and yet watchful and alert, two things which are impossible to combine so long as we cling apprehensively to a self. If we strain to achieve and maintain this alert passivity, we shall fail. We have to learn to 'consent' to it, to let it happen, and the positive aspect of attention consists in our ability to watch, to listen, to wait, observant and detached, yet surrendered to the experience of the moment. This is the kind of action of which the Master, Lu Tzu, said, 'the secret of the magic of life consists in using action in order to achieve non-action.' Though, compared with our previous strivings, it seems actionless, it demands far more positive concentration than the effort we have habitually expended.

In the practice of Mindfulness it is well to begin with the body, as Gautama advised, and particularly is it well for intellectuals or people with lively, restless minds, to do so. For in observing the body we begin, as it were, on the ground-floor, in the humblest class in the school of experience. The lesson we learn here is essentially the same as those we shall learn as we mount higher. But it is less complicated and so more easily sensed directly.

Attention, as I have said, is the solvent of tension and no real relaxation of the body is possible without it. For we cannot relax contractions until we are fully aware of them. Bare Attention in relation to the body begins in an observance of these contractions. We may aid it at first by consciously contracting various muscles, in the arms and legs, for example, or in the brows, eyes or tongue. Thus we may familiarize ourselves with the sensation of tenseness, of which we are largely unconscious. This will help us to recognize its persistence when we suppose that we are relaxed.

In fact, as a faint sensation in certain muscles will inform us, we are not fully relaxed. But the more we detach ourselves from such sensation by observing it, the deeper will the relaxation become, until the sensation altogether ceases. Even then, unsensed residual tensions remain to be resolved by our persistence in observing instead of doing. The same uninterfering watchfulness is practised by Buddhists over breathing. Unlike the *pranayama* of some schools of Yoga, which involves conscious control and spacing of the rhythm of breath, the original Buddhist practice consists in a quiet, unstrained noticing of the breath's natural flow, by which its rhythm is imperceptibly deepened and tranquillized and the whole rhythm of body and mind with it.

By ceasing from all personal effort, except that required for continuing attentive, and by becoming in this way wholly receptive to what is being done and un-done in us, we discover that the habitual fissure between self-consciousness and being which makes us tense is being gently closed. Peace enters and blesses our bodies, not because we have striven for it, but because we have sensitively observed the symptoms of its absence in our muscular system and, by so doing, have allowed ourselves to feel the reality of its presence, like the Jew of old who exclaimed 'surely the Lord is in this place and I knew Him not.'

Complete bodily relaxation includes the muscles of the brow, eyes, jaw and tongue. When these are relaxed, the activity of the lower mind or sixth sense is also stilled. Ordinarily this induces sleep. But it need not. It is possible to remain watchfully alert even when this mental muscle, of which the contraction causes sleeplessness, is no longer tensed. By doing so, we may gain our first experience of a Mind which is not attached to our physical faculties, but comprehends and transcends them. We enjoy in an elementary way, which is no less convincing for manifesting primarily as a sense of bodily ease and well-being, the peace that passes understanding and the nature of union.

Such an exercise in relaxation is, of course, only one example of what Gautama meant by 'contemplating the body in the body.' Nor is it specially Buddhist or even Eastern in its method. It has been taught as a simple form of therapy by more than one enlightened modern healer in the West, notably by Edmund Jacobson in his book, 'You Must Relax,' from the standpoint of an intelligent physiologist.

But it perfectly exemplifies what is basic to Gautama's practice of Mindfulness. Here is Bare Attention at its simplest, directed upon a field of physical sensation and, in the degree that it is maintained and perfected, easing, and ultimately resolving the tension which arises from clinging to the body as if it were a self.

Here we first learn the lesson, which every more advanced exercise in Mindfulness will confirm, that we can only bring unity and harmony to that to which we have ceased to be attached by desire or aversion, hope or fear, whether it be ourselves or another person or thing. For the method of Bare Attention applies equally to the extended body of the world around us, to which we need to bring the same receptive detachment, since upon this all fruitful action and relationship must depend. This is the ground in which a new life of true insight and mindful doing will unfailingly grow.

The practice of Bare Attention in the field of feeling is more inwardly illuminating and reveals subtler and wider implications. But the method and its effects are essentially the same. Every organism lives by alternately contracting and expanding, breathing in and breathing out. And this is as true of man's emotional as of his bodily life. Every physical act he performs contracts and then relaxes his muscles. Similarly every feeling which he experiences contracts and then relaxes what we may call his psychic muscles. If this were allowed to happen without egoistic interference, there would be no false tension. But in all but perfect acts of wisdom and love the ego does interfere to a greater or lesser degree.

The emotive centre in us lies between the negative pole of sensation and the positive pole of thought. When some object excites a sensation, the stimulus is flashed through the emotive centre to the mind which forms an image of it. In this necessary functioning of the psychic organism the emotive centre, like the physical muscle, continually contracts and relaxes as the energy which it has received through the channel of sensation is released in a mental act. If this occurs healthily, there is a balance between the intake and the output, and the emotive centre itself, though continually pulsing with the energy it freely receives and gives, is balanced and stable. It is then a true centre, in which the poles meet and fuse. In other words it is the Creative Heart in Man as in the Cosmos, which pulses steadily as It draws in and gives out what the ancients called the 'Great Breath.'

Tensed and isolated in our selfhood, we seldom live in and through this Heart, but in a false centre through which a short circuit occurs, with a consequent waste of feeling which excites instead of nourishing the mind.[1]

This condition, though obvious, perhaps, only in highly emotional or exclusively intellectual people, is characteristic of everyone to some extent before enlightenment. To be emotionally dissipated is just as harmful as to be emotionally repressed. In either case we deny to feeling its completion in awareness and to thought its substance in feeling.

Feeling is the faculty through which we nourish our roots in the realm of un-knowing. From this realm the mind draws the substance of true knowing, whether instinctive or intuitive. But the self-centred mind which can wholly surrender itself neither to the darkness nor the light, cannot experience truth immediately, but only grasp and store knowledge that is already dying or dead. Meanwhile the feeling which has been denied expression will also accumulate in the sub-conscious, causing those complexes to which the psychologist applies his scalpel of analyisis. Or it will suddenly shatter the defences raised against it by the mind in a violent explosion.

This, then, in crude summary, is the inward situation which we set out to remedy by the practice of Bare Attention. What it enables us to do is to come into direct contact with what is being actually felt by us, at any moment, undistracted by the self-protective ideas and images which ordinarily cloak this from us.

---

[1] For a super-subtle analysis of this the reader is referred to M. Hubert Benoit's *The Supreme Doctrine*.

In Gautama's own words, describing the act of 'contemplating feelings in feelings,'

> *A brother when experiencing a pleasant feeling knows, 'I experience a pleasant feeling;' when experiencing a painful feeling, he knows 'I experience a painful feeling;' when experiencing a neither-pleasant-nor painful feeling, he knows 'I experience a neither-pleasant-nor painful feeling . . .'*

And so on through every gradation of feeling, inward or outward.

This may seem an elementary practice that can have little effect on our mental or emotional habits. But gradually it can alter them profoundly. For through it we learn to cease from subjective feeling and the self-centred mental habits which generate it. Detaching ourselves from these, we discover how much of our feeling is conditioned, if not generated, by the 'wanting' of ignorance and how, through simply watching and evaluating our feeling, this hunger dies, leaving no sense of loss, but rather a sense of relief and clear-eyed gain.

Far from real feeling disappearing in this cleansing process, it is released from the mental cage in which it has been cramped, and the true relation between it and the mind is renewed. To quote again Gautama's own words, 'His mindfulness is established with the thought, "Feeling exists," to the extent necessary for just knowledge and mindfulness, and he lives independent and clings to naught in the world.'

It is important to emphasize again that such 'independence' does not mean selfish immunity from human relationship and affection. Rather it represents a state of inner freedom from selfish preoccupations and demands, without which a creative relationship, at once wise and loving, is impossible.

All emotion which causes ourselves or others pain, whether it be recognized in the moment of experiencing it as pain or disguises itself as pleasure, is falsely centred. The inner task, for which Bare Attention is one important means, is to reunite feeling and thought in their true centre, in which they will manifest as wisdom and love instead of as mentality and emotion. This task does not involve a denial of either sensation or thought, but an abandonment of the tension which cramps them both and manifests, in one form or other, as desire.

We are so lamentably used to this tension that when we are

first invited to relax it or when we begin to observe it loosening its hold, we fear that we are sinking into a lethargy of indifference. This is what Keats called, in a negative moment, 'the feel of not to feel.' If, instead of resenting this condition, we accept it, patiently observing the tides of life and death as they ebb and flow in us, as they do in all creation, we begin to sense the plumbless depths of no-being in which being takes its rise. To be emotionless is not to cease to feel, but to feel in a new way. For it is out of this void of non-individual, untensed feeling, which seems to us to be feeling-less, since we have ceased to appropriate it to ourselves, that the energy of love springs and flows.

When self-interested feeling is at a low ebb, emotion disturbs or excites us less and less. If this is due to emotional weariness or exhaustion, it merely represents a neutral moment in a conflict which will soon be renewed. But if it is slowly induced by the practice of Bare Attention, it will reflect a radical change in our inner being. For the continuous practice of Mindfulness in all its modes, of which that of Bare Attention is one, gradually loosens the knot in which we have bound ourselves. It thus releases us from the self-intoxication which we mistook for the life of true feeling.

In the early stages of this release we may be conscious only of what is taken from us. But in the degree that we trustingly accept this deprivation of what is false, we find something of incomparably greater worth taking its place. The silted channel through which feeling has had to force its way is no longer viable. But what is opening in us, if we persist, is nothing less than the ocean itself, that limitless realm of potential feeling which is united with an equally infinite realm of potential thought.

In the Creative Heart, In which we are beginning to live, this union is consummated instant by instant within the limits of our capacity and attainment. And as we rest in It and the distractions and distresses of the emotional life die away, our first alarmed sensations of indifference and apathy give place to a joyous tranquillity, a sense of being free at last to experience life in depth instead of being tossed upon its surface waves.

Our sensibility, true now to its own nature, is more and more passive to life, and as the mental and emotional film which previously dulled it clears off in the sunlight of Mindfulness, we begin to be continuously aware of the reality, within and without us, of which previously we had at best only fleeting glances.

Only in the moment of complete enlightenment does the fissure between feeling and intelligence close and emotional tension altogether cease. But each reaffirmation of Mindfulness, each act of sensitive attention, makes it possible for feeling and intelligence to come closer together, to interpenetrate each other and resume their native intimacy.

Emotional tension, like physical, is due to our fear of letting go, of ceasing to act, of sinking into silence. By observing this fear attentively, as a prelude to examining and analysing it, we detach ourselves from it and imperceptibly the tension slackens. By repeat ing this act of non-resistence again and again we begin to experience, if only partially, the inner calm in which all our fears are dissolved.

Beneath the habitual fluctuations of our feelings is a continuous uneasiness, a sense of insufficiency inseparable from our attachment to an unreal ego. It is this anxiety which incites us to restless action in a vain effort to lay the spectre within. But as we contemplate it dispassionately, it slowly vanishes and, with it, our wish to be secure and invulnerable. No longer do we need to ensure our individual status by asserting our rights or to increase our power and prestige by dominating others, whether under the guise of loving them or, more honestly, by frankly pursuing our own interests at their expense.

And as we cease to feel the need to assert our will over others, so, inwardly, we are less and less under the necessity of denying any of our faculties. We are free to let life, in all the subtle magic of its serenely changeful being, come to us through them. For we have learnt to experience beyond selfish preferences. We have broken out of what Gautama called 'the cocoon of false discriminations' and no longer '*move along* with the stream of appearances.' We value life for its own sake, not as something to be held under a constant threat of loss, but to be received and given mindfully, as the circumstance of each moment allows. We have discovered what it is to be spiritually open and hospitable and as pliant as a sapling that sways in sympathy with the lightest breeze, but is, also, steadfastly rooted in earth, as we are in the constancy of understanding and of purified instinct.

This release into a life as deeply felt as it is known, awaits us when we have consented to die to the desire which separates our feeling from our thought. This is what is meant by the statement in *The Secret of the Golden Flower*, 'The awakening of the spirit is accomplished because the heart has first died. When a man can let his heart die, then the primordial spirit wakes to life. To kill the heart does not mean to let it dry and wither away, but it means that it is undivided and gathered into one.'

In learning to let the interested heart die the practice of Bare Attention is a humble, but indispensable means.

III

The practice of Bare Attention in relation to the body and the feelings is not confined to what I have written. There is no limit to its application within the field of sensibility. But enough, perhaps, has been said of its method and meaning for readers, who study Gautama's own Discourse, to apply it more extensively to their own physical and emotional experience. But some of the contemplations on the body, traditionally practised by Buddhists and apparently approved by Gautama, may well strike a Westerner as, to say the least, exceedingly dubious.

What are called 'the dissolution factors' in the body, its subjection to decay, are facts which, like all other facts, need to be impartially recognized. So long as we are attached to the body, we tend to evade these facts, except when they force themselves upon our attention in times of sickness or satiety. The glamour which desire casts over the body of life is a perversion of its beauty and in breaking that thraldom it may be helpful to remind ourselves frequently of what such glamour conceals, the sickness, decay and death to which the body is subject.

This was and is the purpose of Buddhist meditation on the body's manifold impurities. Such meditations, however, will defeat their purpose and only invert the bondage they are intended to break, if they encourage the assumption that the body is 'abominable' in itself and that any recognition of its beauty must reflect craving. This is not so, as all the great art of the world, including Buddhist art, attests. The true artist practises Bare Attention habitually.[1] It enables him to cleanse his vision of subjective prejudice

---

[1] So does the scientist, but less organically, since he depends on instruments to ensure it.

and to reveal the creative beauty of which the creaturely body can be the vehicle.

Few of us are great artists and physical attachment in many people, if not a crippling tie, hinders imaginative perception. But in loosening and ultimately snapping that tie it is as necessary to contemplate with undesirous joy the wonder of the body's structure and the spiritual grace which, if allowed, informs it, as to recognize without aversion the factors of physical decay. True Mindfulness is not directed against the transient. It is rather a continuous and joyous experience of the timeless reality of all that passes away.

When we turn to the more complex sphere of the mind and its activities, the practice of Bare Attention imperceptibly blends with the practice of Clear Comprehension, for which it is and must always continue to be the foundation. When we attend impersonally to what is happening around us and within our minds, we find ourselves withdrawn from the current in which we have been, to a great extent, involuntarily immersed. By this simple step we recover something of the pure receptiveness which was ours before self-consciousness had unbalanced us, before, in other words, the heart, by which we breathe, ceased to be at one with itself and so the in-drawing breath was no longer in harmony with the outgoing. The birth of insight depends fundamentally on the restoration within us of this true balance between receiving and giving.

In our self-centredness we are too passive or too active, the two conditions which Vedanta calls *tamasic* and *rajasic*. In the one the mind is clouded or inert, in the other it is agitated. In both we fail to be mindful. The simple readiness to notice, first the condition itself, and then to be attentive to one thing at a time without mental comment or emotional reaction and to maintain such an impersonal attitude until we have literally 'taken in' as much of the object of our regard as we can, eliminates both these conditions.

For, so long as we are attentive, we cannot be either indolent or impatient. To be fully attentive is to be at once actively passive and passively active. As we learn to attend in this way to objects of sense in the outer world and observe them less and less partially, we prepare ourselves for the harder task of studying as dispassionately more complex objects of the inner world, the ideas and images that arise in our minds, such states of mind, too, as anger, envy, fear or restlessness, and, behind these, the mind itself.

The great virtue of this practice is that it gives time for a mutual relationship to be formed between subject and object. This the ego with its tense reactions and anxious, end-seeking haste will not allow. It is always too short of time to experience, too eager to grasp to receive. Attentiveness recalls us to the present, which is the living point of all experience, and holds us there, freed from any distracting concern, until we have taken in the real nature of a fact or a situation, a person or a problem. But we cannot for long be mere spectators in life, however sympathetic. From hour to hour we have to act, to make decisions, to create, maintain, and adjust relationships. For this we need to supplement attentiveness with Clear Comprehension and thus to be 'purposeless through purpose.'

The aim of all the many specific exercises which have grown out of Gautama's original directive is the same. Firstly it is to help us to know our mind, to study its mechanism, its changeful moods and the irrational depths that underlie them, to distinguish between real and pretended motives, and to do all this with the same watchful neutrality with which we have learnt to observe outward objects, so that the gloss of self-esteem or self-deprecation which we habitually put upon our states of mind is removed and we see them, freshly and starkly, just as they are.

The second aim in the practice is to restore the mind, in our active use of it, to its true shape and temper as a sensitive, smoothly functioning instrument of Mindfulness. Here again what we have learnt in observing the body and the feelings is reaffirmed. In particular we refrain from thinking and acting precipitately. However swift and strong the impulse which our contact with life in people and things excites, we do not blindly act upon it. We stop and think. Thus we circumvent what Dr. Conze calls the danger point, 'the impulsive moment' when one snatches at something instead of meeting it half-way.

This arrest of our habitual tendency to react automatically, especially when personal feeling is aroused, is basic to Clear Comprehension. It gives us time, though it be but one neutral instant, to sink from the circumference to the centre, to allow the situation to teach us, instead of imposing our will one-sidedly upon it, to listen to a voice within and, out of a fusion of the outward and the inward, to discover what is really wise in any circumstance, however small and unimportant it may seem, and, if the alternative be to act or not to act, to speak or to be silent, how to do either creatively and helpfully.

But we are continually using our minds when we are alone and our misuse of them in the monologue or dialogue which we maintain within ourselves is, perhaps, even more demoralizing than in our prejudiced reactions to others. Here again we learn to stop and think, to note what is happening to the mind as it drifts in a stream of associative ideas or idle day-dreaming. We withdraw from the stream and observe it from a centre within us which seems to be nowhere. As we do this, the stream of uncentred reflections ceases to flow and we realize how devoid of any real coherence it is.

We will need to do this repeatedly until our mind begins to regain its true tone, as a sick stomach will, when it has been cleansed of the poison of dead food that is clogging it. In the same way the mind, unburdened of the ever accumulating waste-matter of subjective thought and memory, will become light and clear, keen and supple. As the grip of the ego on it loosens, it will be newly energized as an instrument of a Consciousness not its own, and truly tempered to assimilate the vital ideas and images voluntarily presented to it in meditation.

The third and ultimate aim of the practice of Clear Comprehension is the attainment of freedom. All the labour of analysis and discrimination, of regulating and changing mental habits and thereby the kind of action which they determine, culminates in the gift of insight, of unattached seeing. The power of insight may develop slowly or it may come in a flash. But in either case it is conditional on the basic realization of the impermanence, pain and impersonality of Existence. Of these three characteristics, as Gautama revealed them, the realization of the impersonality of every conditioned object of thought, including the incessantly repeated notion of our own separate existence, is the most decisive. To quote from Nyanaponika Thera's *The Heart of Buddhist Meditation*, to which I am much indebted,

Only by training oneself again and again in viewing justly the presently arisen thoughts and feelings as mere impersonal processes, can the power of deep-rooted, ego-centric thought habits and egotistic instincts be broken up and reduced, and finally eliminated.

Little by little as we observe disinterestedly the incessant process of change, the unending sequence of waves that rise and fall,
are born and die in the ocean of existence, of which we, in our
temporal nature, are a part, we lose all desire to cling to something so impersonal. We begin to react to things, as Master Lu
Tzu puts it, 'by reflexes only,' without subjective bias. For now
we know and are ready to accept the kind of world we are really
living in. Through this acceptance we are at last free to act creatively, no longer depending on things to fortify our shadowy self-
esteem or on the light which they partially reflect to relieve the
dimness of our mind. For the Light of Primordial Spirit now
shines clear *within* our mind and through it on all that seems without.

This central Light of Consciousness Which, as self-delusion
dies, irradiates the mind, unites the opposites which previously
divided it. In this centre of Mindfulness the ever-changing and
the ever-changeless are known to be inseparably one, and because
the spectre of a divided self no longer haunts our mind with a
dread of self-loss and a desire of self-gain, we are joyously committed to the dual adventure of being and not-being, free to experience in every moment of mindful life and relationship the
mystery of this Consciousness and Its illumination, Its radiant
showing and Its divine concealment.

This is the life-transforming insight from which all particular
insights derive and upon which they depend. In it the two practices which I have briefly described find their fulfilment.

It must not be thought, however, that the Buddhist emphasis on
Mindfulness excludes the heart. The reverse is true. To be mindful
is necessarily to be heartful. For the Creative Consciousness with
Which we labour to reunite our minds, cherishes as Its very Self
each form It creates, enfolding each one in the dual rhythm of Its
living to die and dying to live, which are the systole and diastole
of Its eternal Heart. Cleansed of the ego by mindfulness, realizing
that all phenomena are essentially an emptiness through which
reality shines, we begin to live wholly in that Heart, Which in
truth has always cherished us so far as we would let It.

Buddhism offers no emotional short-cuts to the kingdom of love
and can seem in consequence cold and calculating to people who
want to indulge in them. It would not deny that every impulse
of love and affection, every desire to help others, weakens momen-

tarily the grip of self. But it insists that until we have become completely conscious of the unreality of such a self, some element of attachment will remain. So long as feeling resists this ultimate purgation of reasoned awareness, its warm generosities will not be free. Love and light will not have fused.

But in insisting upon this Gautama did not neglect the culture of the heart. For Buddhism the four 'Divine Abodes of the Mind' are not mental ivory towers. They are 'loving-kindness, compassion, sympathetic joy and equanimity.' Unbounded loving-kindness *(metta)* is, indeed, the first condition and primary task of Mindfulness without which the practice of Bare Attention and Clear Comprehension and all the exercises associated with it would be sterile. We cannot win enlightenment for ourselves unless we are seeking it for all. Equally, however, we cannot be loving and kind to others, unless we are the same to ourselves.

'First of all,' declares the teacher, 'friendliness should again and again be developed for oneself, "May I be happy, free from ill, enmity, injury, disturbance, and may I preserve myself at ease." Then, as witnesses to such a condition in ourselves and suffused with the distinterested friendliness which sets the heart free, we should extend the same wishes to other people, until friendliness becomes unlimited.[1]'

Buddhism teaches that enlightenment is a universal process which breaks down all false boundaries until it has completed its redemptive task. Yet, in doing this, it reveals the true bounds intrinsic to each created thing in its pure state, bounds within which it can be contentedly itself as a unique expression of the Real within its own limits. As such, it is free to enjoy and value every other particular perfection around it without envy or false emulation. For in seeking what is perfect in its own small ground, it finds it equally, though differently expressed, in all else.

Therefore every form of life is sacred and should be cherished and no violence done to it. But this is only possible if we do no violence to ourselves. For unless we are at peace in our own house, we shall carry our private warfare into our relationship with others and even into well-meant efforts on their behalf. But if, in Gautama's words, reaffirming the Vedantic ideal of *ahimsa*, of harmlessness, 'you hurt neither yourself nor others, nor both yourself and others, you dwell with a self become Brahman.'

[1] Cited by Dr. Edward Conze in his *Buddhist Meditation*.

When we have learnt to be wholly Mindful, the loving-kindness, sympathetic joy and equanimity which we have faithfully
practised as, in some measure, a discipline and a duty, will thus
flower as an inward necessity and a delight, springing up in our
hearts as spontaneously as pure waters welling out of the deeps
of life. Then unbounded compassion and clear-eyed wisdom will
blend in a realization that all life is one, that it flows unceasingly
out of a void of no-self, and the long feud between heart and mind
will be ended in a consciousness of the Supreme Spirit which
unites them.

IV

Buddhist meditation begins in collected thinking; its end is organic
thinking which is knowing. This transition from thinking to knowing is implicit as an aim in the exercises I have briefly reviewed.
It is carried further in the meditations which are known in Pali as
Jhana. It is hard to find an English equivalent for this word, which
is the Pali form of the Sanskrit *Dhyana* and which occurs in China
as *Ch'an* and in Japan as *Zen*. But, as applied to these particular
spiritual exercises, it is best rendered, perhaps, as 'meditative absorption,' or, in the more advanced ones, as 'rapt contemplation.'

The practices I have already outlined gradually wean us from the
tense habit of self-thinking and self-willing, with its servitude to
unconscious impulses. We begin to discover that there is such a
thing as ego-less experience and that it is profoundly more satis-
fying and beneficial than what it supplants. When, by repeated
acts of Bare Attention, we have learnt to be receptive and then to
act in the spirit of such receptiveness with Clear Comprehension,
the mind will become habitually calm and collected and some
depth of inner peace will be established.

It is then possible to extend Mindfulness, which has been largely
concentrated in these practices on the realm of outward observa-
tion and action, into the inner realm. We can thus begin to identify
ourselves more intimately with the new centre of consciousness
to which we are committed. By acts of imaginative realization we
can enter more deeply into its embrace and so dissolve still further the dying illusion of the self. Thus we may prepare the conditions for that consummation of Mindfulness which the Zen

Masters named 'No-Mind,' and conscious recollection find its fulfilment in super-conscious enlightenment.

The inner work required for this emergence from the chrysalis
of self-centred thought is outlined in a series of exercises. These
are named the *Jhanas*. Their number varies in different schools,
but all are designed to raise, step by step, the level of consciousness. Meditation on the four 'Sublime States' or 'Divine Abodes of
the Mind,' to which I have referred, belong to this kind of practice, in so far as our purpose is to become so inwardly absorbed in
the qualities of loving-kindness, compassion, sympathetic joy and
equanimity, and to make them so much our own, that they vibrate
through us into life.

But the series of eight *Jhanas* which are generally accepted as
central to the practice is based upon Gautama's own description of
the succession of 'trances' or 'absorptions' which culminated in his
enlightenment.

The states of consciousness experienced in the higher or more
advanced *Jhanas* transcend altogether a world of forms and so
are indefinable. But we can understand something of the kind of
transformation which these meditations are meant to further by
briefly considering the first four of them.

The concentration required for even the first presupposes an
abandonment, if only during the period of the exercise, of all desire for pleasure as of all mental anxiety. We are not yet sufficiently
unified to think and feel wholly by intuition. But in this meditation we approach such a condition through the practice of disinterested thinking. Gautama spoke of it thus,

> *Now having taken solid food and gained strength without
> sensual desires, without evil ideas I attained and abode in the
> first trance of joy, arising from seclusion and combined with
> reasoning and investigation. Nevertheless such pleasant feelings
> as arose did not overpower my mind.*

Anyone who has acquired the habit of reflecting dispassionately
upon some subject, waiting for it to disclose its meaning and at
the same time thinking round it so that, by seeing it from every
side, he may avoid any partial perspective, will at least recognize
the nature of this first *Jhana*. The ordinary intellect with its habits
of applied and discursive thinking is still active in it, but it is subdued to the theme which is being pondered. It circulates round and

over it, cutting away what is secondary or misleading in its reflections as it approaches nearer to the theme's essential meaning. As it does so, the mind seems to receive an infusion of light that clarifies both itself and the subject it is pondering.

The thinker, in such meditation, handles his mind as a skilled craftsman handles his tool, intent on moulding the material he is working on into a significant shape. He guides the tool, but he also lets the tool and the subject about which he is thinking teach him. Hence his happiness. For he has forgotten himself in a humble readiness for the disclosure of truth, though his mind is not yet sufficiently organic in its functioning to dispense with discursive thought. But the ripples on the pool of his calm reasoning are slight enough for the image of truth to be reflected in it. He thus makes contact, though as yet imperfectly, with what Wordsworth called.

> *An independent world*
> *Created out of pure intelligence,*

a world which Wordsworth himself discovered as a young man in the pure logic of geometry, and, in it, release for the mind beset 'with images and haunted by itself.' But while for Wordsworth at this time relief from self-thought and self-feeling came largely through escape into abstractions, the condition experienced in the first *Jhana* is a preliminary step towards an integration of consciousness in which the actual and the ideal meet and unite in the real.

In the second *Jhana* we cross the threshold into the inner kingdom in which immediate realization of a world known and loved from within becomes possible. To quote Gautama's own words again, 'I attained and abode in the second trance of joy arising from concentration with eternal serenity and fixing of the mind on one point without reasoning and investigation.'

Here the discursive mind is left behind and self-consciousness is correspondingly weakened. Discursive thinking is a necessary bridge between us and the object of our thought, until we can come closer to it. It spans the gulf dug by the ego, and if disciplined, it enables us to achieve a significant contact with 'the other,' if not a really intimate communion. The element of conflict, implicit in the false dualism, may indeed be so much reduced that its stresses begin to be creative. When the first *Jhana* has been fully experienced, antagonism, such as that which lurks in so much critical analysis that claims to be impartial, has altogether passed away. And this explains the happy sense of ease, associated with this meditation, as between two friends who have begun to understand and appreciate one another.

Nevertheless there is still separation. The freedom of the reasoning mind is still cramped by self-consciousness. It has not wholly awakened to faith. In the second *Jhana*, through a voluntary abandonment of discursive thinking and a fixing of the mind on one point, whether it be a particular image or the idea implicit in the image, we begin to experience Mind Itself. And this experience is so convincingly real in revealing to us that our own minds do not depend on their own resources, but are all the time drawing what power and insight they possess from a Consciousness not their own, that faith unfolds in us, not as belief in this or that, but as an intimate assurance of a sustaining presence and inspiration. Our need to cling to our own minds consequently weakens.

In disciplined discursive thinking we had learnt to control and direct our minds. But the concentration of which we now begin to find ourselves capable is of another kind. We are, in short, concentred in a Mind of such infinite understanding that our mental unrest, which was rooted in a baffled longing for just such an 'unknown Knower,' is assuaged and we enter a zone of joy and peace. We are not, however, capable of accepting this joy purely, despite our training in the practice of Bare Attention. The old self has not yet been exorcised. Its grasping habits survive at a subconscious level and there induce a a sort of rapture which differs from pure joy in being tainted by an element of subjective excitement and elation. That unrest 'which men miscall delight' has still to be outgrown.

But in the third *Jhana*, if we persist and deepen our faith and concentration in that creative Mind, the bliss of Whose knowing is utterly transpersonal, we find ourselves ceasing to claim as our own the joy and peace that come to us. They are something that happens in us, that is given and not possessed. The deeper this feeling grows, the more distasteful our previous rapture seems. In rapture there lurks a dread of loss proportionate to the desire for gain. But now our only desire is to lose what remains of the self in That Which is beyond all gain and loss, that undesirous, but infinitely loving Heart of joy, in Which Gautama bid his followers 'dwell mindful, equanimous and happy.'

In the fourth *Jhana* this ultimate self-loss is attained and the consciousness, freed of every constriction, becomes pellucidly clear. No hidden preference for joy or its opposite remains, and so no proneness to elation or depression. The desire which attaches us to the pleasureable or the painful is at last dissolved in a realization of That in Which and by Which all is enjoyed and all is suffered, a realization so immediate, penetrating and transforming that a new world of utter 'purity of mindfulness and equanimity' dawns, and any lingering attachment to the old world of mental or sensuous excitement dies. Joy is ours as something which eternally abides through all the changes of circumstance, of light and shadow, because it is of the very essence of life and at last our minds are lucid enough to see it and our hearts, in consequence, wholly open to receive and give it.

Henceforth we live, not in hungry anticipation of future happiness, but in trustful expectancy of what each moment brings. It was of this calm bliss in the heart of things, which is rediscovered in the human heart when the 'hindrances' to it have been removed, that Coleridge sang so poignantly out of the cloud of his dejection,

> *O pure of heart! thou need'st not ask of me*
> *What this strong music in the soul may be!*
> *What, and wherein it doth exist,*
> *This light, this glory, this fair luminous mist,*
> *This beautiful and beauty-making power.*
>
> *Joy, virtuous Lady! Joy that ne'er was given*
> *Save to the pure, and in their purest hour,*
> *Life, and life's effluence, cloud at once and shower,*
> *Joy, Lady! is the spirit and the power,*
> *Which wedding Nature to us gives in dow'r*
> *A new Earth and new Heaven,*
> *Undreamt of by the sensual and the proud—*
> *Joy is the sweet voice, Joy the luminous cloud—*
>
> *We in ourselves rejoice!*
> *And thence flows all that charms or ear or sight,*
> *All melodies the echoes of that voice,*
> *All colours a suffusion from that light.*

In the consciousness of one who has truly attained the condition of the fourth *Jhana*, joy and peace do not come and go. For they are the inborn qualities of the Unity in which he is now grounded and established. Only then, in this fullness and emptiness of concentrated being or, in Gautama's words, 'with the defilement gone, supple, dextrous, firm and impassible,' is it possible to begin to extend and enlarge the consciousness by a series of deeper contemplations by which the formal limitations imposed on the mind by the physical senses can be transcended and new dimensions of experience open to the inward eye.

Of these formless *Jhanas* or *Aruppas*, as they are called, the first leads the consciousness into the sphere of 'unbounded space,' the second into that of 'unlimited consciousness,' the third into that of 'nothingness.' Beyond this, in the fourth, a kind of awareness dawns in which 'there is neither perception nor non-perception.' These contemplations are only for those who are far advanced in spiritual life. Yet if in our humbler meditations we pass beyond verbal thinking and, though it be only for brief periods, experience immediately the reality of which words are symbols, so that, for example, we know intuitively what the silence in which the Word speaks is, or the emptiness from which the love that sustains and cherishes us flows, we will understand, if dimly, the nature of these advanced contemplations. Nor will we doubt their effectiveness in refining and enlarging the quality of awareness.

This awareness is not a passive thing as mediumistic trance is or fortuitous extra-sensory perceptions. It grows organically in those who succeed in breaking, one by one, the fetters of a self-bound mind. In the Consciousness which unfolds progressively in the *Jhanas* the passive and the active come into ever closer integration and a creative vision ensues in which form does not oppose or deny the formless. All is seen in the moment when the formless takes form and form receives the formless. In such immediate and intuitive seeing form has not hardened, in memory and the grip of possessive mentality, into something not wholly alive, not perfectly informed.

It is thus that the enlightened mind sees the world of nature and of man as it really is. It, also, sees into worlds closed from ordinary vision, and these, too, it sees as they really are and consequently can collaborate creatively with those unseen presences who are ever helping to redeem the darkness of this earth and aiding those who labour to enter more deeply into the Light which they enjoy.

To a mind, in which such vision has opened and thought has

crystallized in sensibility, the unseen is not another worldly loca-
tion. It is just as present in the world immediately around us as in
those more inward worlds we enter in deep meditation. Nor need
spirits be sought or found in séance-rooms. They reveal themselves as clearly in the person whom we meet in the street or who
serves us in a shop, in the friend whom we love, the preacher in
the pulpit, yes, and the flower on our table, as in those visitations
of the mind by beings who respond to our readiness, in 'a rapt
contemplation,' to be raised and guided into realms of new
awareness.

Those, however, who are not practised in meditation and who
have little experience of the realm of reality which it can open
up, are likely to regard the *Jhanas* as dangerous exercises in intro-
version, which are more likely to lead to subjective fantasy and a
fugitive self-absorption than to strengthen and clarify the mind as
an organ of vision.

The reverse, however, is true. They may, of course, be mis-used
and should not be even attempted until stable foundations have
been laid and all desire for personal power or satisfaction has been
renounced. Significantly *Jhana* is named in Buddhism the 'earth
artifice' and it is declared that to 'attain to the heavens of Form' a
man 'cultivates the way thereto, aloof from sensuous appetites,
aloof from evil ideas, and so, by *earth-gazing* enters and abides in
the First *Jhana.*'

Gautama was no fugitive from earth himself and encouraged
none of his followers to be one. He knew that, for those incarnated
here, the Light which is sown in the darkness of the body must
grow and be harvested there. The flesh contains within it both the
promise of spiritual fulfilment and the resistances which make this
fulfilment possible. 'In this very body,' he said, 'six feet in length,
with its sense impressions and its thoughts and ideas, are the world,
the origin of the world and the ceasing of the world, and likewise
the way that leads to the ceasing thereof.'

The release he had gained and taught was not from the body
in which he lived considerately until he was over eighty, but from
the clinging self, a release which ensured a true communion with
all aspects of objective existence, of which the body is one.

It is towards such clarified and enlarged communion that the
Jhanas are intended to lead. The consciousness which has become
capable of it is abnormal only in being more true to the creative

intention of life and the Mind Which informs it than what is at present considered normal.

Nor, of course, are such spiritual exercises peculiar to Buddhism. They correspond closely with the Yoga meditations of Hinduism, known as *Samyama*, of which the three stages are *Dharana*, concentration, *Dhyana*, meditation, and *Samadhi*, pure contemplation. Here, too, consciousness is led step by step out of the cage of self to be recreated in the being and the form of universal Spirit. The Christian mystic and the Sufi tread a similar, though distinctive path.

Even to have practised the first two *Jhanas* faithfully and persistently is to be in no doubt of the realm of light and of inner joy and peace into which they lead. But to describe a meditation can convey little of its reality, as little as a précis does of a poem. For meditation is creative work which transforms experience by changing the centre from which we live.

As the artist recreates nature in the true imaginative form which others fail to see, so he who works inwardly through the self-discipline and the self-surrender of meditation labours to restore to his being the organic form, from which at some stage it has deviated. All meditation is, indeed, based in the conviction that we have only to acknowledge and assent to the Reality from which we have never in essence been separated to awake from the long illusion of the ego. In doing so we shall cease to think about Truth and realize Truth Itself. The transition from thinking to knowing, the fulfilment of Mindfulness in 'No-Mind' will have been effected.

V

It is upon this conviction that the whole technique of Zen Buddhism is based. In this it does not differ from other Schools. Where it does differ radically is in the method it adopts to bring about this awakening. It is known as the Sudden as distinct from the Gradual School, since it rejects the approach to enlightenment through successive stages and aims to break the thongs of self-centred thought in a flash of illumination.

This does not mean that the practitioners of Zen tread an easier path or one which involves less preparation for the 'moment of

Truth' to happen. It seems simpler and more direct. But it is more intensive. And until he who treads it has broken through, he has far less to comfort him or to encourage him to think that he is making progress. For in the view of Zen, there is, indeed, no progress. To realize that and all its implications is to be truly alive. We are either asleep or awake, and until the moment of our awakening, we are as far from Reality as we were when we first began our work, though our sleep-walking may be less worried and worrying.

This rigorous distinction between sleeping and waking, with its rejection of all semi-somnolent states, has certain advantages. The temptation on the path of *Dhyana* (meditation) is a leaning over to its negative side, which is more strongly stressed in Buddhism than in Vedanta. The relief from the more distressing tensions of mind, heart and body which results from a regular practice of even the more elementary meditations which have been outlined, is so great a blessing that many are content to do no more than preserve the tranquillity which has been gained.

It may be that nothing more is required of some for the time being, that they need a peaceful spell before continuing their journey. Gautama, at least, did not blame them. 'The monk,' he declared, 'who is devoted to the recollection of Peace sleeps at ease, wakes up at ease, is calm in the faculties, calm in his mind, endowed with a sense of shame and a dread of blame, amiable, intent on sublime things. . . . Even if he do not penetrate any further, he is at least bound for a happier destiny.'[1]

But this peace is not enlightenment. Indeed it may prove to be further from it than the distress which it has assuaged. For the distress implies the urge of life, while any tranquillity which is not vitally renewing itself, will decline into torpor. We need to live to the uttermost, whether it be with or without a selfish motive. The latter way of life differs from the former only in being a total commitment instead of a partial one, a commitment in which all the faculties, from the humblest to the highest, are devoted to life's service and find eventually the true peace of a vital unity in this common dedication.

The ancient feud, present in all religions, between activist and quietist, the feud which, for example, in the seventeenth century, threw Molinos into the cruel hands of the Inquisition and flared up

---

1 As quoted in *Buddhist Meditation* by Edward Conze.

in the notorious attack of the blunt Bossuet on the spiritually sensitive Fénelon over the writings of Madame Guyon, is more often than not an unreal one, since the activist can be more false to life in his self-assertion than the quietist in his retirement. But the danger, always present on the inward path, of slipping into mere passivity is a real one.

Meditation is in its early stages no more than a means to Wisdom, a practice through which Wisdom becomes possible. To cultivate it as an end or to conceive of any state of tranquillity as an acquisition is to deaden the pulse of Wisdom, if not to become a spiritual and social parasite. The conflict between stillness and movement cannot be resolved by denying either of them. It ceases only at that central point of greatest intensity within us, in which life is at once perfectly active and perfectly passive.

The effortless effort of true meditation will open within us this centre, named sometimes 'the Golden Flower,' and through it a peace, which is wholly alive and Self-renewing, will flow, not as something which we have attained, but rather as something which, because it cannot be grasped or held, is eternally present and available. When we have realized this, a later Zen Master declared, meditation ceases to be a means to wisdom and becomes one with it in a Body which 'remains perfectly quiescent and serene all the time, and yet functions mysteriously in ways beyond calculation.'

But the early Zen Masters tended to encourage a cult of quiescence for its own sake by inviting their pupils to think of the mind as a mirror to be continually cleansed of the dust and stain of erroneous thoughts by controlled meditation. This practice could never of itself open the mind to creative vision. It could reduce its restlessness, even to the point of suspending consciousness for set periods. But where was wisdom and where was life in such trances of empty quiet?

It was this negation that Master Hui-neng challenged by his teaching and in so doing initiated the 'Sudden' method of enlightenment which has been uniquely that of the Zen School, in its various branches, ever since. Previously a pupil had been taught to practise a triple discipline which involved, as 'Precept,' abstaining from evil, as 'Meditation,' purifying the mind, and as 'Knowledge or Wisdom,' doing all that is good. This moral and mental discipline was to be sedulously practised, as all such disciplines are, from the standpoint of someone conscious of his failings and intent on treading the path of virtue.

It was against this familiar attitude that Hui-neng uttered his revolutionary challenge. 'Listen to my teaching,' he declared. 'According to my view, the Mind as it is in itself is free from ills—this is the Precept of Self-being. The Mind as it is in itself is free from disturbances—this is the Meditation of Self-being. The Mind as it is in itself is free from follies—this is the Knowledge of Self-being. . . . When Self-being is understood, there is no further use in establishing the Triple Discipline.'

When asked the meaning of 'no further use,' the Master answered '(The Mind) as Self-being is free from ills, disturbances and follies, and every thought is thus transcendental knowledge; and within the reach of this illuminating light there are no forms to be recognized as such. Being so, there is no use in establishing anything. One is awakened to this Self-being abruptly, and there is no gradual realization in it. This is the reason for no-establishment.'[1]

Previous to this, Hui-neng had declared that 'From the first not a thing is.' This was not an intellectual statement. It was an exact rendering of what he himself had experienced in the moment of his enlightenment. The 'Self-nature,' into which he had looked in that experience, was 'not a thing.' To see into it was to see into no-thing-ness or no self-ness. In such seeing, devoid of inhibiting egoism, Mind in its purity broke through and Wisdom illuminated both the subject and the world of objects, making them one. This true 'Self-nature,' which, in contrast with the self that is displaced, is experienced as 'no thing,' is the unborn original Buddha-nature or divine Spirit, eternally present, and only awaiting recognition and acceptance, in all beings.

This Zen experience is, in fact, akin to that of the advanced *Jhana*, to which I have already referred, in which an awareness dawns that is 'neither perception nor non-perception.' This is only possible when we cease to have any self-conscious thoughts in regard to things. What we ordinarily see as 'things' are dying or dead reality, just as what we entertain as notions or opinions are 'mental things' which have failed to come fully to life or which

---

[1] As rendered, with other quotations from the Zen Masters in this section, by Dr. T. T. Suzuki in his *The Zen Doctrine of No-Mind,* to which and to his other studies of Zen every Western student of the subject is deeply indebted.

have died into systems of thought to which we cling. But when we are inwardy objectless, the reality, of which all objects, regarded as 'things,' are but husks and shadows, becomes visible in forms, born of a true marriage of perceiving consciousness and object perceived.

The Zen Masters called this 'living in the Unconscious.' But to live thus in the Unconscious is not to lose Consciousness which would be death or a least anaesthesia. It is to allow a new Consciousness to spring up, moment by moment, in us, that of Creative Mind or Wisdom Itself, Which hankers after nothing. 'To face all objective conditions and yet to be free from any form of stirring,' wrote a Zen teacher, 'this is the Unconscious. The Unconscious is thus known as to be truly conscious of Itself. But to be conscious of consciousness (e.g. to be self-conscious) is a false form of the Unconscious.' To be thus conscious without being self-conscious is to be no longer divided between perceiving and not-perceiving. It is to enjoy a direct knowledge of the Real, cleansed of all abstraction.

Hui-neng's doctrine, then, condenses into a pungent statement the meaning of the non-dualism which has run like a central thread through the whole pattern of Eastern thought, as we have explored it in this book. His dynamic expression of it is pure of any negative bias. It may seem paradoxical to say this of a doctrine which is grounded in a return to nothingness. 'I establish no-thoughtness as the Principle of my teaching,' he declared, 'formlessness as the Body, and abodelessness as the Source.'

But out of this void, in which all clinging to thought, form and matter has perished, new vision springs up, a true *act* of seeing, intuitive and integral, and the long stultifying conflict between the spiritual and physical side of human nature, between body and mind, the unconscious and the conscious, is resolved in the ever renewed miracle of creative living.

Such a doctrine is hard to grasp, as my efforts to expound it have doubtless shown. But it was meant to be. Its virtue lies in the fact that it evades the grasp of mentality and its dualistic logic. It is against this half-mind that the Zen Masters direct their enigmatic statements, questions and answers, which are called *koans*. A *koan* defies the intellectual analysis which is the necessary instrument of the divided mind. It puzzles, baffles, outrages and finally exhausts this mind as it wrestles with it for meaning. In this sense it is calculated to 'tease us out of thought as doth eternity,' but only to release us into real vision, which is thought of another kind.

A *koan* thus lays siege to the mental citadel of the self and persistently saps its walls. The mentality would like to reject the *koan* out of hand as absurd, but it cannot bear to be defeated by it. Some *koans* do seem to have been intended simply to shock the mind, cluttered up with concepts and logic, out of its complacency by throwing the nonsensical at it. But in most of them a meaning can be divined when the mind has ceased to grasp at it.

For example, the Master declared, 'Empty-handed I go and lo! the spade's handle is in my hand'; or again, 'When I pass over the bridge the water flows not, but the bridge flows.' Both statements affront mentality's habitual logic and fixed way of seeing things. But they can open up an entirely new perspective, when the attempt to apply that logic to them has collapsed. They are not, in fact, intended as mental problems, but express a non-mental kind of consciousness which flashes into the student's mind when he has despaired of making sense of them. This flash of intuitive understanding is named *Satori*.

Our minds are so warped by dualistic thinking that the more earnestly we seek for the truth, the further we are from it. We tie ourselves up in questions about ultimate things and fail to see what is at our feet or in our hand. Yet it is that which can teach and liberate us. The Zen Masters continuously emphasized this. When a pupil asked some sententious question about Buddhist doctrine, they replied with an apparently irrelevant comment on their immediate surroundings, such as 'this ground, where we sit now is a fine site for a hut,' or by some seeming truism as 'when I feel sleepy, I sleep; when I want to sit, I sit.'

But these answers were wholly relevant to their purpose, which was to recall their pupils from abstractions to immediacy and thereby to bring them nearer to 'thinking of that which is beyond thinking.' To be told, 'when hungry one eats; when tired, one sleeps,' might provoke an impatient or cursory 'of course' from the hearer. But in fact, as the Master knew, this was not, at least after infancy or until *Satori* has occurred, the obvious truism it seemed. As he remarked later, 'When they eat, they do not just eat, they conjure up all kinds of imagination; when they sleep, they do not just sleep, they are given to varieties of idle thoughts. That is why theirs is not my way.'

The aim, therefore, of the Zen Master was to initiate his pupil into consciousness as a pure act. That is why he would sometimes teach by a silent bow, by raising or throwing down his staff, by a smile or a cuff. A *koan* is, indeed, a crystallization of silence, a form of words which allows the deeper meaning of silence to penetrate the mind. Until we can hear this silence, all our words are vain and all our acts are half-acts. As a Zen teacher said of a volubly high-minded acquaintance, 'the fellow who talks like that cannot consume even a drop of water.' For to consume is not merely to swallow. It is to taste out of a tastelessness as pure as that of the water itself. It is to drink water and to be drunk by it.

Thus Zen recalls us in countless ways to direct experience. Far from denying nature, it insists, with all the deep-seated obstinacy of nature herself, on a return to simplicity and naturalness. It bids us recover what we essentially are, whatever the stage in apparent development we may have reached. Everything which is irrelevant to that it regards as unimportant and, in the deepest sense, non-existent. Above all it pushes us on relentlessly to the discovery that we lack nothing.

All our mental restlessness and anxiety, all our distracted or discursive thinking springs from the illusion that we are in want of something and must hunt for it and take a fast hold of it, foolishly supposing, to borrow Wordsworth's lines,

> '*mid all this mighty sum*
> *Of things for ever speaking,*
> *That nothing of itself will come,*
> *But we must still be seeking.*

All our work in meditation is to teach us to let things happen in their own right way and at their own right time. When we realize that by our striving we are only increasing our want and rejecting what is given to us if we cease to strive, we are on the way to deliverance and to that pure act which is actionless.

There is thus in the teaching of Zen, as M. Benoit has written, 'no "path" towards deliverance,' since we have never really been in servitude. 'Man has nothing directly to do in order to experience his liberty that is total and infinitely happy. What he has to do is indirect and negative; what he has to understand, by means of work, is the deceptive illusion of all the "paths" that he can seek

out for himself and try to follow. When his persevering efforts
shall have brought him the perfectly clear understanding that *all*
that he can "do" to free himself is useless . . . then "satori" will
burst forth, a real vision that there is no "path" because there is
nowhere to go, because, from all eternity, he was at the unique
and fundamental centre of everything."[1]

The *koan* is only one tool, devised by the old Zen Masters, by
the use of which this understanding may come. Everything that
foils and defeats our self-thinking and self-willing brings it nearer.
Perhaps, indeed, Zen is best conceived as the practice of an art
and a craft, in which we learn to do some specific thing, as if the
Spirit did it through us, realizing that only so can we do anything
as it is meant to be done.[2]

In this way, as the Zen Masters taught and proved, enlightenment would come suddenly, when engaged in some ordinary task,
when digging the soil, for example, arranging some flowers, driv-
ing a nail into a fence, playing a musical instrument, or simply
looking into the face of a friend. One did not require to be withdrawn in solitary meditation. The task nearest to one's hand contained within its limited field the possibility of the miracle, the
achievement of 'purposeless' action, in which pure tension and pure
relaxation combined, as in the Primordial Principle Itself.

A fascinating account of how such action could be learnt in the
struggle to win mastery in a particular art is contained in Eugen
Herrigel's little book, 'Zen in the Art of Archery.' Here, gradually disclosed in the intercourse of pupil and Master, is the whole
secret of Zen and the contest with self which has to be waged to
the bitter end before it is possible to do anything 'spiritually,' that
is 'with a kind of effortless strength.'

Again and again, day by day and month by month through
several years of assiduous effort, Eugen Herrigel strove to
stretch the bowstring to its extreme point of tension and at the
crucial moment let the arrow go without any intrusion of anxious self-will. Yet always he failed to achieve the perfect act.
After instructing by simple example, his Master watched, mostly in
silence. But at intervals, when his pupil was becoming desperate,
he offered advice. Once he said,

[1] From *The Supreme Doctrine* by Hubert Benoit.
[2] cf. Rimbaud's letter to Démeney in which he wrote that, in his experience
it was untrue to say 'I think.' We should rather say 'one thinks me.'

You must hold the drawn bowstring like a little child holding the proffered finger. It grips it so firmly that one marvels at the strength of the tiny fist. And when it lets the finger go, there is not the slightest jerk. Do you know why? Because the child doesn't think 'I will now let go of the finger in order to grasp this other thing.' Completely unselfconsciously, without purpose, it turns from one to the other and we would say that it was playing with the things, were it not equally true that the things are playing with the child.

The teaching of Zen, as of Gautama, of which it is a unique expression, thus confirms with subtle insight into its implications what Jesus taught when he said that except you become as a little child, you cannot enter the kingdom of heaven. For Zen, as for all Buddhism, that kingdom lies at the midmost point between earth and heaven, the pointless point, hard to come upon, which lies between all the opposites. It is, in the words of the *Katha Upanishad*, 'smaller than the smallest atom, greater than the greatest space.' And there the Atman, the Self Which is no self, has its being.

If one tries to reach that point by one's own effort, one falls miserably into an abyss or a narrow defile between the two. But when one has learnt to wait, to be gathered into the inward presence of Mind, and thus to draw on a higher power than our own, the miracle happens. Heaven and earth meet, self-will vanishes in a greater Will, Whose purpose is organic and universal and therefore concentrated but unrestricting, and what we had for so long and so dishearteningly striven to do and could only conceive as an unattainable ideal, 'realizes itself as if of its own accord.' By being self-forgetfully absorbed in the task, the relationship of the moment and, through them, in the mysterious and directive purpose of creation, right doing is at last accomplished as an expression of right being.

To read Eugen Herrigel's account of this moment, so long withheld but at last given, of utterly humble, un-selfconcerned attainment is to see clearly and feel tangibly, if only through transient approximations in our own experience, what the doctrine of 'No-Mind' means as a living act, and also to realize how opposite it is to everything we do and every breath we draw. How such presence of Mind, disturbed by no ulterior motive, manifests in a more

humanly sensitive and subtle art, that of the painters of the T'ang
and the Sung periods in China, has been finely described by Mr.
Iqbal Singh,

> *Here we are in a universe* (he writes) *which is devoid of ten-*
> *sion—not because contrarieties and conflicts have ceased to*
> *operate, but because they have somehow become intelligible.*
> *Here, in the very contemplation of transience, we receive a*
> *measure of eternity. Here the mind manages to realize a stasis*
> *within the flux itself, so that even a waterfall—normally sym-*
> *bolizing incessant movement—emerges as a symbol of stillness.*
> *Here the human soul is at once 'wandering and captive.' Here*
> *the wheel turns and does not turn. Here the paradox is no longer*
> *a paradox, but rather a luminous certitude. Here we are in the*
> *very heart of peace.*[1]

Nevertheless the path of the Sudden School has its own dangers
particularly for the impulsive and the false simplifiers. We are
prone to mistake the shadow for the substance, to believe that we
have achieved creative spontaneity when still some element of
compulsive egoism remains. The surrealist movement in contemporary art was a crude example of this. The temptation to take
short cuts is great for such a prize. We may even cheat in a false
effort to win it. Eugen Herrigel candidly confesses in his book to
having done this. It brought him the sternest reprimand his Master
could have administered, a refusal, only withdrawn after full repentance, to continue to be his teacher.

In *The Secret of the Golden Flower*, in which Buddhism speaks
with the voice of Taoism, as it so often does in China, it is written,
'One must not leave out the steps between and penetrate directly';
and elsewhere, 'Not with one leap can a man suddenly get there.
Whoever is seeking eternal life must search for the place whence
essence and life originally spring.' This may seem to contradict the
central teaching of Zen. In fact it does not.

The moment of re-birth into reality is always instantaneous. How
could it be otherwise? But there are no short-cuts to it, whether
by feeling or by thought. Short-cuts are the delusion of egoistic
desire. The nearer the self comes to its extinction, the more it
strives to perpetuate its existence by persuading us that it is ex-
tinct. The doctrine of the Void can be thus perverted and the en-

[1] From *Gautama Buddha* by Iqbal Singh.

thusiast may be lamentably empty of everything but himself. To disencumber outwardly is not necessarily to enlarge the space within, from which and into which everything can flow.

Enlightenment is not only the art of right seeing and doing, but of right suffering of our own and of other's joys and sorrows, even though both are known to be of the same transient texture; of right caring, too, and sharing, which is relationship. Above all it is the art of right compassion and love. To achieve truth in this art our human sensibility needs educating by exposure to rebuffs as well as caresses, and we must be ready to reject no demand that is made upon it, but to cultivate an ever finer and more alert receptiveness to what life offers for our testing and our reward.

There are, too, certain psychic dangers or trials common to all inward adventures of the spirit, but to which the path of the Sudden School is particularly liable. *Satori* happens in a flash of total awakening, but there are intermediate stages between mental and intuitive living, conditions of partial sleep and partial awakening. These changing phases in the inner life are often difficult to handle wisely. Above all we must not try to force the issue prematurely, but must learn to balance the growing grace and pressure of positive force within us by a correspondingly deeper surrender to the force of gravity, the night of nothingness and not-self, in which we are immersed. Only utmost patience and unassertiveness can render harmless, if not at times disconcerting, the new light which begins to filter into the consciousness and to energize the psychic being and, through it, the mental and physical faculties.

In this respect the prescribed stages of meditation, laid down in the Gradual School, by which the process of transition which leads to transformation is regulated, has obvious advantages which may outweigh the risk of becoming immobilized at one stage of the journey.

Yet if we patiently persist in mindful and loving attentiveness in all we do and refrain from doing, if we allow the change to happen in the knowledge that it is not ours to effect, but only to maintain the conditions that make it possible, keeping our lamps trimmed against the coming of the Bridegroom, all is and must be well.

This is what it means to be a true artist in the spiritual life and only this can bring human life to its intrinsic order of perfection. Such perfection and the attempt to practise it is not merely for the highly gifted with special talents. For this art, as has been said, is the attainment of artlessness. It is the flowering of our true nature, of that which is original in us as sin is not, and which all our misconceiving and misuse have not been able to destroy. The teaching of Zen, as of all Buddhism, is, in its essence, applicable to the simplest routine of daily life and the humblest circumstances. Indeed it is within these that its truth may flower most simply and give its purest scent.

'Walk on,' said a Zen Master, and the phrase has come to epitomise the essence of the teaching. For it is only by moving freely with the flow of the river of life that we enter the stillness hidden in its depths. Our true journey ends, as it begins, nowhere, at that point of intensest peace and rest within the everchanging here and now, where time is timeless and, moment by moment, we become what we are.

EPILOGUE

'WORDS CANNOT EXPRESS,' wrote Whitman towards the end of his life, 'how much at peace I am about God and about death.' So it should be throughout our lives, but particularly in our latter days.

As death was 'the song and all songs' for Walt Whitman, so 'union,' by learning to die a certain kind of death, is the central theme upon which Eastern wisdom plays its subtle variations. The reiteration of this theme is unavoidable in any study of the Eastern mind, which throughout the centuries has remained faithful to the Vedic conception of death as the womb into which the Light descends in every act of creation and re-creation. It holds, therefore, as a self-evident truth, that until death is fully accepted, life cannot be lived in wholeness and harmony.

Doubtless it is or should be easier to accept this truth in the second half of life than in the first. As D. H. Lawrence wrote,[1]...

> Now it is autumn and the falling fruit
> and the long journey towards oblivion.
>
> The apples falling like great drops of dew
> to bruise themselves an exit from themselves.
>
> And it is time to go, to bid farewell
> to one's own self, and find an exit
> from the fallen self....
>
> O let us talk of quiet that we know,
> that we can know, the deep and lovely quiet
> of a strong heart at peace!
>
> How can we this, our own quietus, make?
>
> Build then the ship of death, for you must take
> the longest journey to oblivion.
>
> And die the death, the long and painful death
> that lies between the old self and the new.

[1] In *The Ship of Death.*

But, in fact, from the first breath we draw, we are rehearsing this death. What we need and so generally fail to learn is how to die it willingly and fruitfully. This was the lesson of all lessons that the Eastern sages taught. But many Western minds reject this teaching as being inimical to life and what they term 'personality.' In concluding this book it will be well to try and meet that criticism once again.

For the Eastern sages, our ultimate aim throughout life, recollected in all our activities, artistic, social, religious, or domestic, should be release *(moksha)*. By release they meant a loosening and eventual severance of our attachment to the unreal. To achieve this they taught that we should practise an inner detachment from all that is contingent in life as a means to realizing fully That Which is not contingent. Eventually, if we are faithful in this practice, we shall come to live by the light, love and power of this unconditioned Presence and be made whole. This it is to experience 'Union.'

This teaching did not deny the order and structure of human life as a sphere of social activity and inter-relationship, and it acknowledged that there were many ways in which the lesson of detachment might be learnt and the ideal of union might express itself.

What, however, it did insist was that he who was truly released into the Unconditioned was inwardly beyond that world of struggle and necessity in which the unreleased lived. This was the meaning of Shankara's statement, 'By action a person is bound, and by wisdom he is released. Therefore, the sages who see the goal do no action.' For inwardly, whatever action they may seem to do, they are free from the self-centred compulsion, of which all human civilization is a reflection, varying in degree from the stark bondage of internicine conflict, when a balance of power has broken down, to the comparative release of a well-adjusted relationship.

To-day we are very conscious of the dangers and disabilities of the self-centred life and a new school of psychologists has arisen to study and treat its symptoms as they manifest in the extremes of psychosis and neurosis. Freudian psychology differs radically from the spiritual science of the East or, for that matter, from all traditional religious teaching, in its unconcern with a 'Beyond,' with another order of being than that of temporal individuality and social welfare. The aim of the psycho-analyist of this school is rather re-adjustment within the limits of the dualistic state than re-integration beyond it.

Certainly the encounter of the opposites upon which psychology rightly lays such stress is as essential to the growth of consciousness as to the maintenance of life. But it is meant by degrees to change inwardly from a conflict of self-conscious antagonism into the counterpartal relatedness of imaginative love, in and by which the two who encounter become one in themselves and in each other. This is the true meaning of being 'beyond,' yet within, 'the pairs.'

Similarly the relative ego-stability which we achieve at a certain stage of our development, as we emerge from the collective unconscious, is no more than a necessary basis for fuller and finer being. In the religious view a self, capable of balancing its own claims fairly or even generously against those of another or of society is only a starting-point for re-birth into a new Selfhood in which the illusion of separateness, native to both ego and super-ego, as Freud defines them, is dissipated.

Admittedly the school of analytical psychology, inspired by Jung, has come much nearer to grasping the full meaning of such integration than that of Freud, particularly in its conception of love as, in Erich Neumann's words, 'a travail of the personality, leading through suffering to transformation and illumination.' Jung has always recognized that to be healed, we need to be initiated into a mystery. But the mysteries of even the more enlightened psychologists stop short at the integration of the natural man. The further aim and the higher reality, imaged in the ideal of sanctity, enlightenment or liberation, with its supernatural implications, is generally disregarded, if not deprecated.

And this is because medical science sees man, not as a heavenborn trinity of spirit, soul and body, but as an earth-bound, reasoning animal in dubious travail of a soul. For the Eastern teachers man is essentially a spiritual being on all the levels of his nature, with an eternal 'I' behind and within his evolving personality, from which he derives both his infinite and his unique value. It is this pure Subject, too, which determines his real growth, though temporal conditions play their part as secondary factors and reflect outwardly, if often imperfectly through the 'hang-over' of past errors and their consequences, the degree of Self-knowledge and the depth of being to which he has attained.

For native to this pure 'I' is an integral awareness, which can ultimately penetrate the whole of man's nature and loosen the knots which ignorance and misuse have tied in it and for long continued to tie under the law of *Karma*.

Such a consciousness, a super-consciousness compared with man's ordinary mental state, and the various grades of it which can unfold in those who learn to respond to it, is not acknowledged by modern Western psychology. At best there is a reflected glimmer of it in Jung's 'collective unconscious,' while it is altogether denied in the earth-bound psycho-pathology of Freud.

For the same reason, perhaps, it is not sufficiently recognized, even by psychologists, that breakdown, through failure to adapt to the existing conditions of society, may be due to a legitimate, if misdirected, refusal to accept these conditions. The Eastern sages assume from the start that the existing condition of any society and of the individuals who compose it is one of relative ignorance and servitude to illusory desires, and that it is essential to transcend this condition at any cost. Release, however, has to be won within the mind and body, as, also, within the human society in which we live. This is the conditioned enclosure within which the miracle of transformation has to be sought. But it can be found only through an established communion with That Which is neither body nor mind and Which can create societies in perfect harmony with Itself.

Such ideal community is the primordial pattern which underlies every generation's struggle for social betterment and every individual's wish for brotherhood. For the 'City of God,' which seer and prophet have seen descending out of heaven, like a bride adorned for her husband, the city which, for Thomas Traherne, 'seemed to stand in Eden, or to be built in Heaven,' is no Utopian dream, but the reality of which all earthly cities, even the most beautiful, the Athens of Pericles, the Florence of the Medici, or fabled Babylon with its hanging gardens, are but reflections. Heaven is in them, as it is in all earthly places and all the works of man. But even when its outward form is not blurred and marred by man's blind hands, it is subject to corruption and decay.

Dr. Conze, writing of Buddhist meditations, asserts that they are meant for people who do not want to adapt themselves to any form of social life, 'but to get out of the world altogether.' If this were literally true, it would justify the charges of 'negativism' and 'escapism' which are so often brought against Eastern thought.

I am convinced, however, that this is not a true interpretation of what 'release' meant to the seers of old or to Gautama himself with his unshakable fidelity to the solid ground underlying all human experience, however exalted it might be. For them, as for all the great teachers, 'Union' could only be attained by those who were no longer attached to a world shaped and ruled by desire, however fascinating its civilized disguises or laudable its social organization. But this 'being beyond' consisted in being inwardly free, not in seeking to escape, which was only the old desire in its negative aspect.

The actual world, though a realm of ignorance and illusion, in which human and animal impulse struggle to come to an agreement, has to be accepted as a condition of truly transcending it, but not on its own terms. To see into life's heart we need to look, too, and look long and steadfastly, into its ravaged face. The world about us does not vanish when the true vision dawns. But it is changed. For it is seen in and through the Beyond, in which he who is released perpetually lives.

To live thus in the Real, within the context of the actual, is only possible, the Masters say, to those who have died completely to the illusion of selfhood. And it is upon the meaning of this death and the problem of what, if anything, survives it, that the Western mind most often takes issues with the Eastern.

In one of Elizabeth Taylor's novels[1] I came across the following passage,

> *That little picture of yours,* he was saying, *the lemons lying on some spotted laurel-leaves in a dish, it is so simply, so honourably done. As if you sat down for a long time and looked at the dish and thought about what it was and didn't begin to paint until you knew better than anybody else: and, although you never said 'I,' because you never said 'I,' you shine through it like the sun.*

This illustrates well what the more enlightened Western mind conceives as the legitimate limit of self-transcendence. The 'I,' in the truest moment of an artist's vision, is forgotten, but what distinguishes the artist from every other artist and is recognizable in

[1] *A Wreath of Roses.*

this or that unmistakable nuance of expression, survives. This distinctive focus of being is not annulled by the sun which shines through it. It is purified, but not consumed. Is this what the Zen Masters meant and incited their pupils to become as pure vehicles for the creative act, or is there a subtle and life-denying difference?

In the last three chapters of this book I have been concentrating on Buddhism, in which the negative factor in the equation of life is explicitly emphasized and the positive one only implied. This reiterated emphasis upon what must be denied, if we are to be truly affirmed and affirm, may have distorted a little in my reader's mind the true perspective of the original Eastern wisdom. In Vedanta the balance of 'yes' and 'no' is more explicitly maintained. Yet the same question is asked as was asked of Gautama, a question which he thought that silence could best answer.

It is the question, already referred to earlier in this book, which, in the *Katha Upanishad*, Nachiketa persisted in asking Yama, lord of the kingdom of death, though he begged him not to press it. 'There is this doubt about a man when he is dead: some say that he exists; others that he does not. Teach me of this, that I may know.'

The question is just as applicable to the man who has attained release while still alive here on earth as to those who have doffed the physical body. The truly enlightened, as Gautama showed by his silence, do not need to ask it. The unenlightened can neither answer it nor receive an answer which will satisfy them. For when the soul is fully conscious of its eternal essence, it needs no proof of immortality and no explanation of what will or will not survive the death of self or of the body to which the self clings. That it lives in the deathless by dying to separate existence is as Self-evident a truth of experience as that it lives and dies in each mutable moment.

Such an experience cannot be defined in terms of a persisting entity, named a person, with an indefinite capacity for resisting death and maintaining its limited form and characteristics. For in those who are released from self the conflict or alternative between existing and not existing, has ceased. They can only say 'we *are*,' and in the same breath and by the grace of God, 'we are not.'

But this consent to death as a condition of life is what the unenlightened refuse and 'personality' is for them less a distinctive and qualitative expression of creative living than a buttress against death. Hence their strong recoil from any teaching which suggests that it may be an illusion. As Sri Aurobindo has written,[1] 'it is the extinction or dissolution of the personality, of this mental, nervous and physical composite which I call myself that is hard to bear for a man enamoured of life, and it is the promise of its survival and physical reappearance that is the great lure.' Too often, alas, religions, and Christianity in particular, have indulged this thirst of the self for an immortality which is an immunity from death, a demand to be deathless without that inward dying, of which the body's death is only an outward incident in the eternal drama of becoming as an expression of Being.

What then, to revert to Nachiketa's question, does one who is released from self, in life or after death, experience? Yama would never have consented to answer this question if Nachiketa had not already received 'the knowledge of the sacred flame,' which consumes all the hunger and thirst, the sorrow and fear, by which the self-attached are afflicted. He has thereby qualified to receive an answer and the answer is nothing less than an exposition of the kind of consciousness native to the 'Deathless State' and its correspondence with the Divine Consciousness Which informs it.

Enough has been written of this in earlier chapters. But in brief conclusion it may be said that one who is released no longer gazes outward from an individual centre which is, at least partially, separated from the Heart of being. He has recovered the inner vision, because he is at one again with his Source. He has returned to origin, as the mystics say. So has the outer world in his vision of it. He sees it as the divine Imagination originates it from moment to moment. And seeing it thus, he is in creative communion with it. This experience of ceasing to exist in separation may be interpreted in two ways according as the emphasis is laid on what is lost or on what is found.

In terms of the self which is discarded nothing remains of the previously cherished personality. It has vanished into that neutral stream of becoming in which the force of *Karma* perpetuates the fleeting forms, composed of ideas and sensations, of which the discarded self was one. This was the truth which Gautama stressed, because he knew that until the illusion that self had any substance was destroyed, it was useless to speak of an identity which is real.

Vedanta, however, though just as insistent on the need for the

[1] In *The Problem of Rebirth*.

ego to die, did not hesitate to speak of That in Which we are reborn or to conceive Its nature. In the Presence of That, the *Upanishads* and the *Bhagavad-Gita* declare, we experience, for the first
time in full consciousness, an unshakable sense of coherent identity.

This 'Presence' Vedanta named the Self, the real Man, constant
in all change and difference, in Which we are meant to experience
immortal life in the midst of mortality and to know our fellow
beings for what they truly are. In the knowledge of that One, the
sages said, the 'I' to which we used to cling, in ourselves and
others, is seen to be but a ghost which longs to be laid that it may
cease to wander for ever between life and death. But until we are
in the Sun of that 'Presence,' the shadow of perversity, positive or
negative, remains to personalize or depersonalize life in false
ways.

For what is present when self is absent, we repeat, is neither an
'I,' in the ordinary sense of the word, nor an abstraction. It is
Creative Spirit, inexhaustibly original and expressing its universality in the particular and unique. The more a soul is inspirited, the
more distinctively is it both itself and in communion with each and
every form of life, until, we may suppose, it realizes its ultimate
destiny and blends, in a manner beyond human comprehension,
with the Consciousness which is its creative source. Yet even then,
it may be, in that wordless beatitude of union, we shall 'feel ourselves,' to quote the words of Ruysbroeck, the Flemish mystic,
'living wholly in God and wholly in ourselves,' a distinction without difference.

In the nature of Creative Spirit, Which infinitely loves the finite,
the mechanical and the standardized, the diffuse or disorganic,
have no place. Yet Its originality never intrudes, never forces itself on our notice as does the 'personality' which captivates a fickle
public in a pretty film-star, a forceful politician or a powerful
preacher. What enchants us in real people, as in real works of art,
is the absence of that obvious 'I' with its tedious uniformity or its
equally tedious self-display. In its place is an indefinable quality
of life and being, which is their own and not their own, and which
gives to them the grace of integrity—a grace which at once reveals
and conceals a beauty beyond itself, since it begins and ends in
mystery. Yet there is meaning in this mystery.

For in every form of life an organizing, self-regulating process
resides, an inborn purpose to be a whole in a whole and to main-

tain its distinctive and generic pattern against destructive forces or accidents, even to the extent of re-fashioning lost or injured parts. This organic impulse, which in plant and animal is an unconscious instinct, becomes in man an urge to complete the mystery of Being in the harmony of Knowing.

In 'Union,' as the ancient Wisdom conceived it, this harmony is realized, not by self-mutilation, but in Self-completion. Egolessness, on all levels of the being (and it was this total initiation into the life of Being that the ancient Wisdom sought to confer), alone makes possible an unimpeded activity of the creative impulse in any organism.

We are, however, so unfamiliar with supreme spiritual integrity and so familiar with those who 'personalize' spirit in worthy or worthless ways, that the passionless inner radiance of a fully enlightened man or woman seems to many to lack something necessary to our humanity, if not to be positively inhuman. It must appear thus to all whose thirst for happiness and desire to escape sorrow drive them into sorrow's arms. For such the undesirous peace of the enlightened is at once a reproach and an infidelity to the life they live, though it contains within it all the fulness of life that they unavailingly seek.

Habituated to the glamour and gloom that play for them over the face of life, as over their own faces, they read the words in which Isaiah described the 'suffering servant,' 'he hath no form nor comeliness; and when we shall see him, there is no beauty that we should desire him,' not as a tribute to a beauty of another order, in which joy and sorrow blend and are surpassed in a divine compassion, but as implying a deficiency, a loss of that eager vitality which intoxicates and distracts.

Those whose eyes are opened know otherwise. Truly enough a Master of Wisdom is not tied to this world or any other and for that reason can transform the quality of life of any realm in which he is present or of any person who can receive the light he sheds. Gautama, like Jesus though differently, was so purely Self and not-self that he has left his unique stamp on millions of his fellow-beings. But it is not the kind of stamp which an 'I,' however sublime, imposes. It is a stamp of self-effacement which releases what is real in those who receive it and instead of binding them by any restrictive imitation strengthens the light in their own souls. Rilke wrote of the Buddha, 'it is as though he listened,' and such lis-

tening as his enfolds us in a silence in which, at last, we begin to
hear what we are meant to be.

But most people still want life too much to heed the Light that
beckons to fuller life. For these the absorbed contemplation of
this Light by the Oriental Masters will seem, if they should ever
seriously consider it, a strange unworldly aberration. Many, too,
who do heed and are strongly enough drawn towards the Light
to want to change their way of living, are not yet ready to pass
beyond the dualistic stage in the soul's progress, in which the
dominance of self may be reduced and subdued, even apparently
to its complete abeyance, but the wound of separation is not
wholly healed. Within such a dualism countless lives of devotion
and dutifulness have been lived, but the peace that is won is not
perfect, though it may seem so, because the gulf has not been
crossed which divides a wholly creative awareness from a disciplined, but partial one. Some faculty of the soul, whether of mind,
heart or senses, has been repressed. The awakening is incomplete.

Hitherto, in human history, only the exceptional have been inwardly compelled to transcend this dualism, in that ultimate union
with Brahman in which the veils of separation part and soul and
spirit meet in a total embrace. As Krishna declared, 'Of thousands
of men few strive for perfection. Of those who do strive, few
really know Me.'

Yet this does not lessen the need to affirm for all without quali-
fication the way of perfection. Addiction to the pleasures and
pains of self is not, in fact, fidelity to life, but resistance to it. Little
by little pain breaks down this resistance and teaches us to suffer
life more truly. It is a slow, involuntary way of learning to yield
to reality, but sure and effectual in the end.

Wisdom cannot interfere with this process, if it would. It can
only wait until the hour strikes when mind and heart are ready
to receive news of a more direct and voluntary way. The Eastern
Masters, as I have shown, are particularly concerned to enlighten
the Mind, but not assuredly at the cost of the heart. Subtle-minded
as they were, they knew that the heart dies more readily to a false
independence than the mind. For the heart is feminine and prone
to yield, at least superficially. But the mind is masculine and seeks
to enforce its will.

Yet, in truth, the heart can never be fully surrendered until the mind is fully awakened and each is surrendered in the other to That Which makes them one. Until this has happened, the heart's devotion will be tainted with subjective emotion and sentiment. The mind, on the other hand, will seek in devious ways to impose on life its own undefeated power and prowess. True love is imaginative awareness which, though supremely intelligent and sensitive, is neither a mental act nor an emotional impulse, but is perfectly mindful in its fidelity to the heart's reason. This is why the Masters of Wisdom seem to put the need of Light before the need of Love. For they knew how much labour of inward thought is required before the heart can be wholly mindful and the mind be so cleansed of error that love can deliver it from the prison of merely mental acts.

Then, only, can St. Augustine's words, 'love and do what you will' be accepted and acted on without the risk of self-delusion. For when mind and heart, those two valves in the heart of Being, beat as one, the vision is opened by which everything is seen from within as the divinely imagined universe which it is. Then, only, have we reason to feel with William Blake that 'a man may be happy in this world' and the words of the *Narada Sutra* that 'love is greater than work, knowledge or Yoga, because it is its own end' are fully understood. For what were before but means to the self-renunciation which is the essential nature of love are become pure expressions of it.

Yet those who agree with Ramakrishna that we live in an age, when love must take first place, need also to remember that this is, supremely and more widely, perhaps, than ever before, an age of emerging self-consciousness, and that love cannot and will not take first place until the questioning mind has been satisfied. Impulsive feeling, however ardent its intention, cannot do this, but only humble, patient, concentrated thought. It is in this, above all, that the Eastern teachings give us guidance.

What is true of the redemption of the heart is equally true of the purification of religious belief. There is nothing in the wisdom of Vedanta which need conflict with the essential meaning that all the great religions strive, in their different ways, to recommend to their followers and to encourage them to embody in their lives. But what is partial and interested in institutional religions, what disguises, in doctrine and dogma or in exclusive claims to possess the truth, the spectral selfhood, must fade away in the Light of the new day of disinterested spiritual discovery, of which this ancient teaching has been the guardian down the ages.

As W. B. Yeats wrote, '(we have to) discover in that East something ancestral in ourselves, something we must bring into the light before we can appease a religious instinct that for the first time in our civilization demands the satisfaction of the whole man.'

That has been my experience and it has convinced me that it is not necessary to embrace one of the historical Faiths to fulfil the instinct of which Yeats wrote or to satisfy the whole man.

For many people, doubtless, membership of a Church and acceptance of a creed is still a necessary introduction to the practice of the inward life. But organized religion in its existing forms tends always to become a sanctified, if not a conventional enclosure and, as such, to arrest growth beyond a certain point. This danger is implicit in the vested social interests and the doctrinal framework of ecclesiasticism, as distinct from the vital Brotherhoods in which the inspiration of a Master's teaching first manifests. The creative decline in the Christian Church may, also, be traced back to the fear and repudiation of the ancient 'gnosis' which has haunted it from its early days.

With such matters I am not concerned here nor with the kind of fellowship which inevitably grows out of and enriches a true practice of the spiritual life, reflecting its quality and deepening as it deepens. We are separated from other men in the exact degree to which we are inwardly divided. Union within is communion without, but fellowship between those who share the same religious belief is seldom disinterested brotherhood with all men in the quest of a living truth and a love that unites.

That quest is the only real necessity, and it involves a readiness to respond inwardly to what is constant and what is changing in the spiritual directive of life itself. This fearless response animates all religion when it is true to the voice of the Master it reveres and is unconcerned with power, prestige or self-preservation.

The Eastern Masters make no exclusive claim to divine knowledge, and impose no creed or system of belief upon us. They speak of that which they know and of which, they assure us, we may know, if we put it to the test. They plot the ancient path which leads to ultimate release from the spectral self, and, with it, from all that thwarts communion with life itself and with every struggling, aspiring, joyous or afflicted soul. They leave us to tread this path in our own way, a path which is as flexible and adaptable to our needs and circumstances as is life itself and as constant, stable and enduring.

My task of exposition and interpretation is done. Yet the real task is but begun—the task which long preceded the writing of this book—of concentrating in each living moment the truths of this ancient wisdom. To live intensively with such themes as these, in one's silent hours, by day and night, is in itself to become, little by little, possessed, not of them, but by them, to be invaded and changed by truth, until one knows, beyond all doubt, that consciousness and the rhythm of one's being can be transformed, as the feeling of being at home in nothingness and so in all that is, humbles and enlarges the soul that is willing to comprehend.

Enlightenment, for the Eastern Masters, is the first and last need. 'All other righteousness,' said Santi-deva, a Mahayanist sage, 'fades away after its fruit is cast; but the tree of the Thought of Enlightenment bears everlasting fruit and fades not, being ever fecund.' Its fruit is wisdom which, though absolute in its essence, is always at home in the relative situation in which it finds itself. Thus it is that while the Light which we seek can first reduce and then, in a flash of illumination, banish self-centred ignorance, it in no way arrests the true flow of life. Rather it is into that true current that it releases us, while at the same time committing us to the endless tasks of insight, of imaginative understanding.

For reality in the life about us and in each of our fellows is fathomless, ever surprising us with new revelations, new initiations into its mystery, new invitations to share with others the subtle simplicities of its meaning and the griefs and glories of its life.

O infinite deep, wrote Rupert Brooke,

> *I never knew,*
> *I would come back, come back to you.*

It is to that deep that we return when we cease to want life, when its truth has penetrated to our core and blossomed there in a faith and a love in which youth's unbounded hope and age's utter resignation join hands. 'Two things only do I desire,' protested Fénelon to Bossuet—'TRUTH AND PEACE; truth which may enlighten and peace which may unite us.'

The two are not easily won together, as Fénelon sadly found.
But they cannot exist apart. For though, in men's minds, truth, as
light and life, seems often to be opposed to a peace of darkness and
death, there is, in creation, no conflict between them. In the death
of self-renunciation we find peace. But it is no negative or feature-
less peace. It is the peace of death gathered into the arms of life.
O silence of darkness, wrote Charles Péguy,[1]

> *Such a silence reigned before the creation of unrest,*
> *Before the beginning of the reign of unrest,*
> *Such a silence will reign, but it will be a silence of light,*
> *When all that unrest is brought to an end,*
> *When all that unrest is exhausted,*
> *When they have drawn all the water from the well,*
> *After the end, after the exhaustion of all the unrest of man.*

To-day that 'silence of light' seems very far away, further away,
perhaps, on the surface of the earth and in the sky's space, than
ever before in the history of man. But within, for those who seek
it humbly and patiently, it is as near as ever, nearer, it may be, as
our need of its redeeming radiance grows. We have but to surrender our souls to it and in the darkness of our dying the Light of
the ever-living shines anew, blessing us with Its Truth, Its Love, Its
Power and Its Peace. This is the heart of all that the Masters of
Wisdom throughout the ages teach.

1955-57

[1] In the poem 'La Nuit,' translated by Anne and Julian Green in *Charles Péguy, Man and Saint.*

A SHORT BIBLIOGRAPHY

VEDANTA

Sacred Books of the East. Edited by F. Max Muller.

The Rig-Veda. Sayana Acharya's version, translated by H. H. Wilson.

Hymns to the Mystic Fire by Sri Aurobindo.

The Thirteen Principal Upanishads. Translated from the Sanskrit by R. E. Hume.

Himalayas of the Soul. Translations from the Sanskrit of the Principal Upanishads by J. Mascaro.

Eight Upanishads. Translated by Sri Aurobindo.

The Upanishads. Katha, Isa, Kena and Mundaka. Translated by Swami Nikhilananda.

The Bhagavad-Gita with the commentary of Sri Sankaracharya. Translated from the Sanskrit by A. Mahadeva Sastri.

The Message of the Gita. As interpreted by Sri Aurobindo. Edited by A. Roy.

Bhagavad-Gita. Song of God. Translated by Swami Prabhavananda and Christopher Isherwood.

Hindu Scriptures. Edited by Nicol Macnicol. (Everyman's Library).

The Crest Jewel of Wisdom and other writings of Sankaracharya. Translations and commentaries by Charles Johnston.

The Yoga of the Kathopanishad by Sri Krishna Prem.

The Yoga of the Bhagavad-Gita by Sri Krishna Prem.

The Yoga Sutras of Patanjali. An interpretation by Charles Johnston.

How to Know God. The Yoga Aphorisms of Patanjali. Translated with a New Commentary by Swami Prabhavananda and Christopher Isherwood.

Tibetan Yoga and Secret Doctrines. Edited by W. Y. Evans-Wentz.

Yoga and Western Psychology. A comparison by Geraldine Coster.

The Glorious Presence: a study of the Vedanta philosophy and its relation to modern thought by Ernest E. Wood.

Ramana Maharshi and the Path of Self-knowledge by Arthur Osborne.

Indian Philosophy: 2 vols. by S. Radhakrishnan.

Man and His Becoming According to Vedanta by Réné Guenon.

BUDDHISM

Sacred Books of the Buddhists. Edited by F. Max Muller, Mrs. Rhys Davids and others.

Some Sayings of the Buddha. According to the Pali Canon. Translated by F. L. Woodward.

Early Buddhist Scriptures. A selection translated and edited by E. J. Thomas.

The Quest of Enlightenment. A selection of the Buddhist Scriptures translated from the Sanskrit by E. J. Thomas.

The Dhammapada translated by Narada Thera.

A Buddhist Bible. Edited by Dwight Goddard.

The Path of Light: a Manual of Mahayana Buddhism by L. D. Barnett.

The Lankavatara Sutra translated by D. T. Suzuki.

The Secret of the Golden Flower. A Chinese Book of Life translated and explained by R. Wilhelm.

The Tibetan Book of the Great Liberation. Edited by W. Y. Evans-Wentz.

Buddha and the Gospel of Buddhism by Ananda K. Coomaraswamy.

Gautama Buddha by Iqbal Singh.

The Life of the Buddha as Legend and History by E. J. Thomas.

Essays in Zen Buddhism: 3 vols. by D. T. Suzuki.

Zen in the Art of Archery by Eugen Herrigel.

The Supreme Doctrine by Hubert Benoit.

The Way of Zen by Alan Watts.

The Doctrine of Awakening by J. Evola.

Buddhism. Its Essence and Development by Edward Conze.

Buddhist Meditation: translated selections edited with introduction by Edward Conze.

The Heart of Buddhist Meditation by Nyanaponika Thera.

The Creed of Buddha by Edmond Holmes.

GENERAL

Kabir. One Hundred Poems. Translated by Rabindranath Tagore, assisted by Evelyn Underhill.

Hinduism and Buddhism by Ananda K. Coomeraswamy.

The Meaning of Life in Hinduism and Buddhism by Floyd H. Ross.

Wisdom from the East. Hari Prasad Shastri.

Sadhana. The Realization of Life by Rabindranath Tagore.

Commentaries on Living from the notebooks of J. Krishnamurti.

The Hindu View of Art by Mulk Raj Anand.

From Intellect to Intuition by Alice Bailey.

Living Time and The Integration of Life by Maurice Nicoll.

The Transcendent Unity of Religions by Frithjof Schuon. Translated by P. Townsend.

Founding The Life Divine. The Integral Yoga of Sri Aurobindo.
By Morwenna Donnelly.

The Destiny of Mind: East and West by W. S. Haas.

The Origins and History of Consciousness by Erich Neumann.
Translated by R. F. C. Hull.

The Vision of Asia by L. Cranmer Byng.

The Perennial Philosophy by Aldous Huxley.

An Experiment in Depth by P. W. Martin.

Other Quest books on some religions of the East

WISDOM OF THE VEDAS

by Jagadish Chandra Chatterji

An illuminating presentation of the great Vedic system of thought, India's oldest and most profound religio-philosophical tradition.

THE GLORIOUS PRESENCE

by Ernest Wood

The Vedanta philosophy including what is believed to be the only translation into English of Shankara's Meditations on the South Facing Form (The Glorious Presence).

THE PEARL OF THE ORIENT

by Geoffrey Barborka

The message of the Bhagavad-Gita for the Western World.